Hypnotherapy For Du

Cheat Sheet

Hypnotherapy Terms

Conscious and unconscious

These terms describe aspects of your mind. Think of the range of states your mind experiences as a spectrum. At the right extreme of the spectrum are the super-alert states you're in when you're frightened or excited. At the left end of the spectrum of mind states is deep sleep. Read Chapter 1 for more on the conscious and unconscious mind.

Direct and indirect suggestions

A direct (or authoritarian) suggestion gives an explicit instruction to do something such as 'Stop smoking now'. It acts as a form of reprogramming.

An indirect (or permissive) suggestion allows your unconscious mind to explore a variety of possibilities before coming up with a response. For example, 'I wonder how soon it will be before you stop smoking and start to enjoy a healthy lifestyle?' Indirect suggestions allow your unconscious mind to make change in a way that fully suits you.

Chapter 2 has more on direct and indirect suggestions.

Hypnosis

Hypnosis is a technique. The word *hypnosis* comes from *hypnos*, the Greek word for sleep. People used to think that hypnosis was the same as sleep, but it isn't. Hypnosis is a deeply relaxed state where your mind can help you to focus extremely well on any task that either you or your hypnotherapist suggest to help you.

Hypnotherapy

Hypnosis used for therapeutic purposes becomes hypnotherapy. Many different hypnotherapy techniques and applications exist. This book gives you a good overview of the range of hypnotherapy possibilities.

Hypnotherapy is a way of solving personal problems through reaching a deeply relaxed state of mind called *trance*.

Induction

Induction is the technique used to establish a trance state, usually by fixating your eyes onto something, and counting down from ten to one and becoming more relaxed.

Trance

Trance is a state of mind that involves a selective focus of attention. You are in trance-like states naturally several times throughout the day, such as when you are fully involved in reading a book. Trance-like states are often associated with states of relaxation. Hypnotherapy uses the trance state to access the powerful forces of your own subconscious to make the changes you want.

Post-hypnotic suggestion

This is a suggestion given in trance, for you to make something happen when you are not in trance. Your mind is reprogrammed to respond in a healthier way to something.

Copyright © 2006 John Wiley & Sons, Ltd.
All rights reserved.
Item 1930-1.
For more information about John Wiley & Sons, call (+44) 1243 779777.

For Dummies: Bestselling Book Series for Beginners

Hypnotherapy For Dummies®

Cheat Sheet

What Happens in a Hypnotherapy Session?

Briefly, here are the steps involved in a typical hypnotherapy session. However, bear in mind that a 'typical' session varies widely depending on both the hypnotherapist and the patient.

1. You get acquainted with your hypnotherapist.
2. Your hypnotherapist gathers information about you (mainly completed in the initial session).
3. Trance is induced.
4. Trance is deepened.
5. The actual therapy takes place.
6. You're given post-hypnotic suggestions.
7. You're given feel-good suggestions.
8. You emerge from hypnosis.
9. You're given homework to help reinforce the therapy in between sessions.

Turn to Chapter 13 for a complete run-down of a hypnotherapy session.

Simple Steps to Self-Hypnosis

Serious problems are best dealt with in conjunction with a professional, clinical hypnotherapist, but self-hypnosis is useful for boosting your confidence, encouraging yourself towards a healthier lifestyle, and improving your performance. The basic steps of self-hypnosis are

1. Think about what you want to achieve or change, and state your goal in a single sentence.
2. Choose a place where you can be completely comfortable, whether sitting in a chair or lying down.
3. Set a time limit by mentally giving yourself the following suggestion: 'Exactly ten minutes from now, my eyelids open automatically and I feel calm, rested, and refreshed.'
4. Close your eyes and take a few deep breaths. Progressively relax all your muscles, from head to toe, or toe to head, whichever you prefer.
5. Count down from ten to one and tell yourself that with each number you'll become more relaxed, both physically and mentally, and go deeper into trance.
6. When you're in a deepened trance state, start using the goal statement you devised for your self-hypnosis session. Remember your single sentence goal statement, and make it as vivid as possible in your imagination. Then simply let go. Trust that you have handed it over to your unconscious mind, and that this wise part of you will now solve the problem.
7. Count yourself awake, up from one to ten, and tell yourself that you're no longer in trance.
8. A few minutes after awakening from self-hypnosis, you are still in a highly suggestible state. Use that time to reinforce how relaxed and calm you feel, and how pleased you are that your unconscious mind is helping you reach your goal.

Chapter 14 covers the process of self-hypnosis.

For Dummies: Bestselling Book Series for Beginners

Hypnotherapy
FOR
DUMMIES®

Hypnotherapy FOR DUMMIES®

by Mike Bryant and Peter Mabbutt

JOHN WILEY & SONS, LTD

Hypnotherapy For Dummies®
Published by
John Wiley & Sons, Ltd
The Atrium
Southern Gate
Chichester
West Sussex
PO19 8SQ
England

E-mail (for orders and customer service enquires): cs-books@wiley.co.uk

Visit our Home Page on www.wileyeurope.com

Wiley also publishes its books in a variety of electronic formats. Some content that appears in print may not be available in electronic books.

British Library Cataloguing in Publication Data: A catalogue record for this book is available from the British Library.

ISBN-13: 978-0-470-01930-6 (P/B)

Printed and bound in Great Britain by Bell and Bain Ltd, Glasgow

10 9 8 7 6 5 4 3 2

WILEY

About the Authors

Mike Bryant is an African-American who has lived in England since 1984.

Mike is a qualified psychiatric social worker, counsellor, and hypnotherapist and has also worked as an information technology and project manager.

With extensive experience in both America and the United Kingdom, Mike has established a range of innovative mental health schemes in London as well as having provided senior service development consultancy to NHS Mental Health Trusts across England, Ireland, Scotland, and Wales as a Senior Consultant with the Sainsbury Centre for Mental Health (SCMH). While at SCMH, he published a range of papers and reports on mental health issues.

Mike currently lives in London with his wife and family and has a private practice as a counsellor and as hypnotherapist. You can find more information about Mike's practice at www.londonhypno.com.

Peter Mabbutt is Director of Studies at the London College of Clinical Hypnosis (LCCH) and lectures throughout the UK and overseas to both lay students and medical practitioners. He is responsible for the development of the LCCH's core courses and with his colleagues has introduced many new techniques and subjects to the curriculum, ensuring that it continues to meet the needs of the modern-day hypnotherapist.

With a background in psychopharmacology Peter co-authored a range of papers on tranquilisers, anxiety, and learning and memory before training with the LCCH to become a hypnotherapist. Peter has a specialist interest in the mind-body connection, weight control, the treatment of trauma, and hypertension.

Authors' Acknowledgements

From Mike Bryant: I would like to dedicate this book to my family: My lovely wife Toni, and my gorgeous daughters Jodie and Jessie. Jodie, sorry I couldn't use your working title of *Daddy's Wicked Hypnotherapy Book*. Maybe next time.

A big thanks goes to my parents, and my brother and sister from Indianapolis. Howdy.

Michael Joseph: Thank you for creating some of the best hypnotherapy training in Europe – the London College of Clinical Hypnosis. A big appreciation to my teachers and colleagues there at the LCCH.

I would also like to express my deep appreciation to all of the people who have come to me for hypnotherapy. They have also been my teachers and I owe them a great deal in my development as a clinician, trainer, and author.

Peter: Thanks much for taking on this book with me. Running an international training college (LCCH), I know that wasn't easy! Thank you for providing your expertise and humour to this book. Thanks for also getting me hooked on the BBC's "Dr. Who" - it is indeed fab. But moreover, thanks for being my teacher, supervisor, and friend.

From Peter Mabbutt: This book is dedicated to my parents, Christine and Charles. Though sadly no longer with us, they always encouraged my dreams. Hey mum and dad, I realised another one! To my sister Nadine and her family, ¡Hola! And to the rest of my family a big thank you and hello too.

Thank you Michael Joseph, Principal of the London College of Clinical Hypnosis (LCCH), for guiding me along a path that consistently proves to be exciting and fun and for the many groan-worthy jokes that punctuate the day when you are in the office. On top of this I would also like to say a very special thank you to all my colleagues at the LCCH for their support in all things hypnosis and beyond. We make a great team! To all my hypnotherapy students past, present and future; you may think I'm teaching you, but there is a lot that you teach me. Tom Connelly of the British Society of Clinical Hypnosis, many thanks for searching out those niggling snippets of information for Mike and I.

There can be no replacement for good teaching and good teachers (thanks again LCCH) but the icing on the cake comes when you are out in the field, and with this in mind I extend another set of thanks to all my patients from whom I have learned and continue to learn so much about the wonderful world of humanity.

Mike, a big thanks for bringing me on board this project. It was great fun and you are a joy to work with. Here's to the next one!

To all my friends out there who have been patient with my absence whilst writing this book: I'm free again and the drinks are on you!

To my 'other' family: Sandra, Gerald, and Andrea Winston, thank you for welcoming me in and letting me share in the laughter.

And Elijah (kiddo!) and Dalya (princess!) Winston: Howzit dolls? The laughter you bring is all the therapy I need.

And finally the biggest thank you of all to my partner Steven Winston for your love, enthusiasm, encouragement, support, humour, nags, and glasses of wine. The boy done good!

Publisher's Acknowledgements

We're proud of this book; please send us your comments through our Dummies online registration form located at www.dummies.com/register/.

Some of the people who helped bring this book to market include the following:

Acquisitions, Editorial, and Media Development

Project Editor: Rachael Chilvers

Content Editor: Steve Edwards

Commissioning Editor: Samantha Clapp

Development Editor: Kathleen Dobie

Copy Editor: Martin Key

Technical Editor: Elyse Kassis

Executive Editor: Jason Dunne

Executive Project Editor: Martin Tribe

Special Help: Jennifer Bingham

Cover Photo: © Corbis

Cartoons: Rich Tennant, www.the5thwave.com

Composition

Project Coordinator: Jennifer Theriot

Layout and Graphics: Claudia Bell, Stephanie D. Jumper, Barry Offringa, Heather Ryan

Proofreaders: Laura Albert, Lesley Green, Brian H. Walls

Indexer: Techbooks

Publishing and Editorial for Consumer Dummies

Diane Graves Steele, Vice President and Publisher, Consumer Dummies

Joyce Pepple, Acquisitions Director, Consumer Dummies

Kristin A. Cocks, Product Development Director, Consumer Dummies

Michael Spring, Vice President and Publisher, Travel

Kelly Regan, Editorial Director, Travel

Publishing for Technology Dummies

Andy Cummings, Vice President and Publisher, Dummies Technology/General User

Composition Services

Gerry Fahey, Vice President of Production Services

Debbie Stailey, Director of Composition Services

Contents at a Glance

Table of Contents

Introduction

*H*ypnosis is a subject everyone has an opinion about, but few people have ever directly experienced. Hypnotherapy, on the other hand, is a topic that leaves many people baffled or completely blank. So what exactly *is* the difference between hypnosis and hypnotherapy? That's one of questions this book answers.

An important point to understand is that hypnosis and hypnotherapy are not the same thing. Hypnosis has been around since humans began to speak and involves going into a trance. Hypnotherapy uses the hypnotic trance to help you achieve a goal, or create a positive change in your thinking, to help solve a problem. Whereas hypnosis is centuries old, hypnotherapy, like other talking therapies, is a relatively recent practice.

This book helps you understand how hypnosis works. It also discusses the various problems and symptoms hypnotherapy can effectively treat, and shows you how you can put hypnotherapy to use for you.

About This Book

Hypnotherapy For Dummies helps you understand hypnosis on both a theoretical and a practical basis. Both are useful depending on your interests. You can, for example, use this book simply to find out about hypnosis. You may stop at this level and just be clearer about how hypnotherapists work with their clients.

Or, you may be interested in finding a hypnotherapist to work on problems, or to help you succeed in achieving your goals. If you don't know what sort of things a hypnotherapist can help with, you will be an expert after you read this book!

Hypnotherapy can help people to overcome a surprisingly wide range of habits, emotional problems, and phobias. It can also dramatically improve performance for students taking exams, athletes wanting to improve their game, and creative artists wishing to deepen their abilities.

In many ways hypnotherapy is like counselling, but it is a different approach and much more rapid in producing changes. Hypnotherapists frequently remove phobias within four to six sessions. There is also a body of evidence demonstrating that hypnotherapy is the most effective way to help people stop smoking.

Most people only know about hypnosis from stage hypnotists and movies, which often portray a negative image. This book explores the different ways in which hypnotherapy helps people overcome their problems and achieve their goals.

Conventions Used in This Book

To help you navigate through this book, we set up a few conventions:

- *Italics* are used for emphasis and to highlight new words, or define terms.
- **Boldfaced** text indicates the key concept in a list.
- `Monofont` is used for Web and e-mail addresses.

Sometimes we (the authors, Mike and Peter) use the pronoun 'we' to signify both of us or 'I' followed by '(Mike)' or '(Peter)', depending who the author writing that particular paragraph is.

Also, when speaking generally we use the female pronoun 'she' in even-numbered chapters and the male 'he' in odd-numbered chapters, just to be fair to both genders!

Foolish Assumptions

We assume you picked up *Hypnotherapy For Dummies* for one of the following reasons:

- **You have a general interest in self-improvement techniques.** You're looking for ways to become more the sort of person you'd like to be.

- **You want to break a habit.** You know that hypnotherapy has a good track record with helping people overcome phobias, smoking, eating problems, and other unwanted habits and you have a habit you want to lose.

- **You're curious about various techniques such as psychotherapy, Neuro-linguistic Programming, counselling, and hypnotherapy.** You think that it may all just be psychobabble and want to know what really helps.

  This book tells you about the therapies most closely related to hypnotherapy, how they differ and what they have in common.

✔ **You want tips on choosing the right hypnotherapist.** Chapter 12 is devoted to helping you find a qualified hypnotherapist.

✔ **You're interested in becoming a hypnotherapist.** This book is the equivalent of an introductory course in hypnotherapy so after reading it, you may be interested in learning first-hand. If that's the case, Chapter 19 shares tips on training as a hypnotherapist.

✔ **You're just browsing.** 'Oh, is this a book about hypnosis? I thought this was *Cleaning and Stain Removal For Dummies*!' Sorry, wrong book.

Why You Need This Book

As the authors of this book we, Mike and Peter, are both practising hypnotherapists. *Hypnotherapy For Dummies* emphasises the importance of working with a hypnotherapist to achieve your goals. Developing a working relationship with your hypnotherapist is the key to achieving a positive outcome. We think that this is a significant difference to many introductory books on hypnotherapy. Many of those currently available fall into two main types:

✔ **Specific interest books** aimed at anyone interested in solving a particular problem. These books focus on a single issue, such as the application of hypnosis to achieve weight control, decrease anxiety, develop confidence, or to stop smoking, and so on.

✔ **Scripts books** aimed at teaching a DIY (do-it-yourself) approach to hypnosis. *Scripts* are the phrases hypnotherapists use to conduct therapy, once someone is in trance. These types of books offer techniques you can use to hypnotise yourself or others.

In our opinion, this DIY approach cannot approach the level of trance or range of techniques that a good hypnotherapist can provide. We have seen many clients in our practice who have had nil, or negative results, from amateur hypnosis learned from books alone. A qualified hypnotherapist has a variety of techniques to choose from, and selects the technique uniquely suited to relieving your symptom efficiently and effectively.

We think you need this book, because unlike specific interest books, this book takes a broad overview of the theory and practice of hypnotherapy, examining a wide range of the most common hypnotherapy treatments and looking at these in detail.

And unlike script books, our approach recommends self-hypnosis *after* you've experienced a few sessions with a qualified hypnotherapist. Postponing self-hypnosis lets you understand the depth of trance properly before you try it on yourself. A good hypnotherapist can address your specific needs more directly than a generic script gained from a book or an audiotape. Afterwards, you can approach self-hypnosis with the experience of deep trance.

In short, you need this book to ensure that your hypnotherapy experience is profoundly successful and positive!

How This Book Is Organised

The great thing about *For Dummies* books is that you don't have to read them all the way through. You can simply turn to the bit you're interested in and start at any point within a chapter, within a section, or even just go directly to a paragraph that interests you.

We divided the book into five parts, with each broken into chapters. The Table of Contents and the Index help you pinpoint information within the outline explained in the next sections.

Part 1: Understanding Hypnotherapy

This section defines the terms used in hypnotherapy and what hypnosis can do for you. Here we also explain what hypnotic trance is and what it feels like.

We also describe the techniques a hypnotherapist has to choose from and exactly what you can expect to happen in a typical session. This knowledge lets you know how to set clear and realistic goals for your own hypnotherapy.

We provide practical and useful information to help you make hypnotherapy work best for you.

Part II: Considering How Hypnotherapy Can Help

Ever wondered how hypnotherapy affects the mind and the body? The chapters in this part describe how hypnotherapy can help you overcome unwanted habits and increase your feel-good factor.

We're not pretending to be magicians, but hypnotherapy can help with an impressive range of physical problems. But, just in case you think that hypnotherapy is a cure-all, we devote a chapter to letting you know what it can't accomplish.

Part III: Expanding the Reach of Hypnotherapy

This part focuses on the lesser known applications of hypnotherapy. You may be surprised to know that children are natural hypnotic subjects. The techniques involved in working with children are described here.

Hypnotherapy is also used to work with past-life regression. Whether or not you believe in past lives, this area can still be very powerful in uncovering unconscious themes in how you live now.

We also describe in detail how phobias can be removed through hypnotherapy.

Part IV: The Practical Stuff

This is the part of the book that can help you choose the right hypnotherapist or practice self-hypnosis.

Chapter 13 walks you through your initial session, telling you what to expect and how to prepare – don't worry, it's as easy as closing your eyes! And Chapter 15 introduces you to some of the other therapies you may come across, as you explore the world of hypnotherapy.

Part V: The Part of Tens

You can think of this part of the book as a 'Frequently Asked Questions' section. So you may want to start with these chapters to debunk common myths about hypnotherapy, survey the pioneers who made significant contributions to the field, discover the characteristics of a good hypnotherapist, or find out how to train to become a hypnotherapist yourself.

Appendix

Here we include some very useful books and Internet resources for hypnotherapy training courses and organisations – plus a sample Code of Ethics from the British Society of Clinical Hypnosis.

Icons Used in This Book

This book won't throw lots of questions at you, but it should certainly set you thinking. These icons highlight some of the points you may be thinking about.

Here you'll find anecdotes and examples to illustrate certain concepts, or true life stories we want to share with you.

This icon highlights hypnosis or hypnotherapy terms, or language, which may be unfamiliar to you.

The text next to this icon tries to correct possible wrong thinking or misconceptions.

This icon draws your attention to an important point to bear in mind.

When you see this icon we're trying to emphasise a bit of information that may be useful to you later on.

This icon is saying 'watch out!' This is something to be very aware of regarding the subject you're reading.

Where to Go from Here

You don't have to read this book from beginning to end. Each chapter of the book can be approached individually, depending on your interest. Have a look at the Table of Contents and jump right into any chapter that appeals to you.

If, for example, you wanted to know how hypnotherapy can help break habits like smoking, you could start reading this book by going straight to Chapter 5. On the other hand, if your interest is to understand how a hypnotherapist can help remove your phobias, then Chapter 11 is an excellent starting place.

The most important part is, that after reading this book, you're in an informed position to begin doing the work with a hypnotherapist, and can walk into your very first session with a great deal of confidence and certainty of success.

Good luck to you, and we wish you the best in finding the answers you're looking for.

Part I
Understanding Hypnotherapy

In this part . . .

You find some helpful background information in this part to help you to understand how hypnotherapy works. This part also looks at the terms used in hypnotherapy, the basics of how it works, and what hypnotherapy is used for. You even find a very brief history of hypnosis and hypnotherapy included in this part.

If you want to know exactly what a hypnotherapist does, we describe the techniques and procedures used in a typical hypnotherapy session. In other words, this part is a great place to start if you're new to hypnotherapy.

Chapter 1

Examining Hypnotherapy

. . . .

In This Chapter

▶ Understanding the terms

▶ Realising the evolution of hypnosis

▶ Looking to hypnosis for help

▶ Distinguishing the therapeutic aspects

. . . .

*H*ypnosis is a powerful technique. It can help you change negative beliefs and achieve your goals, treat serious emotional problems, and alleviate a range of medical conditions.

You may hear about a work colleague who was cured of smoking in a single session, or a friend of a friend whose lifelong phobia was permanently removed by a hypnotherapist. A hypnotherapist can also show you how to practise self-hypnosis in order to achieve a seemingly infinite variety of personal goals.

This chapter explains what hypnosis and hypnotherapy are about. It gives you a clear understanding of what is involved, the difference between hypnosis and hypnotherapy, and some of the amazing benefits possible.

Getting to Grips with the Basics of Hypnotherapy

First things first. We want to reassure you right up front that hypnosis is safe.

Being hypnotised is not dissimilar to being sleepy or in a daydream. And, as we explain in the 'Sliding into trance' subsection, you've been in a trance probably every day of your life; hypnotherapy is simply a method of putting your trance state to work solving your problems.

When you're in a hypnotic trance, you are completely aware of the words being spoken to you by the hypnotherapist. And, should a fire alarm go off – or any other physically threatening situation arise – you will immediately take yourself out of trance to respond.

Hypnosis carries an element of risk as do all therapies and activities. But, as long as your hypnotherapist is properly qualified, and operates within a professional code of conduct and ethics (which we discuss in Chapter 12), you needn't worry.

In the following subsections, we sort out the jargon and the basic terms used in hypnotherapy.

Discovering the differences between hypnosis and hypnotherapy

The first useful thing to distinguish is the difference between hypnosis and hypnotherapy. We really want you to understand that there is a big difference between the act of hypnotising someone (hypnosis) and the amazing changes that can happen with the help of a qualified hypnotherapist (hypnotherapy). We hope that after you read this section you will never confuse a stage hypnotist (the person you see getting laughs on TV) with a hypnotherapist (the person who helps you stop smoking, lose weight, or recover from a life-long phobia).

✔ **Hypnosis** is a state of mind connected to deep relaxation, narrowed focus, and increased suggestibility. Hypnosis is an intermediate state between sleep and wakefulness.

Hypnosis can be likened to the state you are in when you act intuitively instead of intellectually. During hypnosis, you basically ask your inner drill sergeant to take a break while your clever, artistic self comes forward. And believe us, everybody has both aspects within them!

✔ **Hypnotherapy** is hypnosis used for therapeutic purposes. Hypnotherapy applies the technique of hypnosis to encourage your unconscious mind to find solutions to problems.

Hypnosis is a state of consciousness. Hypnotherapy is a therapy. Hypnosis itself is not therapy. The therapy part of a hypnotherapy session occurs after hypnosis has been used to induce your trance. Then the hypnotherapist makes suggestions that help your unconscious mind achieve your goals or remove your problems. Just as there are many avenues to hypnosis, including self-hypnosis and self-induced trances (see the next section), there are many different hypnotherapy techniques and applications. (Chapter 2 talks about the range of hypnotherapy tools.)

Stage hypnosis is not hypnotherapy

Stage hypnosis is a form of entertainment. It is not a way to receive help for your problems or to achieve your aspirations. We do not recommend that you become personally involved in stage hypnosis as there is no personal care for your individual needs. It's a stage act where the main aim is to get laughs – at your expense if you get on stage!

Many, many people get involved in stage hypnosis with no bad after-effects. However, some former stage participants have suffered emotional problems afterwards. This is an area of great debate as to whether these people were already predisposed to emotional problems, or if stage hypnosis had a negative influence.

An interesting book that involves a critical look at stage hypnosis is *Investigating Stage Hypnosis* by Tracie O'Keefe and Katrina Fox (Extraordinary People Press).

Sliding into trance

Trance is a state of mind that involves a selective focus of attention. You are in a natural trance state several times each day, usually when you're relaxing.

Examples of times you may slip into a trance include:

- ✔ Being fully involved in reading a book
- ✔ Going window shopping at your favourite stores
- ✔ Becoming anxious or fearful about an upcoming event
- ✔ Playing with an imaginary friend as a child
- ✔ Zoning out while exercising
- ✔ Fantasising about an old love interest

Trance states occur naturally and regularly. Hypnosis utilises these states to access your unconscious mind (see the next section) in order to help you more easily achieve your goal or solve your problem.

The following are the main trance states, and some of the traits a hypnotised person may experience while in each state, listed from light to deep levels:

- ✔ **Light trance:** Eyes closed, relaxed face muscles, deepened breathing.
- ✔ **Medium trance:** Head and body slump, reduced awareness of surroundings, slower responses, deepening of light trance state.
- ✔ **Deep trance:** Deepening of medium trance state, deeper abdominal breathing.

✓ **Somnambulism:** A very rare trance state in which a hypnotised person may experience sensations as if awake. Commonly known as sleepwalking, this is a very rare condition. This state is counterproductive in hypnosis because the person is in too deep a state to retain the hypnotherapy suggestions in either their conscious or unconscious memory!

At increasingly deeper levels of trance, you become more open to your unconscious mind and more receptive to hypnotic suggestions from the hypnotherapist. We discuss the importance of these therapeutic hypnotic suggestions throughout this book.

Examining states of mind

Conscious and unconscious are terms that describe aspects of your mind. Though impossible to prove as a reality, these concepts are widely accepted in the Western world. The *conscious* mind thinks quantitatively using words, numbers, and logical and sequential thinking. The *unconscious* mind, on the other hand, uses images, memories, feelings, intuition, dreams, and abstract, non-sequential thinking.

If you think of your mind as a spectrum, at one end of the spectrum is the super-alert state you're in when you're frightened or excited. At the other end of the spectrum is deep sleep. Figure 1-1 shows the spectrum of consciousness, from the unconscious to conscious states. In the middle of this consciousness spectrum is everyday alert states of mind, in which you're relatively focused on what you are doing. The left of this point, towards the unconscious end, represents an everyday trance state, such as daydreaming.

Interestingly, the word 'hypnosis' comes from Hypnos, the Greek god of sleep. So perhaps the *extreme* left end of the spectrum would be coma, but we're trying to be uplifting here!

Figure 1-1:
The spectrum of consciousness.

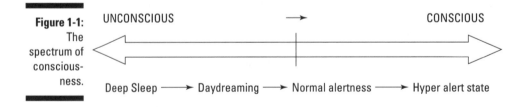

In this admittedly superficial model of human consciousness, the unconscious mind resides somewhere between daydreaming and deep sleep. Conversely, consciousness resides at all points to the right of the midway point.

A brief history of hypnosis

Hypnosis isn't a modern concept, it has been around for a long time. Egyptian hieroglyphics exist depicting the locals experiencing hypnosis as part of religious rituals. Many early practices of hypnosis were linked with a belief in religion, magic, and the occult. These rituals often involved a cure of some illness during what was mistakenly presumed to be sleep. (It was actually a hypnotic trance.) Egyptian priests would hypnotise people to treat illnesses using hypnotic suggestions.

Similarly, in classical Greece, worshippers went to temples to invoke Hypnos, the god of sleep, who brought them healing and prophetic dreams. It is well documented that people would come to sleep in the Temple of Aesculapius, the Greek god of medicine, while priests would speak to them while sleeping, offering suggestions for healing.

Actually, it's impossible to say where hypnosis came from. From the time that mankind developed speech there has probably been some sort of practice where one person expressed words that induced a trance state, in order to alter everyday awareness. Many early cultures have evidence of eliciting hypnotic phenomena for both spiritual and healing purposes.

A modern day equivalent of hypnotic phenomena, such as trance, is seen in religious 'tent revivals', where hands are laid on and people are felt to be 'healed'. However, this is not the type of hypnosis that this book focuses on!

The history of hypnosis is a fascinating subject. If you read about hypnosis over the centuries, different cultures view it differently. It often had a reputation of dubiousness, and/or power, associated with it. The main reason for this reputation is because, until the nineteenth century, the concept of the unconscious was unknown and hypnosis may have seemed like a religious, or possibly supernatural, practice. If you really want to go into the details of the history of hypnosis, one of the finest books on the subject is *Hidden Depths: The Story of Hypnosis* by Robin Waterfield (Pan Books).

No doubt this very simple model will have many scientists in dismay but, if nothing else, it should help you to understand one important thing: that consciousness and unconsciousness are two sides of the same coin. There isn't an either/or aspect to it, but only shades of grey.

Table 1-1 gives you another way to understand the differences between the conscious and unconscious mind.

Table 1-1	Traits of the Conscious and Unconscious Mind
Conscious Mind	*Unconscious Mind*
Logical	Intuitive
Sequential thoughts	Random thoughts

(continued)

Table 1-1 *(continued)*	
Conscious Mind	*Unconscious Mind*
Easily accesses short-term and some long-term memories	Can access most lived memories and experiences since childhood
Uses words/numbers	Uses images/feelings
Analytical	Creative

So, although you may think that your conscious mind is in control most of the time, your hypnotherapist accesses your unconscious mind in order to help you to change your negative thinking, or solve your problems.

Why access the unconscious mind? Because, although your conscious mind is excellent at logical, sequential, and analytical thinking, it can also be quite fixed. Your conscious mind may also develop unhelpful defences in its attempt to protect itself. The unconscious mind is a more flexible friend, and can easily change old habits and defences maintained by your conscious mind.

Getting Past that Old-Style Hypnosis

You've probably seen examples of old-fashioned hypnosis in the movies. The scene usually portrays the hypnotist as a slightly overbearing authority figure and the patient as an unquestioning, sheepish character, totally powerless to resist the hypnotist's commands. The way the hypnotist induces trance is totally graceless and very dominating. He (and it was always a 'he') commands: 'YOUR EYES ARE GETTING HEAVY, YOU WILL GO TO SLEEEEEP . . .' Very boorish indeed!

Although a rather extreme caricature, this scenario is not a million miles away from how old-style hypnotherapists used to operate. But as the times changed, so has the way that hypnotherapists work. Today, medics and professionals are no longer revered for their unattainable knowledge. Most people have access to medical information if they want it. Back then, professionals put themselves above the common, non medical person. And historically, many – though not all – hypnotherapists were physicians or psychiatrists. Hypnotherapy training today is no longer exclusively the domain of the medical profession and a wider, rich range of professions are involved in its practice.

Some common attributes of what we call old-style hypnosis involved:

- ✔ An authoritarian approach and presentation to the patient.
- ✔ The hypnotherapist commanding the patient into trance.
- ✔ A very monotone, artless, repetitive approach to trance induction.
- ✔ The absence of a therapeutic relationship between therapist and patient.
- ✔ A doctor-knows-best approach to treatment. No negotiation.

In essence, the old-style approach was: 'Do as you're told.' Today, people don't accept this type of behaviour from a professional from whom they're seeking help. People expect to have a dialogue, ask questions, and be treated with respect. So clearly, the old style – essentially an authoritarian style – had to be modified.

Understanding the way hypnotists *used* to work is helpful in understanding how modern methods of hypnotherapy thinking and practice developed.

Milton Erickson, a US psychiatrist who started practising hypnotherapy in the early 1900s, helped modernise the field. He developed a variety of new techniques, as well as a more relaxed approach called the *permissive hypnosis style*, traits of which include:

- ✔ Greater respect, gentleness, and support for the patient.
- ✔ Use of any aspect of a patient's beliefs and language to induce trance.
- ✔ Empowering the patient's unconscious mind to find its own solution.
- ✔ The use of metaphor. Erickson developed the ability to improvise story-telling relevant to a patient's life, interests, and/or problem to help the patient's unconscious mind search for its own solution.

It is difficult to convey Erickson's widespread influence. No other single hypnotherapist to date has influenced current hypnotherapy practice as much as Erickson. Not only did Erickson write prolifically about his techniques, but also other hypnotherapists have written prolifically about Erickson, and have even analysed his style of working with patients to create new forms of therapies. (See Chapter 15 for information on cousins of hypnotherapy, especially Neuro-linguistic Programming.)

Finding Help with Hypnosis

Hypnotherapy can help you cope with a wide range of issues, including:

- Increasing confidence
- Breaking bad habits such as smoking, nail-biting, bed-wetting, and so on
- Removing phobias
- Managing pain
- Enhancing performance in artistic, academic, and athletic fields
- Controlling weight and improving eating habits
- Correcting eating disorders
- Curtailing excessive alcohol use

This is just a brief overview of some of the most common hypnotherapy treatment areas. If you're curious about a problem not listed here, speaking to a hypnotherapist can certainly clarify whether the issue you're concerned about is one that hypnotherapy can address. The Appendix offers help in finding an organisation or hypnotherapist to help you.

Understanding the Therapy Part of Hypnotherapy

We write enthusiastically about the potentials for change that hypnotherapy can provide. If you have never experienced hypnotherapy, it's probably a bit difficult to understand how these changes happen when you're in trance, with your eyes closed and in a daydream-like state. Fair enough!

In order to explain how therapy occurs while you're in trance, remember this: during hypnosis your body is relaxed, but your thoughts become very attentive. You are able to focus at an enhanced level when you are in a hypnotherapy session. And what you are focusing on is the therapist's suggestions. This is where the therapy part begins. If your issue is to avoid sweet, fattening foods, the therapist gives your unconscious mind specific suggestions on how to do this very easily. If you are coming to hypnosis to stop smoking, the hypnotherapist gives you suggestions to remove your associations with smoking, so that you no longer have any desire to smoke and no longer consider yourself to be a smoker! Jump to Chapter 13 for a detailed account of what happens during a hypnotherapy session

Hypnosis plus counselling

Hypnotherapists often employ techniques and skills from a wide variety of counselling methods. These skills begin with listening well, in order to accurately understand what you want from the hypnotherapy. Being empathetic, whilst forming a working relationship with the patient, is a skill hypnotherapists have developed since the old days of authoritarian style hypnosis.

There is a huge range of counselling methods, and hypnotherapists may have different theoretical starting points. So do not expect a hypnotherapist to use a specific counselling method. A qualified hypnotherapist should be at least a good listener, and someone who helps you feel confident about the hypnotherapy work the two of you are involved in.

Hypnosis plus psychotherapy

Psychotherapy does not usually focus on a single problem and is about exploring feelings. Psychotherapy does not start with a concept of how many sessions will be required, and places no limits on the number of sessions needed. Hypnotherapists tend to work in a limited number of sessions – usually less than half a dozen – unless additional problem issues arise.

However, the techniques of psychotherapy are sometimes used by hypnotherapists who particularly need to go into past personal history issues. Saying that, most hypnotherapists are very here-and-now orientated and unlike psychotherapists, don't generally spend time talking about your childhood. However, this depends on the problem being brought to the hypnotherapist.

Chapter 2

Techniques: The Tools of a Hypnotherapist

....

....

*Y*our mind is like a complex network of pipes, with each pipe having its own function and route. Some pipes are interconnected, and some pipes run on their own; some pipes are very small, and some pipes are extremely well hidden. In order for the network to run efficiently, all these pipes need to be kept in good working order; occasionally polished, or repaired, or even replaced. Most of the time, you can take care of your own plumbing, ensuring that it flows freely, by giving it a bit of a clean every now and then. Sometimes though, something happens that is beyond your ability to cope, and you need to call in a plumber to prevent the network from collapsing.

Think of your hypnotherapist as that plumber. The hypnotherapist's job is to ensure that your psychological pipework is flowing well, by cleaning and unblocking the pipes; sometimes replacing pipes that have been worn away, or repairing those that are leaking. It may be necessary for the hypnotherapist to go on a search to find a hidden and elusive pipe that is proving to be irksome. You may find that your hypnotherapist has to look at old plans of the pipework with you; or perhaps help you plan a new way to run those pipes. Whatever the job, your hypnotherapist is there to help you return the network to normal or even improve it in some way or other. In order to do this properly, just like any plumber, your hypnotherapist uses an impressive array of tools.

All the techniques we talk about in this chapter comprise only some of the tools available in your hypnotherapist's toolbox. Your hypnotherapist may use some of these tools and not use others. More than likely, you'll find your hypnotherapist using a combination throughout the time you are in therapy, in order to help you achieve your outcome.

Choosing a Tool from the Hypnotherapist's Toolbox

When you visit a hypnotherapist, you're visiting someone trained to carry out a specific job – a skilled craftswoman as it were. And like every skilled craftswoman, your therapist has a range of tools that allows her to efficiently complete any job. The hypnotherapist has tools to take your case history, tools to take you into a trance state, tools to take you deeper into the trance (see Chapter 4 for more on these), and tools to do the therapy itself.

Whatever the job at hand may be, your hypnotherapist selects the appropriate tool for the job. And, as a skilled professional, she must have a full toolbox of techniques from which to choose. After all, you would never employ a plumber who turned up with only a spanner in her toolbox would you?

A plumber has an idea of the job she's about to undertake when she turns up on your doorstep. However, until she actually looks at the pipework, she can't fully assess what tools are required. It's much the same with hypnotherapy. When you book your first appointment, you inevitably let the therapist know why you're coming for therapy. However, your hypnotherapist probably won't decide which techniques to use with you until she meets you.

In fact, many factors determine which techniques the hypnotherapist decides to use, including

- ✔ **Your specific symptom:** Certain techniques have proved to be very effective in dealing with certain symptoms.

- ✔ **Your goals for therapy:** Perhaps you want to know why your symptom started in the first place, or perhaps you don't care about that and simply want it to go away. What you want determines whether your therapist uses techniques that help you explore your past, or works in a goal-directed manner, aimed at moving you towards a healthier future.

- ✔ **Your personal history:** It may seem strange, but your career, hobbies, likes, and dislikes can give clues as to the right technique to use. For example, if you enjoy gardening, your therapist may use metaphors about gardening to help you dig up your problem and plant the healthy seeds of a solution. However, if you suffer from hay fever, your hypnotherapist will avoid using the allergy as a metaphor, so that you don't end up with streaming eyes, sneezing your way through your session!

✔ **Your therapeutic history and personal preferences:** Perhaps you've seen a hypnotherapist before who used a technique you found particularly effective. In this case, let your therapist know. She may be able to use it again to help you overcome your current problem. On the other hand, you may have experienced a technique you hated, or you may have concerns about a technique such as regression, and don't want to use that approach. Again, let your therapist know so that she can avoid using this with you. After all, she doesn't want to put you off your therapy!

✔ **Your belief system:** Perhaps you believe that your current problem stems from something that occurred to you in a past life, in which case your therapist will consider using a past-life regression technique (see Chapter 10 for more on this method). On the other hand, if you strongly believe you haven't lived before, there's little point in taking you down this route.

✔ **Your hypnotherapist's personal preference:** All therapists have techniques they favour. The method your hypnotherapist chooses may simply boil down to the fact that she likes a specific technique, is skilled at using it, and knows it works.

✔ **Your hypnotherapist's training:** As with the majority of psychotherapy disciplines, hypnotherapy offers a variety of training approaches. For example, your therapist may have been trained in the analytical approach, in which uncovering reasons for the development of a symptom is an integral part of resolving it. Or her training may be in the solution-focused approach, in which therapy is focused on resolving a symptom with little or no reference to the past. Or perhaps she uses an eclectic approach (probably the most popular today) that incorporates a variety of systems.

The techniques your hypnotherapist uses may vary throughout your sessions as you work on different aspects of your problem. Even though changing a washer in a tap is a relatively straightforward job for a plumber, they may use several tools to complete this task. The same goes for hypnotherapy. No matter how hard or simple the job is, you may need to use several tools.

Ultimately, your hypnotherapist wants to choose a technique that's right for you. If you want her to use a particular technique but she's negotiating to use another, she will have a good reason for her preference. Be prepared to discuss the matter with her and at the same time allow her to explain the reasoning behind her decision.

Giving It to You Straight and Not So Straight: Direct and Indirect Suggestions

Perhaps the earliest tool created for the hypnotherapist's toolbox is the use of suggestion. In hypnotherapy terms, a *suggestion* is a statement given in trance that something will happen. For example, your hypnotherapist may suggest that your hand is beginning to lose all sensation and become completely numb; or she may suggest that you feel completely relaxed as you think about walking across a bridge.

Simply put, a suggestion is the tool that helps you reprogramme your mind to respond in a healthier way to something. As we write this book, a very pertinent analogy springs to mind: We write what we think is best and submit it to our editors. They may then suggest that such-and-such a paragraph would sound better if it were written in such-and-such a way. We listen to their suggestions, and if we feel that this is sensible and safe, we make the appropriate changes. If we don't agree with what they suggest, we can reject the changes; after all, it's our book, and we're in control. In a similar way, you can view your hypnotherapist as being the editor of your mind. She's there to make suggestions to the way you write paragraphs of your life. You can choose to accept her suggestions, or to reject them if you want; after all, it's your mind and *you* are always in control.

A *post-hypnotic suggestion* is a suggestion given in trance, for you to make something happen when you are not in trance.

Someone who has a problem bingeing on chocolate may be given the post-hypnotic suggestion that they enjoy a sense of self-control whenever they see chocolate, and choose not to eat it.

Like every other discipline in psychotherapy, hypnotherapy has developed over the years. As it has done so, the techniques it uses have developed too. This becomes very obvious in looking at the use of suggestions. Originally suggestions were given in a very direct manner, sometimes called *authoritarian*. After Milton Erickson came on the scene (see Chapter 17 for more on him), a new approach to suggestions was placed in the hypnotherapist's toolbox: that of *indirect* or *permissive* suggestion. Both approaches are still used effectively in therapy, and both form the most basic tools in any hypnotherapist's collection.

Getting direct suggestions

A *direct* (or *authoritarian*) *suggestion* is one that gives an explicit instruction to do something. It leaves no room for error in what it asks you to do – for example, 'Stop smoking now' or 'You have no desire to eat sickly sweet chocolate cake' – and it really acts as a form of reprogramming.

Generally, your hypnotherapist uses direct suggestions if you are trying to give something up or want to make a specific change to a particular behaviour.

Convention has it that direct suggestions tend to be used with people who are used to taking or giving orders (such as soldiers, teachers and policemen for example), and with people who have very logical minds (scientists, mathematicians, chessplayers and so on). However, nowadays this convention seems to have fallen by the wayside, as many therapists use direct suggestion with a broad spectrum of people. It's down to your therapist's judgement as to which type of suggestion (direct or indirect) is most suitable for you.

In ye olden days, direct suggestion was virtually the only approach used in hypnotherapy. Today, most therapists now find only using direct suggestions to be restricting because many other approaches have been developed (as this chapter shows) that complement and enhance their use.

Going the indirect route

An *indirect* (or *permissive*) *suggestion* is one that allows your unconscious mind to explore a variety of possibilities before coming up with a response. For example, 'I wonder how soon it will be before you stop eating sickly sweet chocolate cake, and start to enjoy eating the right kind of healthy food you know will help you to lose weight?' An indirect suggestion induces an expectation of change without explicitly stating it. It also allows your unconscious mind to make that change in a way that fully suits you.

So why choose this approach over direct suggestion? The answer is simple. Some people find the direct approach threatening, and some people don't respond to authority very well, for one reason or another. Also, children are typically more responsive to an indirect approach (see Chapter 10 for more on this). Indirect suggestions are seen to be less demanding and seemingly more comfortable to accept.

This indirect approach can be restricting, and many therapists now favour a mix-and-match approach when using suggestions.

Blending both

You're halfway through your hypnotherapy session and you suddenly realise that your therapist has switched from using direct suggestion to indirect suggestion. Why is this? Well, possibly she realised that you're not responding very well to the authoritarian approach. However, it's more likely that she's using a two-pronged approach in helping you to resolve your symptom.

By using direct suggestion, she's explicitly stating what you want to hear, helping you to reprogramme your behaviour. At the same time, your unconscious mind is allowed to explore a variety of possibilities and options, stimulated by the use of indirect suggestions.

Even when you're in trance, you are still in control throughout your hypnotherapy session. Your unconscious mind will always protect you. You cannot be programmed to accept any suggestions that go against your own moral or ethical framework.

Safely Splitting Your Mind with Dissociation

Have you ever been in two minds over something; one part of your mind thinking one thing and another thinking of something else? Have you ever had the experience of slipping into autopilot when you're doing something, hardly aware of what you're doing, because your concentration is focused elsewhere? These represent times when your mind appears to split into several parts, each seemingly operating independently from the whole. These are times when your mind experiences dissociation.

Some examples of everyday dissociation:

- ✔ Safely ironing whilst being completely engrossed in the television programme you're watching.

- ✔ Talking to a friend in a noisy and crowded bar and editing out the surrounding din as you focus on your conversation. (Or perhaps editing out your friend as you tune into someone else's more interesting conversation!)

- ✔ Driving your car without having to think about how you do it.

- ✔ Daydreaming in class as you tune out the boring drone of the teacher.

Dissociation is a natural phenomenon you experience every day of your life. It helps you to function in the world at large and allows you to cope when things start to get tough. And as your problems form part of your daily existence, it's only natural that dissociation can have a role in the development and maintenance of these too.

Minding your associations

Your mind is like a computer. All your thoughts and behaviours form part of the computer program that is your life. Like all computer programs, your mind contains many subroutines that have specific functions with regard to running certain behaviours. You can say that when these subroutines are running, functioning independently of the rest of the program, your mind is dissociated.

When you're ironing, a subroutine (or dissociated part of your mind) allows you to carry out all the functions associated with ironing automatically, so that you don't have to consciously spend much time focussing on the ironing actions. Running the subroutine frees up the rest of your mind (the main body of the computer program as it were) to watch TV, or listen to the radio, or compose your shopping list, or plan a project.

As any computer programmer knows, a program doesn't necessarily run smoothly the first time you run it. This is true of the mind, too. When you encounter a regular situation in your life, a subroutine in your mind allows you to cope with it in whatever way is appropriate. Many of these subroutines are written, as you progress through life, to incorporate what you learn and experience. Some run smoothly, whilst others have little glitches in their programming (and some have major glitches!).

Whenever you encounter a new situation, your mind has to create a new subroutine on the spot in order to help you cope with it. Your mind may copy elements from older subroutines, or it may have to write the new one entirely from scratch. However your mind does it, it may or may not get it right straight away, so your life may proceed smoothly, or things may go spectacularly wrong.

Even when it does get it right, the new subroutine can sometimes corrupt older subroutines, or end up completely erasing them.

Take the development of a flying phobia. You have comfortably flown many times before. Your mind holds a subroutine that allows you to relax as you are on the plane. Then, on one flight, you experience dreadful turbulence. Your mind has to come up with a new subroutine to allow you to cope in this situation. Part of this new program, rightly or wrongly, causes you to tense your muscles and become fearful. The next time you fly you may find that this new subroutine has either corrupted the old one, or completely overwritten it, and what you now experience is good, old-fashioned fear!

Associating hypnosis and dissociation

As you have probably worked out by now, there is a very close link between hypnosis and dissociation. To put it simply: when you dissociate, you enter into a trance state, and entering a trance state is the basis of hypnosis.

So, the ability to dissociate is very useful for us hypnotherapists, as it provides a means of helping patients into the trance. But it doesn't stop there. Not only can we use it to induce trance, but dissociation can be a very powerful therapeutic tool.

Gaining a more objective point of view

One of the main aspects of dissociation is that it allows you to leave feelings behind. This means that as the mind splits, it can separate you from feelings both good and bad. Okay, so why is this important?

Your feelings colour your experiences in life. How you feel at the time can determine how you respond to a specific situation, which, in turn, can affect how your mind handles that situation. The next time you experience the situation – or even think about it – the feelings you had at the time can come back and once again influence how you experience it this time round. The more this happens, the more likely you are to develop an automatic response to that situation, governed by your unconscious mind. Because your response becomes automatic, you may not understand why you respond the way you do, or be able to control yourself.

For example, when you think about, or meet someone you love, your feelings play a role in determining your behaviour – being soppy and childlike with a big grin spreading across your face, and so on. By the same token, when you meet someone you don't like, your feelings once again shape your behaviour – you become tense, use an aggressive tone of voice, show defensive or aggressive posturing, and so on.

Using dissociation hypnotherapy allows you to separate the feelings you experience with regard to the event, from the event itself. In this way you are able to examine the event more objectively, and consequently alter your response to it.

The words *subjective* and *objective* have a variety of meanings, so it's useful to have an understanding of what they mean when used in hypnotherapy-speak:

- ✔ **Subjective:** Your feelings and emotions intervene and affect the way you assess a situation.

- ✔ **Objective:** Your feelings are put to one side, and you can assess a situation without involving your personal opinions.

Using dissociation in hypnotherapy can help you gain a more objective view of your problem without your emotions affecting your judgement. This separation is important so that you get a clearer picture of what is going on.

Supposing you're very stressed at work. The amount you have to do keeps piling up and you feel completely swamped. When you try to think about ways of managing your workload, those stressful feelings come flooding in and cloud your judgement. You can't see a way round it all and your stress increases. In hypnotherapy, your therapist can use a technique that dissociates you from those feelings, so that you can view that stressful situation as if it were on television. You can see what's going on, but you have none of those awful stressful feelings you had whenever you thought about the situation before. You are now viewing the situation objectively. Because the feelings are no longer interfering with your thoughts, you can see how to prioritise your workload or where you can delegate tasks. You realise that by having some leisure time you can actually work more effectively. The result: your stress levels drop!

Stepping away from yourself in stage dissociation

There are several different ways of working with dissociation in hypnosis. Your hypnotherapist may use it as a method of taking you into trance and as a very powerful therapy tool. One of the most common approaches to using it in either of these ways is an approach that is sometimes called *stage dissociation*. Simply put, *stage dissociation* is imagining seeing yourself – seeing yourself sitting in the chair you are in, seeing yourself enjoying a wonderful holiday, seeing yourself reading this book and so on.

Dissociation is useful in a variety of hypnotherapy situations:

- ✔ **To take you into trance:** Your hypnotherapist may ask that you imagine stepping or floating out of your body, perhaps taking you on a journey to a favourite place. She may even ask you to imagine that you step out of your body and see yourself enjoying that wonderful holiday you are soon going to be taking. In other words, your therapist encourages you to daydream (and you won't get told off for doing so!).

- ✔ **As a therapy tool:** Your hypnotherapist may ask you to imagine seeing a scene projected onto a screen. For example, she may ask you to see yourself handling a specific situation in a certain way. Because you're dissociated from the image (you're watching it), you can view it more objectively, with few or no unwanted feelings.

This isn't all there is to dissociation. Far from it! Another very powerful use is in *parts therapy*.

Adding the Sum of Your Parts: Parts Therapy

How often have you said to yourself 'There's a part of me that...'; or 'I want to quit (some bad habit), but that rebel inside of me just won't let me do it'; or even 'Something just makes me lash out when...'? Whenever you come out with a statement like any of these, you're simply recognising that one aspect of your mind is responsible for a particular behaviour, or for making you feel a certain way, or for stopping you from doing certain things. As hypnotherapists, when we hear one of our patients coming out with a statement like these, we have a very good pointer as to the therapy technique we can use: parts therapy.

In *parts therapy*, the therapist isolates the subroutine that controls a particular behaviour, or emotional response, and does therapy on it. In effect, separating the *part* of the mind responsible for the problem. Why? Because it's the part of your mind that needs corrective action. It's the part of your mind supplying the reason you're going for therapy. It's the part of your mind annoying the heck out of you.

But hang on a moment. You also have a part responsible for your confidence, a part responsible for your ability to focus as you study, a part responsible for your ability to be courageous, and so on. You, or your hypnotherapist, may also want to work with more than one part. For example, you may be going to see your therapist because you have lost confidence when you're driving. Your hypnotherapist may want to help you get in touch with the part of your mind responsible for your confidence and help you to make it stronger; or perhaps just to bring that part back into contact with the rest of your mind so that once again you can enjoy (safely!) getting back behind the wheel.

Communicating and negotiating with a part of you

So, how do you and your therapist work with your different parts? In a nutshell, you isolate the offending part and simply talk to it. The basic process is as follows:

1. **Become aware of the part.**

   Your hypnotherapist may ask you to become aware of the part, perhaps by asking you to float it out of your body, or maybe by asking you to look at the palm of one of your hands and to imagine it resting there. You may be asked to describe what the part looks like. Don't worry if you imagine it to look like something strange, such as a lump of coal or a cute bunny rabbit. It's your perception that counts!

By imagining the part in this way you are dissociating it – splitting it off from the rest of your mind. In this way, you can remove any unwanted feelings that accompany it.

2. **Find out what the part has been trying to do for you.**

   In hypnotherapy-speak, this is called *eliciting the positive intent*, or finding out what function this part has been serving in your life and why it's there.

   The simplest way of eliciting the positive intent is to ask that part what it has been up to and why it was doing that, and to then listen to what it has to say.

   No, we haven't taken leave of our senses and drifted into the mystical world of the arcane. This is all about helping you to gain insight into what that annoying little part of you is up to. The interesting thing is that once you gain insight, your symptom starts to collapse as you gain a measure of power over it.

3. **Thank the part for what it has been doing for you.**

   'What! Thank it! It's been such a pain for so long why should I do that?' Because it was originally trying to do something of benefit for you. Whatever benefit there may have been is long gone, but it is important that you keep a positive state of mind for the rest of the procedure. Ranting at it will hardly achieve that, will it?

4. **Negotiate with the part so that it is happy to change.**

   Your hypnotherapist may then suggest that you explain to the part that what it was doing for you is no longer needed. After this, you can ask it if it's willing to make a change in what it has been doing for you, so that it can do something that is more acceptable for you both. You may find that it says 'yes' straight away, or it may need some resource to help it.

   If the part needs some help, your hypnotherapist will then ask you to become aware of what resource the part wants (for example, more confidence), and to dissociate the part of your mind responsible for that resource in the same way as in Step 1.

   After you do this, you will be asked to give that resource to the first part you dissociated, perhaps by imagining that resource floating into and merging with it.

5. **Transform the part to serve a useful role.**

   The part has finally said 'yes' to making the change and it now has the resources to do that. So now what? Your hypnotherapist will ask you to thank the part for agreeing to make the change – as this maintains the positive state of mind. To further enhance this mindset, your hypnotherapist will also ask you to make the image you have of the part more pleasing to you, perhaps by imagining a smiling face on it, by changing its colour, by changing the way it feels to you, or through some other means.

The part's agreeing to change, and your subsequent altering of its image sets in motion an unconscious process that allows the part to take on a new and more functional role; one that allows you to get on with your life *without* the problem you originally came to see your hypnotherapist about.

6. Bring the part back home.

You're almost done! The final step is to bring that part back home. It is no good thinking 'Oh, I can just chuck this unnecessary part away.' Remember, it is a part of *you!* It may have been unintentionally naughty, disruptive, or whatever, but it has changed its ways and now holds a positive and functional role in your life. Just as the parent of a naughty child, after sending her to her room, gives her a hug and welcomes her back to the family after she has repented, so it is with your errant parts. Welcome them back and let them rejoin the family of your mind.

To accomplish this, your hypnotherapist may ask you to imagine the new, improved part floating back inside you and once again becoming a fully functioning part of your own inner world. Or maybe she'll ask you to pull the part in with your hands, as you welcome it back inside yourself. However you are asked to do it, it is important that you bring the part back home. The next section explains why.

Bringing it all back together again: The importance of reintegration

So, what will happen if you don't bring that part back in or, as we like to say in hypnotherapy circles, reintegrate it? Remember that your mind has been split wide open, and if you don't reintegrate the split part, you're going to feel a little spaced out, to put it bluntly. After a period of time, you would feel normal again. But in the meantime something just as bad as the part you just got rid of may well take its place. So why risk it? Welcome that changed part back with open arms.

If you do come out of a dissociation technique feeling a little spaced out, let your hypnotherapist know. It may be that another part has dissociated without your being aware of it. That part may simply need to be brought back in; a very simple and straightforward process.

Travelling in Time

You may want to play the theme tune to Doctor Who as you read this section! As with the good Doctor (a television time traveller), time can play an important role in vanquishing your adversaries. Unlike the Doctor, your adversaries do not come in the form of Daleks and Cybermen (although the upcoming section on metaphor may turn that statement on its head). Instead, your foes come in the form of phobias, anxieties, and so on. Oh, and it's worth knowing that hiding behind the sofa won't make them go away either!

Your perception of time plays an important role in both the development and maintenance of your symptoms. How you perceive the past, the future, or even the passing of time, influences the way you handle the problems in your life. And with that in mind, your ever resourceful hypnotherapist has an array of tools to help you alter your perception of time: taking you back into the past, forward into the future, or helping you to alter your perception of the very passing of time.

Going back in time: Age regression techniques

Let's start by dispelling a myth: You do *not* have to be regressed for hypnotherapy to be successful! Despite what you may hear or be told, uncovering the past and dealing with it is not an essential part of getting over your symptom. Regression is simply another tool in the hypnotherapist's toolbox that can be very effective, when used at the right time and in the correct manner.

That little rant over and done with, let's get on with talking about what regression is. Very simply, *regression* is a technique in which your hypnotherapist takes you back in time, in your mind, to an event that actually happened or that happened in your imagination.

Considering the reasons for regression

Why does a hypnotherapist consider using regression? For several reasons, that may include:

- ✔ **You want to find out about the origin of your symptom.** You've had your symptom for a long while, but can't remember how, why, or when it started and want to.

  Your therapist may suggest you find the origin of your symptom, believing the origin may well have an important bearing on helping you to finally remove the symptom.

  Several seemingly small events may have compounded together to give you the symptom you're experiencing. And your therapist may suggest that in order to remove your symptom, you need to work through the individual components.

- ✔ **You want to change the way you perceive an event in your past.** You have experienced an event in the past, and as you think about it in the present, you find it disturbing; perhaps feeling disempowered, lacking in confidence, anxious, and so on. Your hypnotherapist may regress you to that time and allow you to change how you remember that event, or how you responded to it.

For example, you may remember being scared as a child by a particularly grumpy dentist who was nasty to you when you cried as you were being given an injection. The sense of powerlessness you felt then contributed greatly to the dental phobia you have in the present. You can be regressed to that time, but this time, as you remember it, you can be empowered to safely tell the dentist exactly what you think of her. Once you're empowered in the past, that sense of empowerment can be brought back into the present and sort out a major component of your phobia.

✔ **You want to remember an event from your past.** Perhaps you hid a particularly valuable piece of jewellery in a very safe place, so safe in fact that you can't remember where you put it!

You may have prevented yourself from experiencing some emotion connected to an event in your past, such as bereavement. Unfortunately, that emotion got locked away inside you, fuelling your symptom in the present. Your hypnotherapist may use a regression technique to let you re-experience the event and let out that emotion in safety. Because the emotion is no longer locked away, your symptom runs out of fuel and disappears.

✔ **You want to access a good feeling from your past.** Perhaps until recently you have always been very focused when you are playing tennis. However, recently your game has been very poor for one reason or another. Your hypnotherapist can use a regression technique to take you back to a time when you had those important feelings of focus; allowing you to once again get in touch with them, and to bring them back to the present and back into your game.

Regression allows you to gain insight into what has gone before. And with insight comes a measure of control over your symptom. Once you have control, it's a relatively simple step to progress forward to finally ridding yourself of the symptom.

Going through the techniques

The time is right and you have agreed to be regressed. So how will your hypnotherapist do this? There are several ways to go about it:

✔ **Counting you back through the years.** Your hypnotherapist may take a formal approach, counting you back through the years as your mind drifts back through time.

Your hypnotherapist may also use a technique that allows you to scan the years to find those times that contributed to your problem; asking your unconscious mind to lift one of your fingers each time you identify an event. The hypnotherapist may then use one of a variety of approaches to let you visit those times.

Defining the terms

It's useful to define some of the terms associated with this process of going back in time:

✔ **Regression:** Going back in time but viewing past events with your adult eyes. Through regression, it's as if you're watching yourself as the event unfolds. And yes, it's a form of dissociation (see the preceding 'Safely Splitting Your Mind with Dissociation' section).

✔ **Revivification:** Going back in time and experiencing an event as if it were happening to you now. Your reference to the present is lost and you act, think, and feel as you did during the event.

✔ **Past-life regression:** An interesting one this: Going back in time to a life you experienced before you were born into the one you are living now.

If you read the hypnotherapy literature, you see that the terms *regression* and *revivification* are often used interchangeably. More often than not authors don't bother with the word 'revivification' and stick to using the word 'regression'. We have often wondered why this is, and apart from it being sheer laziness, have come to the conclusion that it is because 'revivification' is harder to spell than 'regression'!

✔ **Letting your unconscious mind decide where to go.** Your unconscious mind is given the task of taking you back in time to an event that has relevance to the development of your problem.

✔ **Asking you to remember a specific time in your past.** This technique is nice and straightforward. If you know when an event happened, and some of what happened at the time, your hypnotherapist may simply ask you to start remembering that time. As you become more involved in that memory, your recall will improve.

✔ **Being creative.** You, or your hypnotherapist, may have a creative streak and take you back by having you, for example, imagine that you're flicking through the pages of a biography of your life. As you reach the chapter detailing the events that led up to the development of your symptom, you may be asked to step into the pages of the book and re-experience what happened.

And for those with a liking for science fiction, you can always imagine that you're travelling back in time in Doctor Who's time machine, the TARDIS!

You do not have to be regressed if you don't want to. However, your hypnotherapist will always make sure that it is safe for you to go back in time, if you do agree to it.

Going forward in time: Age progression techniques

If you can go back in time in your mind, it stands to reason you can go forward, right? You may be thinking that the past has actually happened, and you have memories of the events in your life, and think that the future is yet to occur, and wonder how you can progress into a future that hasn't happened yet.

Well, the truth is, you go forward in time, all the time. Whenever you start thinking longingly about an upcoming event, you travel forward in time in your mind. Whenever you plan an event or make a date, you travel forward in time. Your hypnotherapist can use this ability as part of the package that helps to resolve your symptoms.

Your mind is goal-directed (we talk more about goals in Chapter 3). This means that you consciously, and unconsciously, set yourself up to achieve things – both good and bad!

When you think about an upcoming event, your mind has a habit of playing out various scenes relating to that event, perhaps creating pictures that almost predict how you're going to look or behave. You also create a wide variety of self-statements that describe how you think things are going to be. In effect, you set goals in your mind that influence the way that you approach an event, subtly altering your feelings and behaviours.

Self-statements are those little things we say to ourselves that confirm our attitude towards some event, person, or situation. They can be positive; for example, 'I can do this' or 'I'm enjoying this'. Or they can be negative; for example, 'I can't do this' or 'I'm fat'.

For example, if you're scared of giving a talk you have to make in the near future, how you view that future talk affects you in the present. You may see yourself as being nervous, stumbling over your words, and panicking. Because of this vision, you feel anxious in the present, which may influence how you behave – becoming snappy with people around you, for example. Furthermore, you give yourself negative self-statements such as 'I'm going to be dreadful when I give this talk' or 'I'm going to be so nervous when I am up there.' When you finally give the talk, you will more than likely have the same negative experience that you have been visualising: you will have achieved your negative goal.

However, if you think about the talk in a more optimistic way, you create more positive goals. Perhaps you can see yourself confidently stepping up to the lectern and clearly delivering your speech. You give yourself positive self-statements such as 'I am going to do well when I give this talk' or 'I am going to remain confident when I am up there.' You feel good in the present and when you finally give the talk, this time you give it well, because you've been focusing on a positive goal that subtly altered your feelings and behaviours in a positive way.

Your hypnotherapist can take this process of looking into the future and use it in a very beneficial way, helping you to create very clear images of what you want to achieve. As she continues with this process, so you break down the negative goals that you have unconsciously set yourself, which have been keeping your symptom in place. By changing your view of the future in this manner, you change the negative feelings and behaviours that you've been experiencing in the present. Both consciously and unconsciously you start to move towards this positive new goal.

So, how does your hypnotherapist send you into the future? Simple! She uses an age regression technique (outlined in the preceding 'Going through the techniques' section), but takes you in the opposite direction. Instead of counting you back in time, she counts you forward; instead of letting your unconscious mind decide where in the past you should go, she lets it decide where in the future you should be, and so on.

Age progression techniques are often referred to as *pseudo orientation in time* or *hallucinated age progression.*

Altering time: Time distortion techniques

'We're preparing to deploy the Phase Shift Stimulator in order to distort the time/space continuum!' Er, no. This isn't how this works (although it would be fun if it were!). What we're referring to when we talk about time distortion is not altering time itself (that does lie firmly in the realms of science fiction), but how human beings perceive the passing of time.

There are two types of time:

- ✔ **Clock time:** This is a constant and is not affected by your own point of view or thoughts because it is determined by an instrument such as a clock (unless you have access to a Phase Shift Stimulator!).
- ✔ **Subjective time:** Your personal perception of passing time, influenced by the way you feel. As such it is variable.

So, why would your hypnotherapist want to help you alter your subjective time? Because subjective time influences how you feel about something, and vice versa.

Sometimes you feel that time seems to fly when you're enjoying something but drags when you're not (and we hope time is zooming past for you as you read this book). Enjoyment and boredom are not the only factors that can affect your perception of passing time; many emotions and feelings – including anxiety, depression, pain, sadness, stress, elation, and interest – and their consequent effects on your perception of passing time, determine how you view situations and events in your life.

If your hypnotherapist decides to use time distortion with you, she will probably do so by reminding you, when you are in trance, of positive times in your past when time seemed to either speed up or slow down. She then associates those experiences to the event you want to change your perception of, by using direct suggestion.

Take the tennis player who feels she never has enough time to accurately serve the ball, and the flying phobic who feels that a one-hour flight seems to last for ten. In both these examples time plays an important role in manipulating feelings. For the tennis player, her perception of passing time causes her to experience anxiety and stress to such an extent that it interferes with her game. For the flying phobic, the experience of time dragging as she sits on a plane serves to heighten her feelings of fear. In hypnotherapy, the tennis player may be given a suggestion that time slows down when she's serving, just as it did when she was waiting to go on that holiday of a lifetime, and that she now has all the time she needs to toss the ball in the air and accurately serve it to her opponent. By altering her perception of time, her feelings change too, and her serve improves. Alternatively, the flying phobic may be given suggestions that time flies by as she sits on a plane, just as it did when she got those wonderful presents on Christmas Day, when she was a child. She's encouraged to experience every minute of the flight as just a second, so that she reaches her destination before she knows it. Contracting her perception of passing time helps break the fear response, allowing her to feel more comfortable as she journeys towards her destination.

Time distortion techniques manipulate your *perception* of events past and future, as well as how you experience the passing of time. You only have memories of what has been, or hopes for what is yet to come. By working with these memories and hopes, you can make positive changes in the way you live your life today.

Scanning a Variety of Other Common Techniques

So far we've discussed the major tools in your hypnotherapist's toolbox. But that doesn't mean that's all there are. Far from it. Your hypnotherapist has plenty of other tools to use; some more popular than others. We explain the most common in the following sections.

Visualising, imagining, or pretending change

Because change always begins in the mind first, your hypnotherapist may suggest that you 'visualise, imagine, or pretend' that you are enjoying the change you wish to make. If you want to be confident taking an upcoming exam, she may ask you to visualise, imagine, or pretend that you are well rested, thoroughly prepared, and actually eager to get the answers out of your mind and onto the paper! Virtually everyone has the ability to visualise, or to imagine, or to pretend. All are valid modalities of representation to achieve the same goal.

Modality of representation describes how you use your senses to represent things in your mind.

When you think, you don't use just words. Thinking is a creative experience that involves your five basic senses – sight, hearing, touch, taste, and smell. Your mind uses these senses as a means of expanding and enhancing your thinking process. For example:

- ✔ **Sight:** As you think you see images in your mind.

- ✔ **Hearing:** As you think you hear sounds in your mind.

- ✔ **Touch:** As you think you experience feelings in your mind.

- ✔ **Taste:** As you think you experience tastes in your mind.

- ✔ **Smell:** As you think you experience smells in your mind.

Most people favour one sense (generally sight, hearing, or touch) as their primary modality of representation, and favour the other senses less – their secondary modalities of representation. This doesn't mean that you only ever think in one modality. For example, when asked to imagine a beautiful garden, some people see the garden in their mind very clearly (visual primary modality). However, they may also be able to hear the sounds of the birds and the bees (hearing as a secondary modality). These modalities colour your thoughts and help to give them meaning and vitality.

Try thinking about your best friend.

- ✔ How do you know you're thinking about your best friend?

- ✔ What comes into your mind that tells you who you're thinking of?

Whatever your answers are, they're proof that you can visualise or imagine! You're representing your best friend in your mind.

In hypnotherapy, this process is used in a variety of ways. It's certainly used in age regression and age progression techniques (see the previous 'Travelling in Time' section) because you need to imagine yourself in your past or future. You may also be asked to visualise and engage in a dialogue with a wise person who has the answers to all the questions you want to ask. You may be asked to pretend that you're digging up weeds in a beautiful garden; where the digging up of the weeds represents digging up and getting rid of your problem.

Using your mind in this way is a powerful tool because it lets you fully represent whatever it is your hypnotherapist is asking you to do. You will find that this technique holds a very important position in your hypnotherapist's toolbox.

Finding out how to forget

What were we going to say about forgetting? We can't remember! Okay, we know it's a very tired joke! However, your ability to forget can play an important role in therapy. How you remember things in your past can taint the way you experience similar events in the future.

A person who has to have a regular and painful procedure carried out by her doctor has a memory of the pain she experienced during that procedure in the past. This memory influences the way she thinks about future procedures, predicting that they will be as painful, if not more so, than those she's already had. As a consequence she'll experience the next procedure as a nasty and painful event! However, if she can forget about the previous pain, she won't necessarily set herself up in a negative way, and can experience the procedure with considerably less discomfort.

If your hypnotherapist decides that it would be useful for you to forget something, she will probably do this by using suggestions that you simply forget it. Because you are motivated to do so, your unconscious mind allows it to happen. It's almost as though you push the erase button on that particular part of the memory. In fact, your hypnotherapist may ask you to visualise yourself doing just that.

You may have an event in your past that you particularly want to forget. Dealing with the emotions that accompany the memory is much healthier than forgetting it in its entirety. In this way you can recall the memory without feeling pain or discomfort. Even if you consciously forget the event, your emotions about it are still there in your unconscious, festering away and perhaps leading to a whole new batch of symptoms.

Another area where you may experience forgetting is when you awaken from the trance and can't remember what went on during the session. This can be because:

- ✔ It is a natural response of having drifted into one of the deeper levels of trance.
- ✔ Your hypnotherapist has asked that you forget what happened during the trance.

It may seem strange that your hypnotherapist wants you to forget events in trance. You may wonder if she's trying to hide something from you. The answer is no. The reason your therapist will suggest that you forget your trance may be because she feels that you're a very analytical person, and that the moment you are out of trance you'll start analysing everything that went on, and in the process undo all the good that the session has brought you!

Even though you will probably forget whatever it was suggested you forget, the reality is that your memory eventually will return. However, as it returns, you will probably find that your perception of the memory has changed to something much more positive.

You cannot be made to forget anything you don't want to forget. If you are in good rapport with your therapist, you're motivated to forget something because you know that doing so will help you to achieve your required goal from the therapy. The result is that your unconscious mind is much more likely to allow you to forget.

Substituting a memory

If you can forget something, surely you can fill that gap in memory with something else? This is very true. You have a great capacity to alter the way you remember events from the past.

If you were to ask a group of people to recall an event they had all witnessed, you would get as many different versions of that event as there are people in the group. This is not because they are all inattentive, and can't remember things very well, but because of the way memory works.

When a digital television signal is sent out, only the important parts are transmitted over the airways. When they reach the television set, the set itself fills in the missing pieces, and creates a representation of the original image. Your memory is a bit like digital television signals. Very few people have 100 per cent accurate recall, which means that most of us store only a variety of fragments of a memory. When you retrieve a memory, you pull up only those fragmented parts stored in your brain. Your brain acts a bit like a television set and fills in the missing pieces so that you can have a reasonably accurate recall.

Your hypnotherapist can use this ability of your brain to create components of a memory as part of the process of resolving your problem. By taking the original memory and forgetting specific parts of it, your therapist has an open canvas upon which to help you create a more acceptable memory through a process of suggestion and visualisation. Don't worry, your therapist won't alter your memory to suit herself. She will have discussed the process with you beforehand, and asked you what you would like to remember – this is the picture that she helps you paint onto the canvas.

Exchanging an old memory for an entirely new one is very difficult. This technique works best when an old memory is subtly altered in some way.

A flying phobic, who has developed her phobia because she had one bad experience of turbulence on a flight, may wish to alter the memory of that flight so that she recalls having remained calm, relaxed, and in control as she sat through the experience. This has a knock-on effect into the present, helping her to feel comfortable whenever she flies, because she does not have the negative reference to the original memory to taint her flying experience.

You are likely to retain the original memory after a memory substitution. However, because you have been playing around with it in a positive manner, your perception of that memory will be radically changed.

Memory substitution is carried out only with informed consent from you. You cannot be made to change a memory if you don't want to.

Telling stories

Perhaps the oldest form of learning is through listening to stories. You teach your children important social and moral truths by reading them fairy tales and various stories found in religious texts. As you grow older, you learn further truths through reading stories in newspapers (hmm! Truths?), magazines, books, television, and films.

The psychotherapy community being the resourceful thing it is, recognised that stories offer an indirect learning method and began to use the concept across its various disciplines, including hypnotherapy. As the listener pays attention to a story, its content creates associations with material already stored in her mind; helping to shape and alter self-perceptions and the way she views the world in general, in a positive or negative way, depending on the story. This means that a positive story can be used in therapy to help you resolve your problems.

In psychotherapy, a story representative of something that holds some significance to the listener is called a *metaphor.*

Your hypnotherapist may use a metaphor during the trance session, or may deliver one when you are not in a state of hypnosis. It may come in the form of a story, or it may come as a reminiscence of the way a previous patient dealt with a symptom similar to yours. Your therapist may tell several metaphors at the same time, one embedded in another, in order to make several different points about the way you can resolve your symptom.

Another way your therapist may use a metaphor is to create a metaphorical representation of something. For example, for a person beset with the problems of premature ejaculation, a therapist may use a version of the following metaphor:

> 'As a child you may remember feeling hungry, enjoying an urge to eat. Perhaps you can remember rushing to sit down at the dinner table and wolfing down your food, paying little attention to anything except the instant gratification of your hunger. But now, as an adult, you can appreciate that hunger in a different way. You can take your time arriving at the table, enjoying looking at the feast that is laid out for you, perhaps complimenting the cook, before you take your first mouthful of food. You can slow down in satisfying your hunger by savouring each and every mouthful you take, pausing every so often to appreciate the flavours and aromas that have been so carefully prepared for you. And slowly, gradually, you prolong your enjoyment, and the enjoyment of others around that table, as you learn to appreciate and control, in an adult way, the satisfaction of your hunger.'

The message contained in this metaphor is to slow down and take your time during sex, as you appreciate your partner more. At the same time there is encouragement to take a more adult approach to making love.

Metaphors can be scattered liberally throughout your hypnotherapy sessions (and they are certainly scattered with gay abandon throughout this book!). They can inspire you by telling stories of how people overcame adversity. They can help you understand something (as we did at the beginning of this chapter where we likened the mind to a network of pipes). They can empower you by getting you to imagine, for example, that your immune system is a Phase Shift Stimulator blasting cancer cells into oblivion. Metaphors can help you overcome a whole variety of difficulties and concerns. However they are used, they provide a very gentle and effective form of therapy.

Chapter 3

Preparing for Hypnotherapy

*Y*ou finally decide to visit a hypnotherapist because you want to sort out that problem that's been bugging you for so long. Getting started couldn't be easier: you phone up, book an appointment and hop along to see your hypnotherapist, at the right time, without having to think too much about why you're going to see him. After all, he's going to sort everything out for you isn't he? Well, let's have a reality check. Many people do approach hypnotherapy this way. But since you want to get the most out of the sessions for which you are paying good money, you can really help the process along with a little preparation and forethought. Oh, and by the way, if you really believe that your therapist is going to be doing it all for you, you had better read Chapter 13, which walks you through a therapy session, straight away!

Keeping Your Individuality in Mind

Preparation is important. In fact, the first goal you can set yourself in advance of your therapy session is to prepare some useful information. Your hypnotherapist will want to know as much as possible about how you experience your problem. And, as hypnotherapy is about gaining answers and creating solutions, your hypnotherapist needs to know what you want to achieve by coming for therapy. The answers here may seem obvious: 'I experience my problem like everyone else' and 'I want to get rid of my problem completely.' To which your therapist can reply in an unconvinced yet sympathetic manner, 'Do you?'

The reason for his scepticism is that, even though he's no doubt treated many people before with your particular problem, the way you experience your problem is entirely individual. People often bite their nails in different ways, their smoking habits may differ, and people who are scared of spiders frequently react in completely different ways to the sight of a spider. So, for example, even if you and your best friend are both scared of spiders, you each experience your phobia in different ways. You may freeze when you see a spider, whilst your friend runs screaming from the room. You may not be frightened of small spiders, whilst your friend collapses into a quivering wreck when one scuttles across the floor.

The same individuality applies to what you want to achieve from therapy. In respect of the spider phobia example, you may want to be able to pick up the spider on the end of a piece of newspaper and flick it out the window, whilst your friend just wants to be able to ignore the wretched thing and let it get on with its little spider life.

In fact, your goal for therapy is as individual as your response to the problem for which you are seeking help. Factors that help shape your goal include the following:

- ✔ **Your personality and attitude:** Are you an optimist or are you a pessimist? If you are an optimist, you may well find yourself setting a goal that a pessimist will consider unattainable. On the other hand, if you are a pessimist then you may set a goal that an optimist will find too low.

    Or perhaps you're the go-get-'em type. If so, you may have the belief that you can attain the world and are therefore more likely to set a much higher goal than the softly, softly type of personality.

- ✔ **Your other goals:** Do you have other goals in life that may influence your therapy goal? For example, if you have a flying phobia, you may have the ultimate goal of going abroad on a nice holiday. That ultimate goal determines that your therapy goal is to feel fine and comfortable on a plane. On the other hand, if your ultimate goal is to be able to meet friends, family, or work colleagues at an airport, then your therapy goal may well be to feel fine and comfortable around planes without having to get on one.

Whatever your goal, in order for your therapy to be effective it's particularly important that your hypnotherapist has all the facts that directly relate to your problem and your goal for therapy.

Identifying Your Problem

Why are you going to see a hypnotherapist? Is it for something specific or for something you can't quite define? Several reasons may have made you finally decide to take the bull by the horns and sort out your life. Whatever your motivation, we recommend thinking over a few things before your first appointment.

Of course, you may not have answers to all the questions in the following subsections. Don't worry if you don't. The important thing is to think about the problem, or problems, you want to resolve and get the issues as clear in your mind as possible. By doing so, you save time and speed up the therapy process. In fact, by thinking about your problem, you are making the first move towards resolving it.

Write down your answers and thoughts inspired by the questions in the following subsections. The act of writing can help you gain a more objective point of view and allow you to see things from a different perspective. Your therapist will really appreciate your hard work, and your notes will provide a very useful reference as well as a discussion point for him, on top of which it will speed up the whole process for you.

'I'm not exactly sure what my problem is'

Being unable to pinpoint your problem is more common than you may think. Many people know they have issues in their lives causing them distress but can't figure out exactly what's going on.

Don't worry, your hypnotherapist can still help. Through a combination of asking you questions and using trance work designed to uncover the specifics of why you're there, together you can reach a true definition of your problem.

You can help the process along by thinking about the following questions before you go for your first therapy session:

- ✔ **What is it about your life that's distressing?** If you had to give a brief definition of your life, what would it be?

- ✔ **How is your life being affected?** Think about how your day-to-day life runs. What is the impact on your home life? Your work life? Your social life? Are you being restricted in what you can do and where you can go?

- ✔ **What thoughts accompany you throughout the day?** What are those niggling little thoughts that constantly seem to hold you back? When are you self-denigrating? What do you tell yourself when you are at work, at home, and socialising?

- ✔ **What is good about your life?** Of course, it's never healthy to focus just on the negative, so think about the good things happening to you. Doing this is important so you can see that your problem is not a constant in your life.

- ✔ **When did you start feeling like this?** What was happening in your life at the time you first noticed you had a problem?

By answering these questions and with further help from your hypnotherapist, you will be able to give your problem a form and shape with which you can both work.

'I know my problem but haven't been able to solve it'

You may well have a very good handle on what your problem is but trying to solve it is causing you frustration. You know that the problem can be solved but you can't see a way to get rid of it. If this is the case, think about the following before going for therapy:

- ✔ **How have you tried to solve this problem in the past?** What solutions have you attempted before? Why did you try them?

- ✔ **What solutions had some effect and what solutions were downright disasters?** What were the reasons for the differing results?

- ✔ **Why did a solution you thought worked suddenly fail?** What was it that triggered the problem again? How did you react?

- ✔ **What are your thoughts about solving this problem?** When you think about solving your problem, what goes through your mind? What are you expecting to happen? What are you saying to yourself?

'I have more than one problem'

It is not uncommon to have a list of issues to attend to. Think about the following before going for therapy:

- ✔ **Are your problems related?** Are there any links between your problems or is each issue completely separate from the others?

- ✔ **When did your problems become troublesome for you?** Have your issues always been a problem, or have they been highlighted only as other issues cropped up?

Communicating Your Problem

In order to get the most out of your hypnotherapy sessions, you need to be able to let your therapist know just what it is you want to work on. Maybe you have only one problem – or maybe several. No matter whether you have one problem or ten, you have to be able to tell your hypnotherapist what they are.

Another useful thing to do is to provide your hypnotherapist with as much information as possible regarding your problem or problems. Doing this certainly makes the whole process of therapy run much more smoothly. The following sections will help you along the way.

Hypnotherapy is not magic. A hypnotherapist cannot simply wave the therapy wand and make everything better. You need to put in some effort too and you can make a start by adequately preparing for your session.

Prioritising your problems

First things first: you can't do it all at once! No matter how skilled your hypnotherapist is and how motivated you are, you need to decide what you want to work on and in what order. Obviously, if you have only one problem, the choice is clear. However, if you have more than one, you need to make a few decisions.

Why can't you do it all at once? The answer is simple. By trying to do too much in one go you will end up watering the therapy down. It is much better to concentrate on one issue at a time because this allows both you and your therapist to focus your endeavours in a specific direction, maximising your chances of success. Of course, if your problems are linked – as may be the case if you're confronting stress issues and a weight problem caused by comfort eating, for example – working on one naturally has a positive impact on the other.

So, where to start? To begin with you can think about the following:

✔ **What problem do you most want to resolve?** Out of the range of problems you have, which one is it most important for you to overcome?

✔ **Do you want to jump in at the deep end and go for the big one?** Tempting, but is it the right thing to do? Are you trying to take on too much too soon? How will you feel if things don't go according to plan?

✔ **Do you want to start with something simple and work up to tackling the bigger issues?** Success in one area of therapy often leads to success in another. It may be best to start with something simple. Once you resolve an issue, your confidence in your ability to change grows. As a result, your chances of resolving any subsequent issues increases.

✔ **Which of your problems are you most confident about resolving?**

By thinking through these questions and discussing your priorities with your therapist, you will come up with an action plan for therapy that fully meets your needs and maximises your chances of success.

Providing as much information as you can

Your hypnotherapist can only work on the information you give him, and your therapy is built on this information. Despite what popular fiction may suggest, your hypnotherapist cannot read minds, so it is important that you provide as much information as you can about your problem as well as your goal for therapy. Of course your therapist can help you by asking many questions whilst taking your case history (see Chapter 13) but it will help both of you if you remember one fact: never leave room to assume. Where you find assumption you find errors. And when you get errors you certainly increase the chances that your therapy will not succeed. So, to help avoid this outcome, provide your therapist with the answers to the following questions:

- **When did your problem first start?** At what point did you first become aware of this problem?

- **When did your problem become troublesome for you?** Did your problem start out as something manageable and then escalate into something that wasn't? Why do you think that was?

- **What was going on in your life when your problem emerged?** Were you experiencing changes in your life when the problem first appeared or became an issue for you?

- **How does your problem affect your life?** How does your problem express itself in your day-to-day life? What does it stop you from doing? What does it cause you to do unnecessarily?

- **How does your problem affect the lives of those around you?** Does your problem have an effect on those around you at work, at home, or when you socialise? If so, what are these effects?

- **What makes your problem worse?** Have you noticed times when your problem appears to become more severe? If so, what was happening in your life at that time?

- **What makes your problem better?** Have you noticed times when your problem appears to ease? If so what was happening in your life at that time?

- **What feelings and emotions can help you resolve this problem?** What psychological tools do you need to help you along the way (for example, more confidence, greater focus, and so on)?

- **How will you know that your problem has gone?** How will your life have changed to show you (and perhaps others too) that you have resolved your problem?

> ✔ **How do you want to be when your problem is resolved?** How do you want to be acting, thinking and feeling when you've resolved your problem?
>
> ✔ **How much do you want to resolve this problem?** How much effort are you prepared to expend to get you to your resolution?

By providing as much clear information as you can you will create a firm foundation upon which the process of change can be built.

Setting SMART Goals and Checking Your Motivation

Simply thinking about and defining your problem only gets you halfway to reaching a conclusion. You're probably not going to see your hypnotherapist just to talk about your problem; you are going to see him so that he can help you find a solution. You have to consider what your motivation is for undergoing therapy as well as thinking about what you want the outcome to be. Just as it is important to accurately define your problem, it is equally important to be able to accurately define your goal for therapy, because you don't want to end up getting something you didn't ask for in the first place!

Just thinking 'Oh! I just want to get rid of my problem' is not sufficient. Unwanted or not, your problem has become a part of your life – probably for quite some time. By simply removing this problem a metaphorical vacuum can result, and nature, which abhors a vacuum, will always try to fill it. Nature being nature, and having a wicked sense of humour to boot, it unfortunately often fills that vacuum with something worse than what was originally there. That means that if you are going to take something away (your problem), you must replace it with something better (your goal for therapy). And that means you need to think about what you want.

Your mind is goal-directed, which means that if you concentrate on something hard enough, you tend to make it a reality. Perhaps one of the reasons you maintain a problem for so long is because you focus attention on the problem, rather than on finding a solution to it. So, all you end up doing is to set yourself up with a negative goal and your problem remains unresolved.

You may be sitting there now thinking 'Aha! All I need to do is to think positively and all my problems will go away.' Unfortunately it is not as easy as that. Certainly positive thinking can be of great benefit; better the optimist than the pessimist! However, the process of hypnotherapy involves creating clear and achievable goals, as well as altering unwanted patterns of thinking. At the same time, your hypnotherapist can help you access psychological resources that perhaps you didn't know you had and to integrate all the techniques and processes as you work towards a successful solution.

Using your SMARTs to set your goals

So, how do you go about setting a realistic goal? The simpler the goal, the easier it is to realise. An acronym that can help you define your goals is **SMART: S**pecific, **M**easurable, **A**chievable, **R**ealistic, **T**ime-oriented.

Make your goals:

- ✔ **Specific:** Your goal needs to have a specific outcome; something defined. Simply thinking 'Maybe I want this' or 'Maybe I want that' is of no use because 'maybe' is not specific and you will end up getting nowhere. Even thinking 'I want to feel better' is not specific enough. What does 'better' mean? It can mean one thing to one person and something completely different to another. On top of this, you need to ask yourself what it is that you want to feel better than.

   However, if you can say to yourself 'I definitely want this specific outcome', you've taken your first step towards achieving it.

- ✔ **Measurable:** Your goal needs to be tangible; something you can witness in your everyday life. Perhaps you want to cope better at work, be able to deal with a spider that runs across your living room floor, or comfortably fit into that too-tight pair of trousers you've kept in your wardrobe because you love them.

- ✔ **Achievable:** Your goal needs to be something that you can attain. It may be nice to think about winning the lottery, however it's very unlikely that you will (more's the pity!). And in any case, thinking about it won't do much to advance your cause in that direction. On the other hand, thinking about losing two stone in weight is something you can achieve.

- ✔ **Realistic:** Your goal needs to be based in reality. For example, 'I want to be happy all the time' is not a realistic goal. It would be lovely if it were, but the reality of life is such that bad things do happen and you would be less than human if you spent your day-to-day existence as a grinning zombie! A much truer and realistic goal would be 'I want to feel happier on a day-to-day basis.'

- ✔ **Time-oriented:** Your goal must be achievable within a specific time-frame. By omitting a timeframe you consciously and unconsciously keep pushing the goal away from you. A part of your mind thinks 'Oh, I can do that tomorrow', and as you know, tomorrow never comes. Put your goal within a timeframe and that laziness is replaced with a positive sense of urgency that will allow both your conscious and unconscious minds to really move towards achieving your goal.

When thinking about time, remember to be *realistic*. If your timeframe isn't realistic, your goal will fall apart. A patient once contacted Peter for therapy in order to lose two stone in weight; a very realistic goal. This all fell apart when asked over what period of time he envisaged losing this weight, as his reply was 'By the end of the week!' This goal was obviously not achievable, nor would it be healthy if it were. However, if Peter were a surgeon skilled in liposuction . . .

Two other concepts to bear in mind when thinking about setting goals are immediate tasks and ongoing tasks:

- ✔ **Immediate tasks** are those you can carry out right now to firmly set yourself on the path of achieving your goal. For example, emptying your fridge of all the unhealthy food and then restocking it with healthier items that contribute to your weight-loss goal.

- ✔ **Ongoing tasks** are those you need to do on a day-to-day basis to carry you along the way towards achieving your goal. For example, remembering to walk a little more briskly and a little farther each day as an aid to losing weight.

Tapping into the power of realistic goals

Because your mind is goal-directed, if you set a goal that is SMART you move towards achieving it both consciously and unconsciously. If you define your goal, make it tangible, make it something you can achieve, ensure that it is realistic, and give it a timeframe, your mind accepts and moves easily towards your goal.

With the help of hypnotherapy, you start noticing subtle changes in your behaviour; you experience changes in the way you think and in your motivation as you become more focused on where you want to be. And as you appreciate these changes, so your motivation improves and before you know it you have realised your outcome.

Compounding your problems with unrealistic goals

If your goal fails to meet the SMART criteria, you may be beset with a whole host of problems, the least of which is not achieving your goal. In fact, you can end up creating an even worse problem for yourself. The person who goal-sets to win the lottery can end up with a gambling addiction, the person who goal-sets to lose an unhealthy amount of weight over too short a period of time can end up with anorexia nervosa.

But don't worry; your hypnotherapist is there to help you and to ensure that you head in the right, healthy direction.

Examining your motivation

Do you have a genuine inner desire to improve your quality of life in some way, or are you going for therapy because your partner/parent/child/boss/doctor wants you to make a change for their own reasons, despite the fact that you are happy with the way you are and don't want to change?

If your motivation is coming from inside you, your chances of achieving your goal are high as long as you are SMART. If your motivation is coming from someone other than yourself, you significantly reduce your chances of succeeding. Why? Because you don't really want to change!

If your motivation is wrong, you may resent having to go for therapy, putting up all sorts of barriers to success. As the old adage goes 'You can lead a horse to water, but you can't make it drink it.' In other words, you can lead a patient to hypnotherapy, but you can't make them do the therapy. Some would say that if you put a sugar lump in the water the horse will then drink. We would say that the horse will eat the sugar lump, getting a bit of the water in its mouth, and then withdraw its muzzle. In the same way, therapy may have some effect, but not to any great extent.

You may need to make a change for health reasons. You may, for example, need to stop smoking or lose weight because of a heart condition. Part of you is aware and understands this, yet there is a much stronger part that just wants to keep smoking or overeating because you enjoy it. Discuss this type of situation with your hypnotherapist. He can help you build up the appropriate motivation. After all, your own health is paramount.

So, when you are thinking about your motivation to change, think about the following:

✔ **What is motivating me to change?**

✔ **Where is my motivation for change coming from?**

✔ **What feelings and emotions do I need in order to motivate me more?**

When you think about your motivation, try to think in positive terms. For example 'I want to give up smoking because I will die of cancer if I don't' is a good motivator, but a very negative one. Rather, think in positive terms such as 'I want to give up smoking so that I enjoy a long and healthy life.' Think of the positive thing you want (life), rather than the negative thing you don't want (death)!

Negotiating Your Goals with Your Hypnotherapist

Even though your hypnotherapist will ask you about your problem in some detail, he also wants to know what outcome you're looking for. Letting him know exactly what you want to achieve by coming for therapy is very important. Try to be as full in your description as you can. The more information you can give the more personal and accurate the therapy will be. Let your therapist know the following:

- ✔ **Your specific goal**

- ✔ **Your timeframe for reaching your goal**

- ✔ **Things that you can do immediately to start you on the path towards achieving your goal**

- ✔ **What you need to do on a day-to-day basis in order to ensure you stay on course towards achieving your goal**

- ✔ **How you think life will be different for you once you achieve your goal**

- ✔ **How you want to be thinking and feeling once you achieve your goal**

- ✔ **What hurdles you think you'll need to climb on the path towards your goal**

- ✔ **What you need to do to ensure that you maintain your goal once you achieve it**

Of course, the answers to some of these may not be immediately apparent to you. Again, this is where your therapist's skill in questioning can help you to formulate an answer. In some cases the answers may not be there at a conscious level at all and can only be accessed when you are in hypnosis. Again, your hypnotherapist's skill will help you to uncover them.

Perhaps you have a variety of possible goals and can't decide which one is the most appropriate. Through a combination of talking and trance work you will be able to select that which is most suitable.

It's also the job of your therapist to ensure that the goal you are working towards is appropriate, so don't be surprised if he questions you about various aspects of the one you want to go for. He is only making sure that he takes you in the right direction during therapy.

Breaking down bigger goals

In some cases, your hypnotherapist may break your goal down into a series of smaller goals to ensure that you are not trying to take too large a step in one go. Take too large a step and you risk tripping and falling, maybe never to get up again.

When a baby learns to walk, he doesn't go directly from the crawling stage to striding purposefully across the room. His goal is certainly to do that, but he needs to achieve several simpler goals – pulling himself up and standing upright, walking whilst holding on to something, walking alone for a few steps – before finally walking competently across the room.

Resolving your problems needs to go through a similar process. If you have the ultimate goal of losing four stone in weight, losing that amount may seem daunting at first glance. Splitting the goal into smaller goals of, say, one stone, makes the task more manageable, less daunting, and, as each of the smaller goals is achieved, much more motivational.

Winning the goal game

Going for hypnotherapy is a bit like playing a game in which you're the team captain and your therapist is a good supporting player. Your aim is to play the best you can and your therapist's aim is to help you win the game. In order to win you need to score that winning goal.

Aiming: Choosing one goal at a time

Don't try to do too much in one go or you'll lose the game. Keep your focus in one direction and on one specific goal. If you don't, you may become confused, and score an own goal, ending up back where you started.

Another sure way to fail is to attempt to score a potpourri of goals all at once. Doing this dilutes the whole effect of therapy and gets you nowhere – you may even start moving backwards.

By keeping your focus in one direction with one aim in mind, you set yourself up to shoot the therapy ball firmly and squarely into the back of the opposition's goal. Win one game and you set yourself up to win the next, and the next, and so on.

Releasing: Developing a winning mindset

Through hypnotherapy you can develop the winning mindset that allows you to overcome your problem, building up and maintaining the motivation that spurs you on to achieve your goal for therapy. This doesn't mean you blindly take one route and stick to it come what may. If that were the case, you could end up like a mindless robot automatically moving forward, possibly achieving your goal, but probably bumping into some obstacle along the way. In continuing your efforts to move forward, you can repeatedly bump into the same obstacle, coming to a grinding halt and not being able to move any farther.

The winning mindset allows you to walk forward and encounter obstacles, as well as to take a step backwards and find another route around them. What we're saying is that the path to change is one that can change itself. Often the path is smooth and relatively obstacle free, but the winning mindset recognises and plans ways around any obstacles. It may even be necessary to change paths completely.

On the surface, this attitude may seem a little pessimistic. On the contrary, it is optimistic because it is realistic. If you try to foresee possible obstacles that may appear on the path towards your goal, you can plan ways of surmounting them in advance.

In the case of weight control, you may be finding out how to eat healthily but know a particular party looms on the horizon where you'll be tempted to overeat. In discussing this with your therapist, you can formulate a strategy that can be given to you in hypnosis in order to successfully help you through this event.

If a goal is wrong, then it is important that you are able to drop it and move on to something more appropriate. However, if you find that you keep chopping and changing your goals without ever achieving any, you really need to go back to the drawing board and start all over again. Something, somewhere, wasn't defined properly from the outset.

The winning mindset also recognises that goals may change as you get closer to realising them. What started out as a good idea may not seem as appropriate as you get closer to achieving it. This is by no means a disaster – the winning mindset recognises that changing the goal is important, because you wish to move towards something that you really do want. Even the efforts you've made so far would not have been in vain; as they will still go a long way toward helping you achieve your new goal.

Your hypnotherapist is there to help you all the way. By discussing your goals at the start of therapy, and by continuing to review those with your therapist, you will end up with the winning mindset that will have you standing in first place, triumphantly and proudly holding aloft the cup of champions!

Part II
Considering How Hypnotherapy Can Help

The 5th Wave   By Rich Tennant

I told you not to stare at yourself in that thing while you're cutting the grass!

In this part . . .

Hypnotherapy is a very powerful therapy, particularly because it not only affects the mind, but also the body. This dual action can produce rapid and lasting changes in many different treatment areas. As you read this part, you may be amazed to discover the range of areas that hypnotherapy can treat, including lifelong habits and deep-rooted phobias.

Chapter 4

Making the Mind-Body Connection

*H*ypnosis doesn't exist and people only pretend to be in trance. Hang on. Before you start writing to our publishers and demanding your money back, take a few moments to read on! This statement has been around for years in various forms, and has proved to be one of the most stubborn sticking points used by hypnotherapy's detractors when trying to debunk our profession. Well, have we got news for them: Hypnosis does exist and people really are in trance!

Over recent years a whole new scientific discipline has come bursting onto the scene: *psychoneuroimmunology*. (Try saying that after a glass or two of wine!) Psychoneuroimmunology is thankfully shortened to PNI, or sometimes mind-body medicine (or even psychosomatic medicine, or behavioural medicine, if you want to be picky!). This discipline proves that there is a very real connection between what happens in your mind and what happens in your body. In this chapter, we highlight how PNI research – in conjunction with other disciplines – shows that hypnosis and trance are very real things. Hypnosis detractors, eat your heart out!

Understanding the Mind-Body Connection

Many years ago the great French mathematician and philosopher, Rene Descartes, put forward the point of view that the mind and the body were completely separate entities, with neither one influencing the other; a theory known as *Cartesian Dualism*. Unfortunately, the medical and scientific world mainly accepted this idea, ignoring or rejecting the concept that the mind can and does influence the way the body works, and that what happens in your body also influences how your mind works.

Fortunately, a few hardy souls steadfastly researched that very concept, and eventually published convincing research that made the scientific and medical world finally sit up and take notice. The research shows that the immune system, which is responsible for protecting you against infection and disease, also influences your moods. In addition, the research shows that chemical messengers, found in the nervous system, help protect the body against illness.

These findings led to a fairly radical new approach to treating patients. Instead of purely symptom-based treatment, in which the symptom and symptom alone were treated, clued in healthcare professionals now use a more holistic approach that treats not only the symptom but takes the patient's psychological state into consideration as well.

Fitting up the connectors: Your nervous system

In order to perhaps understand how the mind and body can work together, it's useful, first of all, to know a little about the nervous system. Think of it as a very complex and intricate system of wiring, controlled by a very advanced supercomputer. It is divided into two parts:

- ✔ **The central nervous system:** This consists of the brain (you know, that squidgy lump of porridge in your head), and the spinal cord (an extension of the squidgy porridge that runs down the centre of your spine).

- ✔ **The peripheral nervous system:** This is made up of the cranial nerves (wires, as it were, that stick out of your brain), the spinal nerves (wires that stick out of your spinal cord), and the autonomic nervous system (the system of wiring that controls all your automatic body functions).

Both the central and peripheral nervous systems work together to keep you going on a day-to-day basis, and it's worth having a closer look at how various bits of them work:

- ✔ **The brain.** This extremely complex grey matter runs the whole show. If you take a closer look at the brain, you find that it's split up into many different bits, each with their own individual function. Some are very primitive and ancient in evolutionary terms, like the amygdala, which is responsible for things such as emotion and aggression. Some are much more intricate and modern, again in evolutionary terms, such as the cerebral cortex – responsible for consciousness, memory, and thought.

  The brain gives you your intellect, emotions, memories, and so on.

- ✔ **The spinal cord.** This is the second part of the central nervous system and dangles from the bottom of your brain, passing down the centre of your spine. Like the brain, the spinal cord is also made up of various bits that all combine together to essentially pass messages back and forth, between your brain and the rest of your nervous system.

  Between them, the brain and the spinal cord control all your body's functions.

- ✔ **The autonomic nervous system.** Found throughout your body, this system basically controls all your body's automatic functions, such as the beating of your heart and your breathing. To make things interesting, the autonomic nervous system is divided into two halves that are basically the opposite of each other:

  - **The sympathetic nervous system.** This part of the autonomic nervous system is responsible for you being active. Amongst other things, it reacts to danger and is partly responsible for the effects you feel when you are stressed or afraid (such as increased heart rate and faster breathing).

  - **The parasympathetic nervous system.** The opposite to the sympathetic nervous system, the parasympathetic nervous system is responsible for the effects you feel when you are calm and tranquil (such as slow heart rate and breathing deeply and calmly).

  In order to keep functioning properly, both the sympathetic and parasympathetic nervous systems must work together.

- ✔ **Nerves.** These carry messages around your body, to and from the brain and spinal cord. They connect your organs, muscles, and skin, to the supercomputer that is your brain, either directly through the cranial nerves, or through the spinal nerves via the spinal cord.

The central and peripheral nervous systems work together. Some of the functioning is under conscious control and some seemingly automatic. For example, if you want to get up out of a chair and walk across the room, your brain makes a conscious decision to do this. Your brain sends messages down your spinal cord and out, via a whole network of nerves, to your muscles, which start to contract to raise you out of the chair. Then your autonomic nervous system kicks in and you start to walk. Your sympathetic nervous system causes some of these muscles to contract (such as those in your thigh and calf), propelling you forward on one leg. Your parasympathetic nervous system then makes some muscles relax as the leg is lifted (such as your calf muscles, because they're not needed for a few moments).

The act of walking is under the control of your peripheral nervous system and your spinal cord, whilst the decision to start or stop walking is under the control of your brain.

A similar process lets you experience emotion. Your peripheral nervous system registers information from the outside world through your eyes, ears, nose, and skin. Those messages are relayed to your brain via your nerves and your spinal cord. Your brain then interprets these messages.

If for example, your brain interprets something as scary, then the amygdala – that primitive part of your brain that is partly responsible for emotions such as fear – becomes active and you feel fear. Messages are sent out via your spinal cord, and the sympathetic nervous system kicks in causing your muscles to tense, your heart rate to rise, and your rate of breathing to increase. When your brain registers that the scary thing has gone, messages are sent to your brain that are interpreted in a way that lets you know not to be scared. The amygdala turns off and you feel calm. Messages are sent out, again via your spinal cord, and the parasympathetic nervous system kicks in and your muscles relax, your heart rate and breathing slow down and hey presto, you are calm again.

Making the connection with hypnosis

Hypnosis happens in the brain, that's for sure. Studies show that the brain wave activity of a person in a trance is very different to when that person is alert, asleep, or pretending to be in trance.

Brain waves are a measurement of the electrical activity of the brain. This activity changes very distinctly when you're sleeping, being alert or experiencing trance. And for those of you who like big words, the machine that measures these brainwaves is called an electroencephalogram. For those who don't, you can call it an EEG!

A number of studies confirm that brainwaves are measurably different when you're in trance. Alpha waves, theta waves, and something with the very grandiose title of the 40-Hertz band, are all altered when we are in hypnosis. These waves and bands have nothing to do with the sea or popular music; they refer to the frequencies at which the electrical activity of the brain is operating. When you are alert the electrical activity is running at a certain frequency, when you are asleep it changes to another frequency, and when you are in trance, to yet another.

Further evidence can be found in PET studies. No, not the study of how Fido is behaving, but something called Positron Emission Tomography. This very interesting technique allows scientists to look at your brain and work out what parts of it are active when you are experiencing something. And guess what? The brain in hypnosis shows different activity than the awake brain or the sleeping brain.

A study was carried out on how the brain reacted to hypnotic pain control (for more on hypnosis and pain control see Chapter 6). In a non-hypnotised person experiencing a painful stimulus, two areas (amongst several others) were 'lighting up' as it were: the *somatosensory cortex* – the rather posh name for the part of the brain that processes painful stimuli – and the *anterior cingulated cortex* – an even fancier name for the area of the brain that is involved in your perception of suffering. In a hypnotised person being given a painful stimulus, the researchers noticed that the somatosensory cortex was still lighting up; however the anterior cingulated cortex wasn't. In other words, the pain stimulus was being processed, but the brain did not perceive any suffering. Proof positive that hypnosis directly affects the brain.

When you're awake and alert, your sympathetic nervous system is very active. It helps you walk, talk, exercise, and sometimes feel stressed. On the other hand, when you enter into trance, the good old parasympathetic nervous system comes to the fore, turning off the sympathetic nervous system and allowing you to go into a state of relaxation and rest.

So to pull it all together, when you enter into trance, your brainwaves alter, various areas of the brain change their activity, and the parasympathetic nervous system becomes dominant. Small wonder that many patients report that they feel wonderfully relaxed when they are experiencing hypnotherapy.

Considering How Your Emotions Affect You

Everyone experiences emotions. These emotions are products of your brain; they are mental states and as such mean that your brain is active in promoting them. If your brain is active, the rest of your nervous system is too. That means that when you experience an emotion of any kind it will have a knock-on effect in your nervous system. And, by extension, other physical parts of you – remember that the nervous system controls your entire body.

If this emotion that you experience is having an effect on your body, is that a good thing or a bad thing? The answer is that it's a little of both. It all depends on the type of emotion that you are experiencing. The good ones – such as happiness, elation, and joy – have a beneficial effect on your body; helping you to feel relaxed, keeping your immune system healthy, and so on. Positive emotions help you to recover when you're ill by boosting your beleaguered immune system. On the other hand, negative emotions such as anxiety, stress, and depression have a detrimental effect on your immune system.

Your body is quite a resilient thing and can take a fair amount of punishment before it starts to fail. It takes a good old battering from such things as physical knocks, the environment, and your negative emotions. Between these bouts of battering it does need to rest and recuperate. If it is not allowed to do so, then the pressure of keeping you going builds and builds, and if you are not careful, your body eventually starts to fail. It may seem obvious that physical and environmental factors can do this to you, but how do emotional factors figure in this? Read on to find out.

Depressing the effects of low moods

When you are in a good mood your body is in a state of balance in regard to the various biochemicals coursing through it. These biochemicals all have their own specific functions that help to keep your body in tiptop condition.

When you are down or depressed your mind is in a very negative state. You end up having bad feelings coursing through your body, which in turn puts a myriad of hormones and biochemicals out of balance. As a result, your body no longer functions as it should.

For many people these low moods are transitory, you perk up and your resilient body gets a bit of a break – no harm done. In some cases though, these moods persist and your body doesn't get any respite from the imbalance, ending up in a descent into bad health. In fact, studies have shown that people who stay in prolonged low moods, like depression, are more likely to fall ill than those who don't. Now that's a depressing thought! That's because the imbalance in your body is having a negative effect on your immune system – the part of your system that is responsible for keeping you free from infection and disease.

Stressing about fear and anxiety

Even the most chilled out people in the world experience anxiety once in a while. It's one of those annoying moods that you can't escape.

In this chapter, we use the words *stress* and *anxiety* to describe the way that your body and mind respond when you experience something that you perceive as threatening to your physical health. You may call this *fear* – we prefer the terms stress or anxiety.

Whatever the word used, your body reacts to this state by releasing a whole host of biochemicals that are usually kept in balance. The quantity of biochemicals released determines the strength with which you experience these feelings – the greater the volume, the stronger the feeling. In an ideal world, this response – mild to intense – should only last a short while. However, this is not an ideal world – more's the pity – and this response is often left switched on for long periods of time in many people.

Moderate anxiety is good – without it the human race would probably not exist. No, we haven't lost the plot; all we are saying is that anxiety has a very functional role within your life. It helps to keep you focused on things in your life that need to be attended to. The only time you really need to worry about anxiety is when you experience too much of it, and for too long a period of time. Then it can become a downright liability by increasing your risk of having a heart attack, or lowering your immunity to disease, for example.

Your body has a wide variety of warning and alarm systems that help to keep you safe and out of harm's way. Anxiety is one of them. Anxiety warns you that something is a potential threat to your safety. It keeps you wary and away from harm. Should you decide to explore whatever it is that is potentially dangerous, then feeling anxious will mean that you approach whatever it is with caution. What we are talking about here is what anxiety is *supposed* to do for you, and what it *actually* did for your ancestors. You'll see what we mean by going back in time for a few moments.

Fighting or fleeing: Facing the fear response

Experiencing anxiety, stress, or fear is also known as the *fight-or-flight response*.

Several things happen the moment you feel anxious:

- ✔ Your sympathetic nervous system becomes over active.
- ✔ Your heart rate increases.
- ✔ Your breathing rate increases.
- ✔ Your muscles become tense.

✔ Blood is diverted to the muscles in your arms and legs.

✔ Your digestion slows or stops.

These physical responses happen whether you're confronted by a bear, or just a beastly boss warning you that your job is at risk.

Unfortunately, the biochemicals that help you to run away and fight also end up damaging your body and immune system if they're left active for a prolonged period of time. If you don't get a chance to take your system off high alert status, the effects of your flight-or-fight response can cause physical damage: an overactive sympathetic nervous system can cause your body to shake; an increased heart rate wears down your heart muscle; increased breathing may end up as hyperventilation, which in turn can lead to a panic attack; muscle tension can cause tension headaches and muscle pain; diverted blood may cause hot flushes; and decreased digestion can result in a number of problems associated with your gut.

Staying alive in caveman days

This response proved very useful to your ancestors! The anxiety response has kept the human race from being eaten into extinction by predators. Imagine one of your ancestors wandering along nonchalantly through a forest, when a sabre-toothed tiger jumps out in front of him with the intention of picking up a caveman takeaway. Your ancestor's immediate response is to fight for his life or to run away: His fight-or-flight response is turned on as a reaction to a perceived personal threat. His body is flooded with a whole variety of chemicals that prepare him for action. After saving his own life (and possibly picking up a sabre-toothed tiger takeaway in the process), his fight-or-flight response is turned off and his body returns to normal.

Just imagine that the human race evolved without an anxiety response. Ah! Nirvana! Or is it? Imagine your everyday caveman hunting for some animal that has the potential for being a pot roast. As he is walking through the forest he hears the sound of branches breaking behind him. Without an anxiety response, he turns nonchalantly around to see what it is that is making the sound, perhaps striding boldly over to investigate. Before he knows it, a bundle of fur, sharp claws, and very long teeth comes hurtling out of the undergrowth and sends him into oblivion.

The moral of this story: no anxiety equals no caution equals no life! Add anxiety back into the equation, and the moral changes: anxiety equals caution equals staying alive (with a nice lunch too!).

During periods of real danger, your stress response can actually save your life by giving you the energy to defend yourself or run away.

Surviving in the modern jungle

You don't meet very many sabre-toothed tigers today, but you do have nagging bosses, threatening bullies, troubling financial concerns, and so on, which are the modern day equivalents. However, in today's society you do very little fighting or fleeing in response to your anxieties (unless you are in a war zone or a dangerous inner city area). In fact, all you tend to do is to let your feelings grow and grow. This is not good, because you have a body that is ready for action, but isn't doing anything.

When your body switches to the fight-or-flight response it prepares to become explosively active. Today, you don't often actually fight and you don't actually run away. As far as your body is concerned, it's a bit like having your foot pressed down on the accelerator and brake at the same time – your engine is revving and going nowhere. The result: breakdown.

All of these responses are like revving your car. Take your foot off the brake and away you go! In this day and age, you tend to keep your foot firmly on the brake, risking damage.

Integrating Hypnosis into the Mind-Body Connection

If your mind can affect the way your body functions, and hypnotherapy can affect the way your mind functions, then it stands to reason that hypnotherapy can ultimately affect your body's responses. Using hypnotherapy to change the way you think about and respond to situations and events that affect your life can ultimately change the way your body reacts. This effect can be a by-product of therapy or an actively sought response. For example, if you are coming for therapy to help reduce your levels of stress, a by-product could be better health. Or perhaps you are coming for therapy to help manage and reduce the pain you are experiencing. In this case, you are actively seeking to alter your body's response to whatever is causing the pain (see Chapter 6 to find out more about pain control using hypnotherapy).

Whatever you are seeking therapy for, the hypnotherapy process makes a variety of positive changes to your body. The next sections highlight some of these.

Hypnotherapy does not cure disease and should never be advertised as doing so. Hypnotherapy does help to make changes to the way you think and feel, and the way your body responds in certain situations. De-stressing may, in itself, reduce or eliminate any stress related ailments you may experience such as headaches, ulcers, and rashes. But any effects on a disease state are lucky by-products that may or may not be attributable to your therapy, and can never be guaranteed.

Relaxing mentally and physically through hypnosis

Even though you often don't know how to handle stress, anxiety, or fear, that doesn't mean that there is nothing you can do about it. In fact, you can take a lesson from your primitive ancestors. After any burst of activity that resulted from a fight-or-flight response (have a look at the previous section, 'Fighting or fleeing: Facing the fear response' for more on this), your caveman ancestor would probably seek out a quiet and safe place and take time to rest, to sleep, to perhaps enter into a trance-like state. By doing so, his mind would calm down. As his mind calmed down, it would communicate with his body, which would release all the muscle tensions and turn down the biochemical responses that resulted from the fight-or-flight response. In effect, he would relax.

The key to combating that excess of anxiety, stress, or fear is to relax. How your body responds when you relax is much the same as when you enter hypnosis. The most common body responses are:

- ✔ Your heart rate slows down.
- ✔ Your breathing rate slows down and becomes deeper.
- ✔ The muscles throughout your body become less tense.
- ✔ Blood is evenly distributed throughout the body.
- ✔ Your digestion system works efficiently.
- ✔ Your thoughts become less concrete and more abstract – more image and feeling based

Of course, you will always have periods of anxiety. It's how you handle that anxiety that is important.

If you can get into a regular pattern of relaxation and exercise, you can minimise the nasty effects of long-term anxiety. It's also worth mentioning that if you stop smoking, eat healthily, and cut down on the amount of alcohol and caffeine you drink, then you will be on tiptop form to beat that anxiety firmly into the ground.

Manifesting the mind through the body

Many of your body movements are the result of conscious decisions to move a specific part: perhaps lifting your hand to pick something up, or maybe shutting your eyes to block out an unpleasant sight. However, many of your movements, such as walking, are unconscious (see the previous section 'Fitting up the connectors: Your nervous system'). You make a conscious decision to start walking, however the movement itself is controlled by your unconscious mind; you don't actively have to concentrate on the mechanics of lifting first one foot and then the other.

This unconscious response is very useful in hypnotherapy as it can help induce or deepen hypnosis, or it can be used as part of your therapy. The suggestions given by your therapist create ideas in your unconscious mind. These ideas stimulate the connection to your body, which acts on the suggestions being given.

In the following sections, we refer to closing your eyes, lifting fingers, and moving your hand or arm – all actions that can be carried out by your conscious mind. However, the movements we refer to are all examples of the mind-body connection, because they are automatic and result from ideas that are suggested to your unconscious mind. In other words, the movements are not under conscious control.

Shutting out the external world with eye closure

When you go into trance, there is a good chance your eyes will become droopy, feeling heavy, and wanting to close as a result of the suggestions your therapist is giving to you. This shows that you're entering a relaxed and receptive state.

When you close your eyes you become a little removed from the outside world. Sure, you still hear and feel things, but removing your sense of sight encourages you to focus inward. Try it as you read. Put this book down, close your eyes and take a few deep, slow breaths. You will probably experience a slight (and hopefully pleasant) sensation as a shift in your consciousness begins to occur. This is the first movement towards a trance state. And it all comes from simply closing your eyes.

The simplest way to get a patient to close her eyes is to ask her to do so! However, hypnotherapists being what we are, also use a host of other methods. Here are a couple to be getting on with:

- ✔ **Prolonged fixation of the eyes on a single spot:** If you stare at one spot for a period of time your eyelids become tired. They want to close. And when your therapist directs you to do just that, you experience a sense of relief and relaxation that moves you towards the trance state.

- ✔ **Eye rolling:** Looking upward, without moving your head, produces a small level of discomfort and tension in your eyelids. When your hypnotherapist asks you to relax and close your eyes, again the sense of relief and relaxation moves you towards trance.

Your eyes are closed and you're nice and relaxed, so how do you keep from falling asleep? In our experience it is rare for a person to fall asleep during a hypnosis session. By altering the volume, tone, and pitch of her voice your therapist will keep your unconscious mind sufficiently interested to prevent you from drifting off!

Letting your fingers do the talking: Ideo motor response (IMR)

During a hypnotherapy session your therapist may need to communicate with you by asking you questions that require 'yes' or 'no' answers. Your treatment may necessitate your responding to these questions on an unconscious level in order to avoid too much conscious thinking, intellectualising, or second-guessing the answer.

So how do you communicate at this unconscious level while in trance? While it is perfectly possible to have a verbal dialogue while hypnotised (though some people struggle to maintain the trance when they are talking), a more elegant solution is to use ideo motor responses.

Defining IMR

The term *ideo motor response* literally means a physical (motor) response to an idea (ideo). In a hypnotherapy session, an IMR is a slow, hesitant, jerky movement of any limb or muscle of your body controlled by your unconscious mind. IMRs are used to signal an answer to a yes/no question.

IMRs can also be used as a *ratifier,* which simply means a way of proving you are hypnotised. The mere act of having your fingers respond, seemingly independent of your conscious mind, firms up your belief in the trance state, leading to a deepening of the trance itself.

Flexing your fingers

So how does an IMR work exactly? Your hypnotherapist assigns your unconscious mind to lift different fingers to indicate different responses.

For example, while in trance, your hypnotherapist may suggest that when you need to indicate a 'no' response you will lift your left index finger. They may also suggest that lifting your right index finger would signal a 'yes' response.

Additional fingers can be assigned to indicate other responses, such as one of your middle fingers could be assigned an 'I don't know' response. Another finger, for example, could be assigned as an 'I don't want to answer' response, allowing you to maintain privacy. However, most hypnotherapists may choose to keep it simple with this technique, choosing only a 'yes' and 'no' finger. In this case, if you really don't want to answer, then either both fingers will rise, or nothing will happen at all!

Communicating without talking

Have you ever watched a card game involving high gambling stakes? A professional card player can easily spot an inexperienced or bad card player. The bad card player will unconsciously signal what type of hand they are holding. They are like an open book to a trained observer and it will be easy for the gambler to take their money. The inexperienced player will invariably give something away on an unconscious level through facial expressions, hand movements, and other unconscious body movements. In effect, the novice player is communicating unconsciously with the seasoned pro.

You probably observe many similar examples of this on a daily basis. Unconscious movements made by others communicate a lot of information about that person: how they are feeling, the direction in which they are thinking, and so on. How often have you heard someone say 'I'm fine!', yet you know that they are far from fine? The reason that you know is because you have picked up on physical factors generated by that person's unconscious mind, such as muscle tension or an unhappy expression. Even though they wanted to convey a happy exterior, that person's unconscious mind is very aware that they feel bad. Their autonomic nervous system responds to this unconscious reality by automatically generating the physical factors you pick up on.

Treating with IMR

Your hypnotherapists can use IMRs to achieve unconscious communication with you while you're in trance. Here are a few examples of the different uses IMR can be put to:

✔ **Treating phobias:** IMRs might be used to indicate whether or not you feel comfortable with a potentially anxiety provoking scene you are imagining, that relates to your phobia. See Chapter 11 for more on phobias and their treatment.

✔ **Regression hypnosis:** This involves a fair bit of questioning while you are hypnotised. Your therapist may need to ask a series of yes/no questions and may use IMR to ensure a good level of communication.

✔ **Replacing a symptom with something more acceptable:** It is never wise to just help someone remove their symptom. Take it away and you leave a gap in that person's life. That gap needs to be filled with something. IMRs can be used as part of the filling process. Your therapist could ask your unconscious mind to come up with a healthy alternative to your unwanted symptom, and to indicate when it has done so by giving a 'yes' IMR.

Raising your hand

You may be aware from stage hypnosis shows that it is possible to hypnotise someone to 'levitate' their entire arm unconsciously. This concept is not just an entertainment technique – there are also very valid uses for it in a therapeutic setting.

Hand levitation – or sometimes arm levitation – is primarily a way of inducing or deepening trance, with the entire arm being made to rise unconsciously.

One way to demonstrate the process of hand levitation is to give you a couple of examples of what a hypnotherapist might say to induce hand levitation in a patient not yet hypnotised.

> ✔ **The 'I don't know which hand will lift first' technique:** *'Now, when I tell you, I'd like you to lift your left hand or right hand deliberately and consciously . . . but your unconscious mind can lift the other hand . . . before we start I'd like you to look at both of your hands, and I'm going to ask you a question . . . you do not know the answer to that question, but your unconscious mind does . . . so you'll just have to wait and see what the answer is . . . I'm going to ask you which hand your unconscious mind is going to lift up first . . . the right hand or the left hand? . . . and you really don't know . . . but your unconscious knows.'*

> ✔ **The lifting balloon technique:** *'Imagine that a balloon filled with helium is tied to the wrist of your left hand. Imagine the feel of the string on your wrist. Now let's say that this balloon has a particularly strong pull as it floats upwards. It is really pulling on your wrist, lifting, lifting your hand. Imagine the balloon is now lifting your hand higher and higher.'*

So what is the point of hand levitation? How does it help you with your therapy? The main aim of hand levitation is to induce an *unconscious* movement of the hand and arm.

Activating your unconscious is what hypnosis is all about. The process of hand levitation also activates that part of you that keeps you breathing, keeps your heart beating – and all other life sustaining, *unconscious* bodily activities. So the deeper you go into trance the better for hypnotherapy purposes, as you turn down your consciousness and turn up your unconscious. This will in turn help you to absorb the hypnotherapeutic suggestions being given by your therapist more deeply and effectively. That is the how the therapy 'sticks' with you.

Hand levitation may be used to treat problems that involve using your hand, such as:

✔ Smoking

✔ Nail-biting

✔ Hair pulling

✔ Eating disorders such as bulimia and overeating

The rational for using hand levitation is that with these problems the conscious mind 'switches off' and the hand movements become unconscious. Mimicking these unconscious movements in therapy with hand levitation helps bring the unwanted behaviour to conscious awareness when it is being carried out, subsequently helps stop the habit. Pretty ingenious, eh?

Chapter 5

Breaking Away from Old Habits

In This Chapter

▶ Understanding your habit and how hard it can be to change it

▶ Fighting nicotine and food

▶ Getting a good night's sleep

▶ Talking with confidence

▶ Chewing away at nail-biting

*W*e all have habits. Some are good, some are not so good and some are downright dangerous to your health. Your habits are part of what makes you who you are. They're a part of your personality; part of those quirky little things that draw some people to you and repel others. On the whole, you happily live with your habits. Happily, that is, until habits go bad! In this chapter, we address the most common bad habits and tell you how hypnotherapy can help you change them.

Examining Habits and How to Change Them

The word habit has several different meanings, but we use it to refer to any pattern of behaviour you carry out time and time again with little thought or effort.

A habit is not an addiction. Having an addiction means that you depend on some form of drug – such as nicotine, alcohol, or cocaine – to help get you through the day. When you're addicted to a drug, your body *needs* it to be present in your system. If it is not, you tend to feel awful – something known as withdrawal. In order to get back to feeling normal, you have to take some more of whatever it is you are addicted to.

Of course, habits can be part of an addiction. Just look at the smoker who habitually lights up when he talks on the phone, or reaches for his packet of cigarettes, the moment he steps out of his office. His body is addicted to the nicotine and he also has habits that maintain the addiction.

Hypnotherapy is a very effective way of helping you to overcome those annoying bad habits that interfere with your life. Even habits associated with addictions can be effectively treated. However, it is important that you realise that certain habits/addictions can be treated using hypnotherapy – such as smoking – and certain habit/addictions – such as those to do with heroin, cocaine, and alcohol – should be treated by a doctor. Of course, hypnotherapy can play a very important role in helping you stay drug-free, after you successfully beat a serious addiction.

Where do habits come from? In general, you learn them. You start a pattern of behaviour for one reason or another and after a while it becomes so ingrained in your mind that you carry it out almost unconsciously. Aha! *Unconsciously!* This word should give you a pretty hefty clue as to why hypnotherapy can be so effective in treating habits. If habits are stored in your unconscious mind, and hypnotherapy can help make changes to what is stored in the unconscious mind, then it stands to reason that hypnotherapy can help to change habits.

So, why would you want to change your habits? After all, your habits are a part of your personality aren't they? Of course they are, but that doesn't mean to say that you're happy with every aspect of your personality. And by extension, it certainly doesn't mean to say that you're happy with those habits that are harming your health, or making your life less pleasurable to experience.

'Right, I'm unhappy with my habit so I am just going to change it. Simple!' For some people, changing habits can be as straightforward as that. Make the decision and then make the change. But for many other people, changing isn't that simple. The habit has become a part of your life, something you're used to doing on a day-to-day basis. Changing a habit means removing something that has been an integral part of your life.

You may miss your habit. Quite strongly! You may associate certain activities with the habit and feel at a loss when you carry them out. You may erroneously associate the habit with reducing your stress and feel even more anxious when you are under pressure because you can't turn to your habit. In the end you give in to your feelings and suddenly the habit is back with a vengeance.

When giving up an old habit, you must replace it with something else: a new and healthy habit or a suitable strategy for coping effectively without the old habit.

After a while, the new habit or strategy becomes part of your make-up and the old one is left safely in the past. And it is with this process that hypnotherapy can play a huge role.

You acquire your habits from somewhere. If you can learn bad ones, you can certainly learn good, healthy ones too.

Quitting Smoking

Smoking is bad for you. You know it, and you know what it can do to you in the long-run – make you very ill and kill you. No point in mincing words here. So, why do people do it? Why do people, when they know the consequences, continue to puff on the old coffin nails? Probably because:

- ✔ **Smoking is addictive.** Nicotine is a drug that causes your body to become addicted to it. This means that after you have been smoking for a while your body gets so used to the nicotine coursing through your veins and invading your nervous system that in its absence your body misses it. Because your body is missing it, it throws a metaphorical temper tantrum and you experience the effects of withdrawal. To make yourself feel better you grab another cigarette, light it up and take a long drag (Cough, splutter, wheeze!), and hey presto! You give your body what it wants and, just like a child, the tantrum subsides.

- ✔ **Smoking is a habit.** Oh boy! Is smoking a habit! Every smoker knows about this. Every smoker associates their smoking with various activities they carry out during the day. It's not that they need the cigarette at that point, it's just that they always have a cigarette when: they talk on the phone, have a cup of coffee, walk to the station, read a book, sit on the loo, watch television and so on. The list is endless. They do it for no other reason than this is what they have always done at this time. It's a habit. And if they don't do it at these times they feel uncomfortable because they feel something is missing; they don't know what to do with their hands and so on. To fill that missing gap, or give their hands something to do, they light up.

  If you ask a smoker to tell you which cigarettes they need to smoke during the day because of the addiction factor, you probably find that there are only a very few. All the other cigarettes are smoked simply out of habit.

Preparing to quit: What to do before visiting your hypnotherapist

Okay. You want to quit. And you want to do it through hypnotherapy. So here's some useful advice for you to think about:

- ✔ **Plan the right time to quit.** Think about a good time to quit. Make sure that you plan to quit at a time when your life is going to be reasonably stable – when you have no major events over the coming month or two such as getting married, birthday parties, exams, holidays such as Christmas, and so on. On the other hand, many people find that quitting just before they go on holiday is a great time to do it, as the change of scenery and lack of all those familiar smoking triggers can reinforce their new non-smoking habit. Fix an appointment with your hypnotherapist and mark it in your diary. Oh, and keep to the date!

- ✔ **Tell people, who you know are supportive, that you're quitting.** It's always nice to have support and encouragement. These are the people you know you can turn to when your resolve is wavering, or who you know will give you those little words of encouragement just when you need them. Avoid at all costs those who would delight in your failure!

- ✔ **Get rid of all your smoking paraphernalia just before your hypnotherapy session.** Throw out your ashtrays, your lighters, and your stash of emergency cigarettes. You won't need them any more. Once they are gone they won't be there to tempt you from the straight and narrow. And ensure that your home becomes a strict no smoking zone.

- ✔ **Do something that you know will increase your motivation to quit.** You're motivated, but what else can you do that cranks up that motivation? Half-fill a jamjar with water and drop your old dog ends into it after you smoke each cigarette. Every so often, shake it up and smell the mixture. Nice! That's what's going on in your body each time you smoke. Or take another jamjar and each time you buy a packet of cigarettes put the equivalent amount of money into it. At the end of the week count it up and see how much you are spending on ruining your health. And then think how much you save once you have stopped. Plan to do something nice with that money.

At your first hypnotherapy session your therapist obviously asks you about your smoking habits. It can be helpful to think about these in advance. You can think about:

- ✔ Why you want to quit.
- ✔ How many cigarettes you smoke a day.
- ✔ The cigarettes you feel you need each day.
- ✔ The cigarettes you have just out of habit.

✔ How smoking affects you.

✔ How you think being a non-smoker benefits you.

✔ How old you were when you first started smoking.

✔ Why you first started smoking.

✔ Why you haven't quit before.

✔ If you have quit before, why you started smoking again.

✔ How much you spend on smoking each week and what you are going to do with all that extra money once you are a non-smoker.

✔ Any fears you may have about quitting.

This last issue often proves to be a sticking point when it comes to helping people quit.

Addressing your fears about quitting

Hypnotherapy for smoking is not just about helping you to stop. After all, you stop smoking between each cigarette you have. No, it's also about helping you to remain a non-smoker. That means it should not only address the process of stopping and keeping you stopped, but also those fears that you may have of what happens when you've done so. It's often these fears and concerns that prompt a person to fall off the healthy wagon and go back into the tarpit of smoking. So it is very important that you talk through any fears or concerns you have with your therapist to enable him to create strategies to help you get around them.

Some of these fears and the way your hypnotherapist can help you deal with them could include:

✔ **'I'm scared that I will put on weight.'** This is perhaps the most common fear. It is a fact that some people put on weight after they quit smoking. But hold on. That doesn't mean to say that nothing can be done about it. Far from it. It just means that these people have probably traded one habit – smoking – for another – eating. Not to worry, your therapist can give you suggestions designed to help you gain greater control over your eating habits. In fact, you should find that you only replace the habit of smoking with the wonderful habit of healthier living!

✔ **'Smoking helps me manage my stress, so what do I do once I quit?'** This old chestnut! If this is one of your fears, then think about this: nicotine *causes* the physical effects of stress. Nicotine increases your heart rate, increases your blood pressure, and causes your nervous system to release various stress hormones such as adrenaline.

So why do people associate cigarette smoking with stress relief? Probably because when a stressed smoker lights up, he's distracting himself away from the stress by the very process of lighting up and smoking the cigarette. He may also remove himself from the environment where the stress is occurring by having to go outside to smoke.

If you use cigarettes as a stress management tool, discuss this with your hypnotherapist. Through a process of suggestion and strengthening your ego (see Chapter 13 for more on ego-strengthening) your therapist can help you manage your stress in a much more healthy way. And perhaps you might like to book a session of stress management with him too! (Chapter 7 addresses stress.)

✔ **'What do I do with my hands when I'm in a bar?'** This is a very common fear among smokers who want to quit. Picture this: You're in a bar, holding a drink. What do you have in the other hand? A cigarette! It's as much a part of your drinking as raising your glass to your lips. Take away the cigarette and you take away part of your drinking behaviour. This can leave you with a sense of loss, a sense that something is missing and because of this you can feel a little out of sorts; perhaps a little anxious because you don't know what to do with your hand. This is easily dealt with in hypnotherapy by the use of suggestion. Suggestions that you forget about your hand and focus on what you are doing, the people you are talking to and the people around you help you to divert your focus of attention away from the empty hand. Another suggestion that may be used if you do notice your hand, is to replace that thought with a sense of pride that you are now a non-smoker and that your fingers no longer reek like a week-old dirty ashtray.

✔ **'I find it difficult to say no, so how do I react when I am offered a cigarette?'** You react by saying 'No thank you. I don't smoke.' Your hypnotherapist will give you suggestions to respond in this way when you're in a situation like this, and to feel proud about doing so! At the same time your therapist helps you to build up your willpower to resist through a whole variety of suggestions.

✔ **'I don't know if I can cope with the withdrawal symptoms.'** Some people give up smoking with no withdrawal symptoms whatsoever, whilst others go through the mill with them. Why is this? The answer probably has something to do with the psychological resources accessible at the time a person gives up. What is meant by psychological resources? Well, things such as beliefs (a strong belief that you won't have withdrawal symptoms), or positive feelings (a strong sense of confidence that giving up is straightforward). Whatever it is, your hypnotherapist will do his utmost to try to reduce any withdrawal symptoms you may experience, by strengthening your own psychological resources through the use of direct suggestion and other techniques.

You're quitting smoking. And that means ALL types of smoking. You can't quit cigarettes and start smoking a pipe or cigars, because you're still smoking and before you know it, you are back on the cigarettes again. Oh. And that also means you can't (and shouldn't because it's illegal) smoke the, er, 'herbal' variety of cigarettes either!

Using hypnosis to become smoke-free

How many sessions is it going to take you to become a non-smoker? Well, hypnotherapy can help you to quit in as little as one session.

Just as in medicine, several approaches can help you become a non-smoker. The approach your therapist uses with you could simply boil down to how they have been trained. Some schools teach a one-session approach to quitting, during which all your smoking issues are dealt with in one go. On the other hand, some approaches take three or four sessions to complete. In these, each session deals with a separate aspect of your smoking habit. Each is as good as the other, though we both favour the one session approach as it is immediate and takes into account that at your first session you are perhaps most motivated to quit.

So, what can you expect during your therapy session? First of all, your therapist will take a complete case history (see Chapter 13) and ask you questions that allow him to fully understand your smoking habits. From your answers to these questions he will then be able to design a therapy session (or sessions) that is personal to you, allowing you to take control of the habit whilst breaking your daily associations with smoking.

What happens if you have had your therapy sessions but still have a strong urge to smoke? Don't worry; pick up the telephone and call your hypnotherapist rather than pick up a cigarette. Any reputable therapist will make an appointment for you as soon as possible, so that they can help you through this crisis.

Before you go in for your hypnotherapy session, have that last cigarette. Enjoy it, as it will hopefully be the last one you will ever want.

Using hypnotherapy to quit smoking is not magic, and very much relies on building up your willpower. If you enter into your therapy session with the right motivation and a genuine desire to quit, then hypnotherapy is extremely effective in helping you to become and remain a non-smoker.

Never think that just because you have successfully managed to quit through hypnotherapy that means you are now so in control of your smoking habit, that you can allow yourself to have the occasional cigarette with impunity. Sorry, it doesn't work that way. One cigarette leads to another (after all, you're in control aren't you?), and then another (Hmm! Not so in control now), and then another (Ooops! Control has completely gone), and before you know it you are back where you started (and probably back to forking out for another trip to see your hypnotherapist).

Cessation suggestions

In general, a hypnotherapist helps you quit smoking through the use of suggestion. He gives suggestions that link your desire to quit to the various times of day that you smoke. For example, he may suggest that *'You have no desire to smoke when you first wake up in the morning'* or *'You have no desire to smoke after a meal'*.

Sounds too easy, doesn't it? Well, it's not that straightforward. What your therapist helps you do is a form of reprogramming. By associating your problem times with having no desire to smoke, the suggestions break the old unconscious associations you have with smoking; they reprogramme you. You may well find that you go through the day and, because of these suggestions, you forget about smoking for long periods of time. Why? Because your mind is no longer focused on the smoking behaviour. The association of various points in the day with smoking has been broken.

Of course, the issue of cravings and withdrawal will be taken into account. Many people who quit smoking through hypnotherapy say they have very few cravings and very little in the way of withdrawal. That doesn't mean to say that everyone gets off this lightly. Your hypnotherapist will give you suggestions to help you cope with any cravings – after all, they only last a very short time – as well as suggesting that you have the willpower to get through any feelings of withdrawal.

Aversion associations

Some therapists use aversion therapy as part of the process. In *aversion therapy*, your hypnotherapist reminds you of all the terrible harm smoking does to your body, or perhaps associates the smell and taste of tobacco with something like dog poo in an attempt to scare or revolt you out of the habit.

Your hypnotherapist may even use age progression (covered in Chapter 2) to let you see how you damage yourself in the long run if you remain a smoker; then show you how great your life will be as a non-smoker. What a wonderful motivator!

Analytic techniques

A few therapists (more and more in the minority) use analytical techniques such as dissociation and regression (again, discussed in Chapter 2) to discover why you have been a smoker and to then move you away from the habit. They feel that understanding why you became a smoker in the first place plays an important role in your becoming a non-smoker. Our own personal view is that this isn't necessary. Most smokers know why they started – peer pressure, rebellion – and are quite content with simply getting on with the process of moving on into a healthier future.

Managing Your Weight

We have a hefty problem with obesity in the Western world. And this means that more and more people are trying to find an effective way to lose weight. They hop onto the passing bandwagon of each and every fad diet that rears its head, only to fall off again later and to then bounce back onto the next . . . and the next . . . and the next! Sound like anyone you know?

The plain and simple fact is that many diets probably do little more than make money for the people who invented them. (Is that the sound of a contract being taken out on our lives for uttering such heresy?). The majority of diets rely solely on restriction of food intake and therein lies a problem. By relying solely on food restriction, these diets do not teach people to eat healthily, nor do they help them to modify their lifestyle. So, once you are off the diet you return to your old eating habits and the next thing you know all that weight you have lost is piling itself back on. In fact, studies show that around 95 per cent of all people who lose weight through dieting alone subsequently put it back on again! Not good news.

So why bother in the first place? Well, your health for one thing. People who are overweight are at a greater risk of developing:

- Heart disease
- Type-2 diabetes
- Stroke
- Joint problems
- Breathing difficulties
- High blood pressure

It's well worth shedding those pounds then!

Taking the safe route to the body you want

So, how can you lose weight safely and effectively (and that means keeping the weight off too)? Of course you need to look at what you eat and how much you consume, but weight loss and weight control do not solely rely on restriction of food. For effective weight management, the following should apply to whatever route you take to shed the pounds:

✔ **It must not be arduous.** There is nothing worse than having to force yourself to do something. If you are forcing yourself too much it becomes a drag. In the end it is much easier and enjoyable to slip back into your old ways, and any weight you may have lost slips back on. Remember that losing weight is your choice and that means you have to put in some effort to accomplish it. However, with the help of hypnotherapy, the whole process can become something that you can enjoy.

✔ **It must be flexible.** Don't be rigid. Just because eating chocolate can make you put on weight doesn't mean you have to give it up completely. Control the amount you eat. Reduce it, but don't ban it. Prohibiting something leads to desire. As the desire grows, you may find that you lose control and end up bingeing on the chocolate.

✔ **It must be realistic in terms of weight loss and time.** Most experts agree that 1 to 2 pounds a week is a safe and effective amount to lose.

✔ **It must be nutritionally balanced.** Basic common sense here. Ideally you should be eating as much fresh, organic food as possible, but not to the extent that you put weight on. This means that you should be including portions of all the food groups in your diet. Yes, that means fruit and vegetables too. Eating fresh and healthy food provides your body with a quality source of fuel. That means your body runs more efficiently and burns up that fat with more gusto. Oh, and you feel fitter, have more energy, are less prone to illness – the list of positives goes on and on.

✔ **It must include exercise.** No, this doesn't mean having to take out a membership to your local gym (though that would be a positive step), but rather it means that you should be prepared to increase your levels of daily activity. The more active you are, the more fat you burn off. Simple steps such as walking more, climbing the stairs rather than taking a lift, and walking up the escalators all help you to lose weight and keep that weight off, not to mention the good it does your heart (you know, that thing in your chest that keeps you alive!).

✔ **It must promote behavioural change.** This means that your lifestyle needs to change. If you take on board all the preceding points, you find that behavioural change occurs naturally and your weight drops. Remember it was your old behaviours and habits that led to that weight piling on in the first place!

If you haven't taken much exercise before and are thinking about starting to work out at the gym, or go running, or whatever, get checked to make sure that you are fit enough to do so. Also, get advice on how much exercise you should be doing. Suddenly going from a sedentary lifestyle to running ten miles a day won't do you, your heart, your muscles, or your joints any good at all. However, with some sensible advice and by building up the amount of exercise you do, you could eventually be running that marathon as you run off that excess weight.

Feeling hungry? Then you must be thirsty! No, you haven't read that wrong, nor have the proofreaders of this book missed a glaring mistake. In this day and age many people don't drink enough fresh water. That means many of us are dehydrated. Unfortunately, your brain sometimes gets mixed up when interpreting those messages from your body that say you're thirsty; and mistakenly registers that you're hungry. Consequently you eat to satisfy a non-existent hunger instead of drinking water to satiate your thirst. In fact, you should be drinking at least two litres of water each day. And that means water alone. Not in a cordial, tea, or coffee. These drinks are all *diuretic*, which means they cause your body to urinate out more water than it should. Drink water and you feel far fewer hunger pangs, eat less and lose more weight.

Eating yourself thin

We've said it before and will say it again – hypnotherapy is not magic. You cannot go in for a hypnotherapy session and come out ten pounds lighter; it just doesn't work that way! What hypnotherapy does is help you make changes to your eating and exercise habits, as well as help you enjoy the process of managing your weight. All in all, it helps you to change your lifestyle to one that keeps you slimmer and fitter and looking great.

In order to make sure you get the most out of your hypnotherapy sessions, think of the following before your first visit:

- ✔ **What weight do you want to achieve?** Make sure it is something sensible for you. Perhaps discuss this with your doctor if you don't know.

- ✔ **Over what period of time do you want to achieve this?** Again, make sure it is sensible. Remember that experts recommend 1 to 2 pounds of weight loss per week.

- ✔ **What is your motivation?** Do you have a genuine desire to lose weight for health reasons or your body image – a good motivation – or is someone bullying you into it – the 'I won't marry you unless you drop 2 stone' brigade, which is a not so good motivation. With a good and healthy motivation your chances of success increase.

✔ **How should you be changing your diet?** Examine your diet and see where you can make changes. For example:

- Grill instead of fry

- Cut down on portion size

- Eat more fresh produce including fruit and vegetables

- Cut down on eating sweets, biscuits, fatty puddings, and so on

- Drink more water!

✔ **Should you cut down on alcohol?** Sorry folks, but alcohol is *fattening*! We're not saying that you need to cut it out completely – after all, a small amount is good for your heart (thank goodness!). Rather, reduce the amount you drink and have a couple of alcohol-free days each week.

✔ **How can you improve on the amount of exercise you take?** Remember to be sensible. Think of times during your day when you can be more energetic (and to put the smutty minded in their place: yes, sex *is* a great calorie burner!).

✔ **What hurdles do you need to overcome?** Let's reality check. There are times when it is difficult to remain in control, at parties for example. How do you want to respond to the situation when temptation rears its fat, ugly head?

✔ **How do you want to look?** Hey, we all have a streak of vanity. Why not pander to it? But again, make sure what you want to achieve is realistic.

✔ **Do you binge on anything?** Are there any foods that when you eat them, you lose control of how much you are eating? You know, opening that box of chocolates and simply having to eat its entire contents!

Armed with the answers to these and other questions that you'll be asked at your first session, your hypnotherapist creates an appropriate plan of action for you. And that plan of action is probably constructed from a variety of techniques that certainly include direct suggestion. For example, '. . . *You have no desire to eat sickly . . . sweet chocolate . . . in fact . . . you only enjoy the wonderful flavours of the right kinds of healthy food . . . that you know are right for you . . .* '

Your hypnotherapist may put your imagination to use. For example, he may ask you to imagine that you are shopping for food and that all you buy are small amounts of healthy fresh food. He may take you into the future in your mind, so that you can experience what it's like having lost that weight and maintained its loss too. This mental picture can help you to stop thinking of yourself as a fat person; rather, you can start focusing your self perception on being a thin person. Very motivational!

Some therapists may use analytical tools such as regression or dissociation, though we feel that these analytical tools should be left alone and used only as a last resort. Why? Because for the majority of people coming for weight control it's a simple case of too much of the wrong kind of food into the stomach, and not enough energy out through the muscles! Of course, there are some people for whom being overweight is a symptom of something deeper, and in these cases the use of analytical tools is entirely justified.

However he works, your hypnotherapist aims to help you to:

 ✔ Take control of your eating habits.

 ✔ Improve your levels of exercise.

 ✔ Deal with any issues you may have with regard to losing weight.

 ✔ Build up and maintain your motivation.

Getting a Good Night's Sleep

Sleep is something you normally look forward to. A time to rest and recharge your batteries, to take you into the next day alert and full of energy. However, sometimes the process of sleeping may be arduous and less than restful. If you fall into this category, then perhaps a visit to your hypnotherapist is in order.

Solving your insomnia

Most people experience periods when they find it difficult to sleep. Perhaps you're stressed, or travelling from a different time zone, or just don't know why you can't sleep. These times are transitory and are little more than an inconvenience. However, your periods of sleeplessness may become more than transitory and develop into a recurring pattern when you are trying to get to sleep.

There are basically three types of insomnia:

 ✔ **Initial sleep difficulties:** You have difficulty falling asleep when you first go to bed.

 ✔ **Intermediate sleep difficulties:** You fall asleep when you first go to bed, but awaken in the middle of the night. Once you awaken you find it difficult to return to sleep.

 ✔ **Early morning awakening:** You sleep throughout the night, but awaken much earlier than you normally would, feeling unrefreshed and sleepy. Typically you're not able to return to sleep.

There could be many reasons why you are experiencing insomnia, but eventually the insomnia becomes a habit – a faulty sleeping strategy, as it were. Hypnotherapy helps you:

✔ Develop a healthy sleeping strategy

✔ Deal with any underlying issues contributing to your insomnia

As with any trip to see your hypnotherapist, a little forward thinking goes a long way (and may mean you don't have to see them in the first place!). Think about the following:

✔ **What was happening in your life when the insomnia first started?** Was there a trigger point for the insomnia, and is this still an issue for you?

✔ **Do you eat a meal too close to your bedtime?** Going to sleep on a full stomach is not a good idea. You can feel uncomfortable and the process of digestion may interfere with your ability to fall asleep. Ideally, you should not eat for two to three hours prior to going to bed.

✔ **Do you drink a caffeine drink before bed?** This may seem so obvious, but you may be surprised by the number of people who come for therapy for insomnia who drink coffee or some other caffeinated drink just before going to bed. Remember – caffeine is a stimulant that keeps you awake. If you have a drink before going to bed, make sure that you look at the label of what you are drinking to ensure that it is caffeine free.

✔ **Do you nap during the day?** If you do, you could be using up your quota of sleep before you get to bed. Try cutting out the napping and see what happens to your sleep.

✔ **Do you drink alcohol close to your bedtime?** You may think that a little night-time tipple helps you to sleep. Wrong! Even though alcohol is basically an anaesthetic, it can act as a stimulant in small doses. So have your last alcoholic drink a couple of hours before going to sleep. Oh, and don't think that you can drink more alcohol so that you are anaesthetised into sleep! Alcohol-induced sleep is not the same as natural sleep and you still wake up unrefreshed in the morning.

✔ **Are you overestimating the amount of sleep you think you need?** Try going to bed a little later. See what happens.

Hypnotherapy techniques centre very much on helping you to re-associate bed with sleep. With this in mind your hypnotherapist may give you some advice that could include:

✔ **Banning anything except sleep from the bedroom.** That means no eating, drinking, watching TV, reading, or sex when in bed. You want to re-associate the bed with sleep and only sleep. Any other activity can be done elsewhere – and that includes sex, so why not spice up your relationship and get amorous in the kitchen or the living room? And don't worry, once you're sleeping well then all these activities can once again return to the boudoir.

- ✔ **Going to bed at the same time each night.** Develop a regular pattern.

- ✔ **Getting up and doing something else if you can't sleep.** If you awaken and aren't able to get to sleep again, get out of bed and go and do something else. The great hypnotherapist Milton Erickson had his insomnia patients polish their kitchen floor over and over again, no matter what the time of night it was! When you're feeling sleepy again, return to your bed. By doing this you associate your bed with sleepiness and eventually sleep.

- ✔ **Writing down any worries or concerns before you go to bed.** This is called *externalising*. Writing down any worries or concerns helps to remove them from your mind, increasing your chance of focusing on sleep, rather than stress.

Trance strategies to help you to sleep

Okay, so what happens when you are in the trance? Well, a very common technique applies: the *Law of Reverse Effect*. This law basically means that the harder you try to do something, the more difficult it is to achieve. For example, your hypnotherapist may try the following suggestion: '. . . *When you go to bed at night . . . you will try to stay awake . . . and the harder you try to stay awake . . . the drowsier and drowsier you will become . . . until you fall into a deep and refreshing sleep . . .* ' You may be thinking 'Go to bed and try to stay awake? Are you mad?' Actually, no we're not. All your hypnotherapist is doing is taking a strategy that you already use – going to bed and trying to sleep. The harder you try to sleep, the more awake you become – and turning it round, putting the Law of Reverse Effect into play.

Your hypnotherapist may use direct suggestion to help you become less aware of disturbances such as the ticking of a radiator as it cools down, or the barking dog outside your house. Of course, he'll give you a suggestion that you hear your alarm when it goes off in the morning!

If your insomnia is pretty stubborn, then an analytical technique such as dissociation may be used to help you work with the part of your mind that is responsible for your inability to sleep, helping you to understand it and to then get it to change.

Of course, where there is an underlying cause for the insomnia such as anxiety or depression, these are dealt with as part of the therapy process.

Your therapist may also want to teach you self-hypnosis so that you can practise it in bed at night (Chapter 6 explores self-hypnosis). This allows you to relax and to enter a state of mind that is very close to sleep. In fact, it is a state of mind (called the *hypnogogic state*) that is a natural part of the sleep process anyway. You can use self-hypnosis to help you deal with any unwanted thoughts as you lie in bed; perhaps imagining that as each thought comes into your mind, you pluck it out and put it into a magic box that keeps it safely locked away until the morning.

Sweet dreams are made of this – turning your nightmares into nothing

Dreams are great: a time to let your unconscious mind revel in frivolous fantasy. But what happens when dreams go wrong? Anxiety. Sweating. Waking up terrified in the night. In a word: nightmares! We all have nightmares at one time or another, and they pose little more than an inconvenience to us. However, if you have them repeatedly, they can disrupt your sleep and make you fear the very act of going to bed. With hypnotherapy, you can find a solution, so that you return to dreaming those sweet dreams that have so sadly been lacking. A visit to your hypnotherapist helps you to alter the mindset driving the nightmares. Your hypnotherapist may use several approaches:

✔ **Direct suggestion:** Your hypnotherapist can give suggestions that as soon as a nightmare begins, it changes into a different, more pleasant dream. Your therapist probably discusses with you the type of dream you would like so that it can be as close to what you want as possible.

✔ **Lucid dreaming:** Some therapists may teach you how to *lucid dream*, which means experiencing your dreams in a way that allows you to control them. Through lucid dreaming you can eradicate nasty characters from your nightmares, fly away from bad situations, or just delete the entire thing and replace it with something else.

Lucid dreaming does require some practise, though. However, for those who do, it proves to be very rewarding and useful. More information on lucid dreaming can be found at www.lucidity.com, the Web site for the Lucidity Institute.

✔ **Dealing with the underlying cause:** Dissociation again! Your therapist encourages you to become aware of the part of your mind that is driving the nightmares. You enter into a dialogue with it to find out what it's up to, why it's doing it, and how you are going to change that. During this process, you may come up with issues that need to be treated with other techniques such as regression (if, for example, there is something unresolved from your past) or direct suggestion (if, for example, you need to manage your stress levels more effectively).

However it is done, your nightmares can become a thing of the past; just a dream that gradually fades into nothing!

Sorting out snoring – for both you and your partner

Maybe your partner's snoring keeps you awake and causes your insomnia. Or perhaps your snoring has driven your partner to sleep in another room. Whatever is happening, snoring can be a problem for any couple (and the whole household, if the snoring is loud enough!).

A hypnotherapist can do several things to help alleviate snoring. Here are the facts:

- ✔ **Most people snore when they are lying on their back.** When you are lying on your back your airways are less open, restricting the passage of air through them, causing the tissues to vibrate and therefore creating the sound of the snore. When you move onto your side, your airways open up and reduce the chance of vibration.

  Direct suggestions can be given to alert your unconscious mind when you are lying on your back, and encouraging it to shift you onto your side. For example, '. . . *As soon as your unconscious mind is aware that you are lying on your back . . . instantly and immediately you will move onto your side . . . as you remain deeply asleep . . . breathing freely and easily . . .*'

- ✔ **Many people who are overweight snore.** The fact of the matter is if there is an accumulation of fat around your neck or chest, it puts greater pressure on your airways when you sleep. Moving onto your side helps, though losing those pounds improves things no end! And obviously hypnotherapy has a major role in helping you do this, as we explain in the 'Managing Your Weight' section earlier on in this chapter.

- ✔ **Smoking causes mucus to build up in the lungs and airways.** Ugh! If you are a smoker your lungs produce mucus to get rid of the tar and other nasties you inhale. When you go to sleep at night, as you breathe, the air rattles through that mucus causing the sound of the snore.

  If this is the case, book a session with your hypnotherapist and quit the habit!

- ✔ **Drinking alcohol causes the muscles in your neck to relax.** Not only is alcohol an anaesthetic, but it also makes muscles relax (part of the reason people fall over when they are drunk!). If you're in the habit of having an alcoholic drink or two before bedtime, you may find that your neck muscles relax, causing the air you breathe to vibrate the tissues of your airways. The result: you snore! Think about cutting down on your drinking, or if drinking is a problem for you, see your hypnotherapist for help in sorting things out.

You snooze; your partner loses

We mustn't forget the snorer's partner. It may be worth their while coming in for a hypnotherapy session too. The therapist can help them to distract their attention away from the snoring in several ways. Perhaps by suggesting that '...The sound of your partner's snoring just fades into the background... as you find yourself focusing on those enjoyable feelings of drifting off into a deep... deep... and refreshing sleep... and I wonder how soon it will be before you... forget completely about that snoring?...' or '... as you become aware of your partner's snoring you find that in a very strange and contradictory way... it just helps you to drift into an ever deeper and refreshing sleep...'

But before you go and see your hypnotherapist, it's a wise idea to get checked out by your doctor first. This ensures that there are no physical causes for your snoring such as overly large tonsils or a problem with your adenoids. If this is the case, then a surgical procedure may be required. And if you have a problem about going in for an operation, guess what? Hypnotherapy can help you here too!

If your partner tells you that you stop breathing every so often when you are asleep, and that when you do start again you do so with a loud snore, then you may have a condition known as *obstructive sleep apnoea*. It is important that you see your doctor so that it can be sorted out. Studies show that people with obstructive sleep apnoea are at much greater risk of having a heart attack or developing a stroke.

Controlling Your Words: Stammering

Stammering (or to use the medical term if you want to, *dysphemia*) is a very common condition that appears in approximately one person in every hundred. It can be expressed in several ways:

- ✔ Some people become blocked when trying to say certain words or sounds.
- ✔ Some people repeat certain words, phrases, or sounds.
- ✔ Some people have long pauses in sentences.
- ✔ Some people prolong the sounds of certain words.

One of the central features of stammering is that the stammer is often accompanied by a sense of a loss of control. This can lead to fear and anxiety building up around the pronunciation of certain words. In fact, many feel that there aren't any words that are impossible for a stammerer to say, only those that they have come to fear!

Stumbling over anxiety

Fear and anxiety certainly promote a stammer. Overcoming these twin hurdles is hard enough for anyone meeting someone new. But for many who stammer, the situation is worsened as the anxiety of the situation increases the worry of saying certain words, which then starts off the stammer. If the person is someone in authority, then the situation gets even worse (something known as *Headmaster Syndrome*). Add time pressure, excitement, or fatigue to the equation and things get completely out of hand.

However, when a stammerer is speaking to someone they know well, many are able to talk quite fluently. Why? Because their levels of anxiety are well down, no longer fuelling the fears that lead to the stammer in the first place.

Relaxing your speech through hypnotherapy

Hypnotherapy can help you to speak more fluently, and your hypnotherapist works in conjunction with any advice you have been given by a speech therapist.

The main aims of therapy are to:

✔ Help you to enjoy a greater sense of self-control.

✔ Help you to reduce anxiety in general and in specific situations.

✔ Help you to reinforce your speech therapist's recommendations.

✔ Help you to interact with strangers more confidently.

In order to do this, your therapist uses a variety of approaches that include:

✔ **Direct suggestion:** You're given suggestions to direct your attention away from how you're saying a word, and to focus more on what you're saying. You may also get suggestions to help you feel calm and relaxed as you say certain words, or enter into certain situations.

Where it is appropriate, your therapist also reinforces your speech therapist's recommendations.

✔ **Self-hypnosis:** This is very useful, because with a regular pattern of practice, self-hypnosis helps you to reduce your general levels of anxiety. Also, you can imagine yourself in a whole variety of situations, speaking calmly and fluently (see the upcoming Rehearsal bullet point, as well as Chapter 5 on self-hypnosis).

✔ **Ego strengthening:** If you're feeling demoralised, then ego strengthening can help you to feel much better about yourself. Your therapist gives you suggestions themed around enjoying greater self-control.

Ego strengthening also helps you to cope more effectively with your stress levels and can be directed to help you feel calmer, more confident and relaxed in specific situations.

✔ **Rehearsal:** If you fear a situation, you almost always think about that situation in advance, imagining all sorts of dire consequences. What you're really doing is practising a form of negative self-hypnosis. The result is that you end up having the bad time you predicted you would have.

In hypnosis, you can break this nasty habit and start to set yourself up for a good time. Your therapist helps you see yourself coping and speaking much more fluently at these times. By doing this, you set yourself to have a positive experience.

✔ **Paradoxical advertising:** Many people who stammer often fear that the person they are talking to notices their stammer. By adding this fear, you put yourself under pressure to try and hide your stammer, succeeding only in making the situation worse!

If you fall into this category, your therapist may advise you to advertise the fact that you stammer by saying something on the lines of 'Bear with me, I have a stammer'. By doing so, you immediately reduce one of your concerns and help to improve your fluency.

Reaching a Nail-Biting Conclusion

For someone who doesn't bite their nails, nail-biting can seem quite trivial. However, for those who do, it is an issue that preys on their minds and adds a sometimes considerable inconvenience to their lives. They sit watching TV and munch away at their fingers, they get stressed and dine out on their cuticles, they stop to think and chew away at their problem through their digits! The result is ragged, excessively short nails and, in some cases, bleeding fingers. Not very pleasant.

Biting your nails is a habit that may be associated with some other activity. And, as any nail-biter can tell you, it is often something you do quite unconsciously. It may only be sometime after you have started that you become aware that you are, in fact, biting your nails.

So, your goal is to have fabulous nails. What's your hypnotherapist's goal? Well, obviously the same as yours, but therapeutically he attempts to take your unconscious habit and make it conscious. That means handing you control of your habit. Once it is brought into your conscious awareness and you gain control, you're able to finally stop biting your nails.

And by the way, don't expect to hear your hypnotherapist saying '*. . . Stop biting your nails . . .*' as part of your hypnotherapy session. Why? Because you have probably been hearing that most of your life, and has it ever stopped you? No, we didn't think so. That is why hypnotherapists avoid using this suggestion.

So what do they use? Well, something called *reverse suggestion* – suggestions designed to give you conscious control over a particular behaviour, by suggesting that you can carry out the behaviour – but only if you want to. Your hypnotherapist may deliver suggestions something along these lines: '*. . . As soon as your hand moves towards your mouth in order for you to bite your nails . . . . it will instantly and immediately STOP . . . and you will become aware of what you are about to do . . .*' This brings the unconscious behaviour to conscious awareness and is followed by the reverse suggestion '*. . . In fact . . . you will only be able to bite your nails through a deliberate . . . and conscious . . . act of will . . .*' They may then finish off the suggestion with '*. . . And you choose to have beautiful . . . healthy . . . shiny nails . . . of which you can be proud . . .*'

That sounds straightforward, doesn't it? However, there is a lot more to it than that. Your hypnotherapist also gives suggestions that associate all this with specific times in your day-to-day life, when you know that you bite your nails. And to cap it all off he also wants to take you into the future in your mind, so that you can see yourself enjoying these wonderful new nails. In other words, really firming up a good and strong goal image that motivates you to succeed in your quest for the perfect manicure.

Biting off more than you can chew: Why you bite

First things first. Nail-biting is *not* a symptom of some deep-seated neurosis! So you can put your mind to rest; you're not some psycho serial killer because of your habit! In fact nail-biting is simply a remnant of an old childhood behaviour that gave you pleasure: thumb sucking.

To explain this further, we need to take an extremely brief journey into the world of psychology. When good old Sigmund Freud was pondering his theories of psychosexual development, he identified a stage that he termed the 'oral stage'. In fact, it is the earliest developmental stages and lasts from birth to 18 months of age. During this period we are said to gain pleasure and gratification through putting things in our mouth (stop sniggering at the back!). As we develop past this stage, our pleasure and gratification is derived from, er, other areas of our body (we said STOP SNIGGERING!!!). Freud thought that some of us don't fully move on from the oral stage and end up going through life with habits directly linked to gaining gratification through the mouth (oh, come on now!), which could include non-stop chattering, chewing the ends off pens, smoking, eating, and nail-biting.

For most people who come to hypnotherapy for nail-biting, this is all that is needed. However, the wonderful diversity of the human mind means that for some, for whatever reason, it may not be this straightforward. If you fall into this category you may also find that your hypnotherapist uses an analytical technique such as dissociation (explained in Chapter 2), to help you work with the part of your mind that is responsible for your nail-biting.

Anything else? Well, yes! How about doing something to help yourself along the way. Set yourself up for success by:

- Buying yourself a nail file
- Buying yourself a decent pair of nail scissors
- Booking yourself in for a manicure in a month's time

And yes, that means men too! Come on, this is the 21st century after all. Oh, and if you bite your toenails, then perhaps a pedicure would not go amiss either!

Chapter 6

Touching on Body Matters

· ·

· ·

*H*ypnotherapists have to restrain themselves when describing the range of physical ailments hypnotherapy can help with. The challenge is to not oversell the incredible variety of treatments possible, nor in any way to imply that hypnotherapy is a substitute for medical care.

Hypnotherapy is a wonderful complementary adjunct to medical care and it can alleviate an amazing range of physical problems. Patients often seek help from a hypnotherapist *after* a doctor has ruled out any physical cause for a complaint and relegated it to the area of 'it must be emotional'.

Common areas of treatment that people come to hypnotherapists with include:

✔ Pain management

✔ Skin problems

✔ Pregnancy related issues

✔ Irritable bowel syndrome

✔ Bulimia

This is in no way a complete list, but rather the areas of physical treatments we discuss in this chapter.

Letting Go of Pain

Nobody likes to talk about pain – except maybe sadists and masochists. When you're healthy, pain probably never crosses your mind. However, when you experience pain, it takes up some part of your awareness and can affect your mood. If the pain is serious enough or becomes chronic (long-term in duration), it can make you feel irritable and depressed. Chronic pain can even weaken your immune system, making you susceptible to other health problems.

Although the American Medical Association listed hypnosis as an approved treatment for pain as early as 1958, it is a sad fact that medical science has been very slow to acknowledge the powerful pain relief that hypnosis can provide. The evidence of how effective hypnosis can be is available to anyone who wishes to review it.

People who deal with people in pain recognise two types of pain:

- ✔ **Acute pain:** Pain that is severe but lasts for a relatively short period of time.

- ✔ **Chronic pain:** Pain that ranges from mild to severe and is present for more than three months.

Both acute and chronic pain can involve periods where the sufferer is pain free.

If you have chronic pain that inhibits you from pursuing normal, everyday activities, consult your doctor. Obtain a physical examination from your doctor before seeking any help for pain. It is important to eliminate any medical issues before seeking a psychological cure, such as hypnosis. A qualified hypnotherapist will always gain confirmation and permission from your doctor, prior to using hypnosis, to work with pain related issues.

Experiencing pain

Simply put, pain is your body's warning system that protects you from hurt or provides a warning that something is wrong somewhere in your body. We all react differently to pain. No two individuals are likely to have the same response to a similar pain-inducing event. But how do you describe something as subjective as pain? The experience of pain can be put into two broad components:

- ✔ **Sensory pain:** This tells you the location of the pain and its sensory quality – whether the pain is an aching, burning, cold, stabbing, or tingling sensation.

✔ **Affective pain:** This refers to your personal, subjective experience of pain – how much it bothers you.

An athlete may experience injury during her performance but isn't bothered by the pain while she focuses on winning. After finishing the competition, she may gradually, or suddenly, become more aware of the pain.

Perceiving pain

There's a distinct relationship between your perception of pain and how you experience it. If, for example, you're having fun playing football and experience a minor cut on your finger, you are likely not to feel the pain until the fun ends. However, if you are sitting in a quiet office, slightly bored and irritated and a little unhappy when you get a paper cut, the chances are that cut will really hurt because you have nothing to distract you.

The mind perceives pain subjectively. If you are distracted from your pain, you are less likely to focus on it and less likely to register it. For example, you have probably had the experience of suffering some minor injury, like a bruise or a paper cut, without realising it and then, suddenly, when you see it, only then do you begin to feel it. So pain does not necessarily cause suffering. How you perceive pain plays a large part in how you experience it.

Doctors cannot help you to have greater control over your perception of pain. Interestingly, hypnosis can. Your unconscious mind, however, has the power to alter your experience of pain.

Hypnosis can help you manage a variety of pain including headaches, muscular pains, dental operations, and childbirth. Hypnosis can even be used as a supplement to, or complete replacement for, anaesthesia used in surgery!

Relieving pain

During hypnosis, you relax and your mind focuses on something other than pain, possibly even something pleasurable. The combination of these two events – lowering your anxiety through relaxation and moving your focus away from the pain – lets your nervous system register less pain, or no pain at all. It is mainly through relaxation and removing fear that hypnosis pain reduction has its greatest advantages.

Two options in dealing with pain management are:

✔ **Analgesia** refers to the partial loss of pain sensation.

✔ **Anaesthesia** refers to the total loss of any pain sensation.

Theorising about how hypnosis manages pain

There are many theories about how hypnosis is effective with controlling pain. Until recently, it was believed that being in a hypnotic state produced *endorphins* – the body's natural pain-killers. This theory now seems to have been disproved, or at least placed in dispute, by a number of researchers. Currently a more popular idea about the theory of hypnosis and pain control involves the 'gate control theory'. This theory was proposed in 1965 by researchers Melzack and Wall, and modified in 1978 by Professor Wall. It states that the brain and the spinal cord pass information about pain in the form of continuously flowing impulses. These pain information messages are sent via the central nervous system to the peripheral nerves.

According to the theory, certain cells and nerves within the body register any signals of injury or pain. These signals are then directed (or not) through a system within the body, not unlike a gate, that lets some message pass onto the brain. The messages allowed through the gate are then received by the brain and interpreted as pain. Because hypnosis can directly influence the nervous system through relaxation, it can decrease the amount of pain signals that are registered.

Research shows that the hypnotic management of pain is not a placebo effect, but has a physiological action that explains its effectiveness. Through PET (Positron Emission Tomography) scans, it has been demonstrated that hypnosis directly affects areas of the brain involved in the perception of suffering (the anterior cingulate cortex). Activity in this brain area decreases during hypnotic pain control.

Analgesic and anaesthesic techniques

Hypnotherapists may suggest using either the analgesic or the anaesthesic approach to your pain control. You may wonder why they don't use anaesthesia in all pain control work. After all, why not lose all the pain instead of just some of it? The reason is that it is usually a good idea to leave just a small amount of the pain behind after a hypnosis session. For example, if you suffered a badly sprained ankle, it probably wouldn't be a good idea to hypnotise all the pain away so that you could go out and run the Boston marathon!

Hypnosis to induce anaesthesia – the total loss of pain sensation – may be useful in a situation such as a surgery, where having an anaesthetic drug is not possible, or unwanted. In such a situation, hypnotherapy can be an alternative where a total absence of pain is required.

Using hypnosis to induce analgesia – the partial loss of pain sensation – may be useful for treating conditions such as migraines. In this situation, the migraines may be occurring for a reason, such as providing an indication of an underlying problem; a food allergy or a yet undiagnosed medical problem. Leaving a trace amount of pain serves as a reminder that more investigation may still be needed. Of course, the approach on whether to use hypnotic analgesia or anaesthesia is negotiable with your hypnotherapist.

Your hypnotherapist may very well avoid the word *pain* and substitute the word *discomfort*. Discomfort sounds much less serious than pain, and by deliberately reframing your perception of pain and subtly changing it, your hypnotherapist encourages your unconscious mind to shift your perception of the pain that your body is registering.

The level of trance directly correlates with how much pain can be made tolerable. Broadly speaking, the deeper the trance you experience, the deeper the pain you are able to endure. However, it's possible to undergo minor surgical procedures even in light and medium-deep trances.

With practise, you can use self-hypnosis to undergo routine dental procedures. Dentists with minimal hypnosis training can use it to perform minor procedures on their patients.

Glove anaesthesia has nothing to do with mittens

Glove anaesthesia is a hypnotherapy technique in which the entire hand is made insensitive – from the fingertips to the wrist. This area is numb, wooden-like, and lacks feeling – as if an anaesthetic had been injected. I (Mike) first saw this demonstrated as a student at the London College of Clinical Hypnosis. Michael Joseph, a master hypnotherapist, used a fellow student on our very first day in class – without inducing a trance. He simply spoke a few words and asked the student if she could imagine wearing a glove on a freezing winter day. The student said 'Yes' and he asked permission to test her hand. He then pinched her skin – very hard. She didn't flinch! But this was for demonstration purposes only. Your hypnotherapist will always work slowly, inducing a trance and being very careful with you!

Glove anaesthesia can be effective in a variety of uses, including treating arthritis and rheumatism, glaucoma, migraine and tension headaches, obesity, and skin disorders. It can be used to ease the pain of dental procedures, childbirth, cancer, and the phantom limb pain amputees feel. Psychological disorders may benefit from glove anaesthesia, and it can be used before and after surgery.

The *ice bucket technique* involves your hypnotherapist asking you to imagine placing one of your hands in a bucket, full of crushed ice, up to the wrist. The hypnotherapist vividly describes how your hand feels as it gets colder and colder, eventually becoming numb. She then tells you that she's going to test your hand for sensitivity – gently – by pinching your hand with various degrees of strength.

This technique can be demonstrated without trance induction and still be effective. However, for deep and sustained levels of anaesthesia, such as for surgery, trance induction is required. In surgical hypnosis, several hypnosis sessions will typically take place prior to surgery. These will involve helping the client practise self-hypnosis, and experiencing sustained periods of trance and hypnotically induced anaesthesia.

Additionally, the hypnotherapist may inform you that the absence of sensation in your hand will remain even after awakening. She awakens you and tests for sensitivity by pinching the hand, with various degrees of strength. She then re-induces trance and places your 'anaesthetised' hand over your other hand, and informs you that the sense of numbness will be transferred to the non-anaesthetised hand.

You are then told to remove your hand only when the numbness has been transferred. This newly numbed hand is tested as before and then both hands are restored to normal. Your hypnotherapist teaches you self-hypnosis – *while in trance* – and awakens you. Then you are asked to hypnotise yourself, and while in the trance you are asked to anaesthetise one of your hands and to then transfer the numbness, to the part of your body affected by pain. The hypnotherapist then suggests that you will be able to do glove anaesthesia at any time in the future, and that you will be able to use it to reduce pain. You are awakened with the new skill of being able to conduct glove anaesthesia on yourself!

Helping Your Skin Look Good

Care to guess what your body's largest organ is? (Men, be very careful with your answer!) Actually, your skin is the largest organ of your body, and what a protective organ it is! Skin acts as a defence against bacterial and viral attack, as well as protecting you from heat, cold, physical injury, and ultraviolet radiation. Skin regulates your body temperature, detects potential harm before injury can occur, provides input to the brain regarding the physical nature of the environment, and even allows you to become sexually aroused.

Since both the skin and the nervous system share a common organ – the *ectoderm* – it is not surprising that stress and anxiety can adversely affect the course of any skin disorder. Conversely, once skin disorders develop, they often produce and prolong the mental and emotional disturbances that can perpetuate symptoms. Hypnosis can be a wonderful adjunct to conventional medical treatments in providing relief from a variety of dermatological problems.

In the following sections we talk about three of the four main types of dermatological problems – eczema, psoriasis, and warts.

Hypnotherapy can't do a lot for someone with acne, the fourth type of skin problem, other than bolster their sense of self-worth. Acne is best treated by dermatologists as it has fairly serious medical implications.

Scratching away at psoriasis and eczema

Both psoriasis and eczema are also known to be stress-related diseases that respond well to reduction in stress levels. Hypnotherapy can help to alleviate stress and thereby factors that may exacerbate both conditions.

Relieving the rash of eczema

A common condition, *eczema* is a very itchy, peeling, thickened, sometimes weepy area of inflamed skin, typically found in the creases of joints and the trunk of the body. The rash may fluctuate both seasonally and over the course of a day. Scratching may lead to bleeding and infection.

Eczema may have physical causes, such as with varicose eczema, in which swollen or twisted veins may influence the condition, but eczema is thought to be a stress-induced condition.

Scaling back psoriasis

Psoriasis is characterised by plaques of red, scaly, easily bleeding skin, often over the knees, elbows, trunk, and back. Finger and toenails may develop pitting. Some people with severe arthritis are prone to getting psoriasis as well.

The disease varies widely from one patient to another and in rare, severe cases, may be life-threatening because wide areas of skin are exposed to infection.

The cause of psoriasis is not known, although genetic factors appear to play a role. Environmental factors such as injury, stress, cold climate, and other illnesses are known to adversely affect the condition with some patients.

Stop kissing frogs: Treating your warts

Warts are overgrowths of skin cells caused by the human papilloma virus. The major symptoms are cosmetic, and treating warts is primarily a matter of preference, although warts in certain locations (the sole of the foot, for example) can cause pain.

You can spread warts by person-to-person contact and you can increase the number of warts you have by scratching or picking at them.

Whether you develop warts depends on your immune response to the virus. Though people with known immune deficiencies are more susceptible, most sufferers have a normal immune system.

About 25 per cent of warts go away on their own within 6 months, 50 per cent within a year, and 65 per cent by two years.

Easing skin problems with hypnotherapy

Skin conditions are often exacerbated by anxiety as well as through scratching. Hypnosis – as you know by now – is excellent for lessening anxiety. A hypnotherapist working with someone with a skin disorder would make suggestions to address any emotional problems that may be causing anxiety, and would pay particular attention to the patient's everyday circumstances.

If a client's anxiety is linked to issues of low self-esteem, part of the treatment would include direct suggestions for ego-boosting.

Approaching techniques

For skin problems linked to psychological or emotional problems, your hypnotherapist can choose from a range of techniques, based on your individual needs, such as

- ✔ Suggestions to decrease the perception of itching sensations. For example, 'You might still feel itchy, but you no longer have any desire to scratch.'

- ✔ Post-hypnotic suggestions providing practical techniques to alleviate the desire to scratch. For example, you may imagine breathing through the itchy parts of your skin with sensations of 'calmness' and 'coolness', and feel relaxed as you do so, or 'You have no desire to scratch'.

- ✔ Symptom substitution to eliminate scratching. The hypnotherapist may suggest substitute feelings, such as numbness or pressure, instead of itchiness.

- ✔ Analytical techniques similar to doing counselling or psychotherapy in trance. These techniques may be used when the previously mentioned techniques are deemed ineffective. Analytical techniques are more of an advanced treatment approach and may involve a deeper application, not dissimilar to psychoanalysis. Don't worry – they're not physically painful!

  These analytical techniques may involve such approaches as:

  - **Regression:** Using hypnosis to take you back in time to before you had the problem. This allows the therapist to demonstrate to you the link between your mind and body, thus giving you control over the symptoms.

  - **Dissociation:** This involves working with any unresolved issues that contribute to the skin condition. Dissociation techniques allow you to gain insight into your condition, as well as develop strategies to resolve your problem. Chapter 2 has in-depth information on dissociation.

Glove anaesthesia (see the 'Glove anaesthesia has nothing to do with mittens' section earlier in this chapter) is an effective treatment for burning sensations and can be used to 'freeze' a wart. How does this work? In a word, *dissociation*. The hypnotherapist creates a split between your conscious awareness of pain sensation and the normal response of reacting to pain, thus dissociating your normal reaction to pain. It's like watching a film of yourself having the wart frozen. You wouldn't react with the pain sensation if you were simply watching yourself having the wart removed (although you might cringe!).

Sampling scripts for treating skin problems

In this section are some typical scripts a hypnotist may use for skin problems. The scripts are phrases that broadly represent what a hypnotherapist might say as part of post-hypnotic therapy; that is, after you've been hypnotised and are still in trance.

Keep in mind that these scripts are worded generally, and in a real session would be specifically tailored to your particular problem. Your hypnotherapist won't use the exact words we use; she tailors her words to be meaningful to you and your situation. Still, you can get a good idea of the various approaches from reading the following scripts.

Stopping scratching

In this script, your hypnotherapist would identify the specific areas most affected by the rash, to personalise the suggestion for you.

> '. . . and you have no desire to scratch . . . if at any time . . . your hand moves toward your skin in order to scratch . . . the moment your fingers touch your skin . . . you will instantly . . . and immediately become aware of what you are about to do . . . and your hand will move away from your skin . . . and because of this . . . your comfort will increase . . . and your skin will continue to heal . . . and any rash will begin to disappear more and more rapidly . . . even while you sleep at night . . . the moment your fingers touch your skin in order to scratch . . . instantly and immediately your hand will move away from your skin . . . and your skin will continue to heal . . . as you sleep . . . because of this treatment . . . you will be able to exercise enough self-control to . . . allow your skin to heal . . .'

Improving circulation

A hypnotherapist may treat itching by suggesting that your blood circulation is improving. Research shows that the mind can directly affect circulation.

> '. . . your heart will beat more strongly . . . so that more blood will flow through the little blood vessels in the skin . . . carrying more nourishment to the skin . . . because of this . . . your skin will become well nourished . . . it will become healthier . . . and the rash will gradually diminish . . . until it fades away completely . . . leaving the underlying new skin . . . perfectly

healthy and normal in every way . . . and . . . as your circulation improves . . . and you become stronger and steadier in every way . . . so . . . the unwanted itching and irritation of your skin will subside . . . and disappear . . . the comfort increasing each day . . .'

The next brief script is for lowering blood circulation:

'. . . as a result of this treatment . . . you are going to feel fitter and stronger in everyway . . . your circulation will improve . . . particularly the little blood vessels that supply the skin . . .'

The above script would actually allow your circulation to improve and allow blood vessels to become healthier.

Solving skin-caused insomnia

If you have a severe skin condition, you may have trouble sleeping, either because of the pain, or the itch. Your hypnotherapist can use your discomfort to ease you into a restorative slumber, through a reverse suggestion:

'. . . the more you notice the discomfort . . . the drowsier you become . . . until you fall into a deep . . . refreshing . . . healing sleep . . .'

So you can see that the suggestions leads you into a feeling that healing is taking place, even as you become progressively sleepier.

Working on warts

In assisting you in ridding yourself of warts, your hypnotherapist may give you suggestions including:

- ✔ The blood flow to the wart has stopped. You then imagine your wart shrivelling and dropping off, leaving an area of healthy skin behind.

- ✔ Your wart becomes smaller and smaller until it disappears.

- ✔ Your wart is an unwanted building. You then imagine that your immune system is a demolition company, taking apart the unwanted building and carting it away.

Relieving the Pressure of Hypertension

Hypertension (high blood pressure) affects millions of people every year, and is a major contributing factor to coronary heart disease and stroke. Until recently the main treatment approaches involved pharmacological intervention and lifestyle changes. However, more eclectic approaches have been developed involving clinical hypnosis.

Hypnosis can play an important role in maintaining a healthy heart as well as aiding recovery from a variety of cardiovascular diseases. When entering trance, a shift in the autonomic nervous system from sympathetic (responsible for activity) to parasympathetic (responsible for rest) control occurs. When the parasympathetic nervous system is dominant the heart rate decreases, thus reducing the burden on the cardiovascular system.

For anyone experiencing cardiovascular disease, the following lists ways hypnotherapy techniques may be useful:

- ✔ Mastering self-hypnosis for relaxation
- ✔ Using hypnosis to cope better with lifestyle issues such as stress management, weight control, diet, alcohol consumption, and smoking
- ✔ Using hypnosis to engage in appropriate exercise
- ✔ Working with issues of depression related to health problems

Relaxation techniques are an important part of helping to alleviate feelings of stress, which are often contributing factors to hypertension.

Let's get things straight, right from the start. Your hypnotherapist will *not* give you suggestions that your blood pressure becomes lower and lower. It just doesn't work that way. However, the very act of going into trance lowers your blood pressure. In fact studies show that people who have regular experience of trance, either with a therapist or through practising self-hypnosis, can achieve a significant lowering of their blood pressure, with some being able to come off their antihypertensive medications. So, when your therapist asks you to practise self-hypnosis, make sure that you practise it. And regularly!

Going into trance isn't the complete story. An important part of managing hypertension is making some important lifestyle changes according to your doctor's recommendation. Many external factors influence hypertension, and working with a hypnotherapist can help you by looking at strategies designed to control these. Your hypnotherapist can strengthen your resolve to carry out your doctor's orders.

These changes are not just for the short term. If you keep them up, you can definitely help to reduce your blood pressure to a much safer level. And if you need a boost in your determination, pick up your phone and call your hypnotherapist!

Never stop taking your medication without your doctor or consultant giving the go-ahead. You're taking it for a reason, and that is to keep you healthy! If you make the required lifestyle changes and stick to them, you have a very good chance that you'll be able to either cut down or stop taking your meds – but *only* with your doctor's say so!

Taking a Pregnant Pause for Childbirth

Hypnosis is useful for a range of issues around conception, pregnancy, and childbirth. Many people are unaware that hypnotherapy can help in this area, but hypnotherapists are regularly involved with helping couples conceive and also get through childbirth with minimum difficulties.

Conceiving options

How does hypnosis help someone become pregnant? Mainly through helping decrease the anxiety associated with having sex with the goal of conceiving. *The Law of Reversed Effect* states that the harder you try to do something, the more likely you are to fail at it. The body works this way too. If you're desperate to conceive each time you have sex, your body may activate hormones that kill off the very sperm that you want to fertilise your ovum. So hypnosis simply helps you to relax, and may offer suggestions of you becoming extremely fertile.

Hypnosis can help only those people who can't conceive due to *psychogenic infertility* – infertility without a physiological cause. Put another way, hypnosis may be able to help if there's no known biological or physical obstacle to pregnancy, and the problem is most likely emotional. Around 17 per cent of all couples experience psychogenic infertility, with psychological stressors possibly playing a central role.

However, hypnosis can help a significant percentage of people with psychogenic infertility conceive. The scientific community is still trying to explain exactly *why* hypnosis is effective in this area, but if you have been unsuccessful in conceiving, and your doctor has found no medical reason why you shouldn't be able to have a baby, you can have hope that there is a good possibility that hypnosis may help you. Given the choice between hypnosis and expensive and complicated *in vitro* fertilisation (IVF) treatments, there really is no competition.

For many people who are having difficulty in conceiving, it becomes an arduous task for both sides of the parental divide: making sure you do the act at the right time, when the woman's temperature is right, having to lie back for 20 minutes with your legs in the air to let gravity do its job, and so on. It takes all the fun out of it and more importantly, on a biological level, it adds stress into the equation.

When you're trying to conceive, stress puts a major biological spanner in the works! When you're stressed, your body's biology switches from long-term survival priorities to immediate survival priorities. And the last thing the body wants at this time is for its all-important biological resources to be drained by having a baby growing inside it! Changing the biological balance of the body makes it a much less welcoming place for the sperm and egg to meet and unite. Think how you feel when you meet someone in a warm and inviting environment. The lights are low, soft music playing in the background, and love is in the air. Turn a couple of spotlights (playing the role of stress) onto the scene and turn the music up loud, and the last thing you think of is romance!

We've all heard the tales of couples who spend years trying to conceive a baby. In the end, they give up and adopt. The next thing you know, the woman is pregnant. The stress of trying to conceive prevented the very thing the parents were after. Take away the stress and the body reverts to long-term survival priorities, the biological lights and music are lowered, and the next thing you know, a baby is on its way!

Both the male and female in a couple experiencing psychogenic infertility should undertake treatment. Women who are stressed out because of this problem experience chemical changes in their pH levels that make pregnancy more difficult, and men who are stressed may experience decreased sperm counts.

Hypnosis does not work in cases where there is a known medical problem. A qualified hypnotherapist will always ensure that you have a thorough medical examination prior to seeking hypnotherapy.

Delivering the goods

Many mothers have discovered that hypnotherapy can dramatically improve their ability to enjoy the experiences of both pregnancy and labour. If you are pregnant and considering hypnosis, we encourage you to try hypnosis and enjoy your child's introduction to the world.

In the 'Relieving Pain' section earlier in this chapter, we describe *hypnotic analgesia* – the loss of the sensation of pain. Analgesia can also be successfully applied to childbirth, with no problems for you or your child. Many studies consistently show that hypnosis can be effective in pain management, as well as in improving the birth experience.

The main goals for hypnotherapy are to help the mother-to-be achieve control over her pain and develop a greater sense of self-control throughout labour and delivery.

To make this happen you schedule a series of hypnosis sessions when you're pregnant – for you and your birth partner, if possible. Your hypnotherapist takes you through the stages of self-hypnosis – probably during your first session – so that you can practise pain control techniques (Chapter 14 is devoted to self-hypnosis). You may also benefit from visualisations that increase your confidence and ability to relax.

Your hypnotherapist will help you, while in trance, visualise going through the stages of labour and delivery safely and easily, and give you suggestions to enable you to conduct self-hypnosis and induce a loss of sensation of pain as you experience these stages. The hypnotherapist may also suggest that during all this you are in constant, reassuring communication with the child in your womb.

During your sessions with her, your hypnotherapist will take you through all the stages of labour and delivery. Keep in mind that the hypnotherapist will help you and your partner reach a level of skill in self-hypnosis (for the mother), and skills for the partner to make simple, post-hypnotic suggestions to ensure that the mother is relaxed and able to cope with any situation that arises. The following list offers a stage-by-stage approach to how this occurs:

- **Pre-birth stage:** Your hypnotherapist addresses any specific concerns you may have, and helps increase your confidence about the birth and post-birth period. This is when you become familiar with pain control techniques.

  Your birth partner can find out how to cue you on relaxation and trance responses.

- **Birth stage:** Your hypnotherapist will probably suggest that, no matter what level of relaxation or trance you are in, you will always respond to your midwife's or doctor's instructions.

  You will probably also be given suggestions that, no matter what happens, you will remain calm. This will prepare you to cope well with anything unexpected that may arise.

- **Post-birth stage:** For the post-birth stage, you may receive suggestions for healing and recovery. Also helpful for this stage are suggestions for confidence and helping you, as a new mother, to feel able to cope. Further hypnosis pain control techniques appropriate for this stage may also be helpful. See the 'Letting Go of Pain' section of this book to understand more about pain control techniques.

Examples of what a hypnotherapist may say at this stage are:

- *'As the process of bringing your baby into the world begins . . . you will find that the contractions will be weak.'*

- *'You will feel the contractions merely as pressure in your stomach . . . and you will feel calm . . . relaxed . . . and in control throughout.'*

- *'As the contractions continue . . . you will always follow the advice of your midwife or doctor . . . and as soon as you feel the urge to bear down . . . tell the midwife . . . but do not give way until she tells you to . . . when she does . . . take a deep breath . . . hold it as long as you can . . . and push down as hard as you can . . . as long as each contraction lasts . . . if you have to breathe out before the contraction is over . . . take another deep breath as quickly as possible . . . and continue to hold it and push down . . . since it is usually the last part of the contraction that produces most progress . . . you will find that this will greatly reduce any discomfort.'*

Improving Irritable Bowel Syndrome

Irritable bowel syndrome (IBS) is a disorder of the intestines. When your gut is working normally, you hardly notice that it moves food through its long passageway, through a series of muscular contractions known as *peristalsis*. Problems with these contractions are classified under the broad heading of IBS.

Hypnotherapy is a recommended treatment for IBS and most people respond rapidly. Usually three sessions are all that are required.

Before going to see a hypnotherapist for IBS treatment, get a proper medical diagnosis of IBS confirmed by a GP. The symptoms may indicate a potentially serious condition, and a qualified hypnotherapist will never work on a patient's self-diagnosis.

Problems with IBS can potentially extend throughout your entire digestive system, which includes the area from your mouth to your anus. Hence, a great number of different conditions come under the heading of IBS.

Some of the symptoms that people with IBS may experience, and that hypnotherapy can help with, include:

- ✔ Abdominal distress or pain.
- ✔ Cramps or pains in the lower abdomen or rectum (often after eating).
- ✔ Variations in bowel movements, including constipation and diarrhoea.

   Bowel movements may alternate between constipation and diarrhoea. Even after a bowel movement, you may feel that the rectum is still full.

- ✔ A feeling of urgency. People with IBS often need to rush and open their bowels, usually soon after eating. Incontinence may occur if a toilet is not nearby.
- ✔ Bloating. IBS sufferers may experience flatulence or painful trapped wind. You may have rumbling noises in your abdomen.
- ✔ Back pain associated with irregular bowel movements.
- ✔ Nausea, belching, and vomiting.

Dealing with your IBS anxiety

Many IBS sufferers feel ashamed of their condition. They may experience extreme incontinence, or extreme constipation, or both. This may lead them to feel that this problem has to be kept secret, even sometimes from their own doctors. If their problem is a long-term one, it may lead to psychological problems such as anxiety and depression. Ironically, anxiety and depression exacerbate the symptoms of IBS. Relieving anxiety can be an immense help to IBS sufferers, and confidence and relief from anxiety are areas in which hypnosis excels.

Conventional medical treatment of IBS involves stress management and dietary awareness, along with pharmacological intervention when needed.

✔ **Diet:** Avoidance of foods that irritate the gastro-intestinal tract is recommended, including spicy food, cabbage, turnip, caffeine-containing drinks, and alcohol. Hypnosis can help to maintain good, healthy eating habits.

✔ **Pharmacological intervention:** Bulk-forming agents and anti-diarrhoeal medications may be used. Antispasmodic drugs may also be used in severe cases, to regulate peristalsis. Hypnosis can help with overcoming any resistance to following the medication schedule.

✔ **Stress management:** Guess what we recommend for an excellent stress management tool? Hypnosis of course! Through hypnosis-based stress management, IBS sufferers may experience significant relief.

Coping with constipation and diarrhoea

IBS sufferers may fluctuate between constipation and diarrhoea. So what exactly does a hypnotherapist do to help?

Depending on the individual, a hypnotherapist can provide a variety of areas of help, including:

✔ **Stress management:** IBS is often related to stress and worry. Hypnosis offers other ways to see the problem as not so overwhelming. This can help to provide new coping skills and a sense of managing better.

✔ **Relaxation:** A person with IBS invariably associates the toilet with anxiety. A common hypnotherapy approach is to ask the IBS patient to practise hypnosis while using the toilet, in order to be relaxed.

✔ **Metaphorical imagery:** While in trance, a hypnotherapist can help to offer metaphorical images that provide relief. For example, to help with constipation, a hypnotherapist may tell you to imagine logs flowing freely down a river; for diarrhoea, imagining logs jamming up a river flow. These can be very effective if given while in trance.

Offering an ice-cold example

Imagine that you come to a hypnotherapist for treatment for IBS. Your session may go something like this:

> '... I would like you to imagine that there is a large bucket of very cold water, filled with lumps of ice ...'

At this point your hypnotherapist will vividly describe the bucket to you, using all modalities of sensory representation such as touch, imagined vision, and so on.

> '... and now ... you are dipping your fingertips into the surface of the water and you can feel the ice against your skin ... you will notice that the sensation is changing in your fingertips, as they become more and more numb, and you start to lose all feeling in them ... I now want you to immerse your whole hand into the bucket of water and ice, and notice how the numbness starts to spread over your hand ... as your hand becomes ... and continues to become ... colder and colder ... you are aware that all sensations are now disappearing from that hand ... including any response that may arise from a painful stimulus ... it will seem as if a thick leather glove has been placed on your hand ... and the colder it gets the more like a piece of wood your hand becomes ...'

When the hypnotherapist is convinced that your hand is numb, she instructs you to transfer the numbness to your belly, to help calm your overactive colon. She then gently places your hand on your stomach and tells you that you are going to transfer the analgesia from your hand to your colon.

> '... I want you to imagine that your numb hand is very cold ... and that this cold is stored in the form of a blue dye ... and when I count to three I want you to start transferring this dye to your abdomen ... you may notice how the coldness and numb feeling begins to spread over your abdomen as the dye flows from your hand ... ready ... now ... 1 ... 2 ... 3 ...'

When the numbness has transferred, the hypnotherapist continues:

> '... Observe how free from discomfort your abdomen is and how your colon is quiet and free from tension ... and unnecessary contractions ... it just continues to do very little as far as you are concerned ... you notice that your hand is now a normal colour and all sensation has returned ... and ... the numbness only persists in your abdomen and colon ... as the days and weeks go by ... and your unconscious mind is more and more able to control your inner feelings ... you will feel less bloated as your inner tensions and anxiety flow from your body ... leaving you calm and able to live your life in a way that is more satisfying to you ... free from pain ... free from your problems ...'

Before awakening you from trance, your hypnotherapist may teach you to automatically hypnotise yourself, and to use pain control techniques whenever needed in the future. Then they awaken you from trance in the usual way.

Loving the Dentist!

Hands up those who look forward to going to see the dentist. Hmmm ... very few hands seem to be appearing! Well, that can all change with a little hypnosis.

Various applications for dental hypnosis exist, including:

- ✔ Controlling pain
- ✔ Treating phobias
- ✔ Controlling excessive salivation or bleeding
- ✔ Controlling the gag reflex
- ✔ Adjusting to orthodontics, such as dentures, braces, and so on
- ✔ Stopping smoking (it adversely affects gums, and so is a dental concern)

I (Mike) work as a hypnotherapist within a London dental practice, and help a range of people overcome various psychological issues prior to receiving dental treatment. Some people fear even the simplest dental procedures, and would otherwise require an expensive anaesthetist to give them a general anaesthetic. Usually a couple of sessions of hypnotherapy can overcome life-long phobias.

Dentists and medical doctors are now beginning to learn hypnotherapy themselves. Since the 1950s and 1960s medical staff – admittedly in small numbers – have used hypnosis, or employed sessional hypnotherapists. Additionally, some training courses exist, such as at the London College for Clinical Hypnosis, aimed specifically for medically trained staff.

Drilling away at your problem

Many people have a fear of dental drills. This is understandable due to the noise, and occasional pain, that may accompany the use of a drill. The fear of drills for some patients can be extreme.

Hypnotherapy can help get rid of the fear of the dentist's drill. Chapter 11 deals with phobia treatments in detail, so here we only briefly mention some of the approaches that a hypnotherapist may use to help you receive a treatment that involves the dentist's drill. Some of these approaches are:

- ✔ Hypnotising you to float out of your body during the drilling.
- ✔ Hypnotising you to speed up your subjective sense of time, so that the procedure seems to be over in seconds.
- ✔ Hypnotising you to forget about being afraid.
- ✔ Dealing directly with the fear itself through more extensive phobia treatments.

Grinding down your bruxism: Teeth-grinding and hypnotherapy

Bruxism is the unconscious grinding and/or clenching of the teeth, when a person isn't eating. It's often associated with high stress levels, anger, or rage. Bruxism can happen day or night, though most people experience it while asleep. Problems bruxism causes may include:

- Fracturing and/or erosion of the teeth.
- Breakdown of the bone supporting the teeth.
- Fracturing of the jaw if bruxism is severe.
- The jaw may 'click' (frequently audible) when eating.
- Problems in the joint connecting the jaw to the skull, which may lead to a condition known as myofacial pain dysfunctional syndrome, a chronically painful condition affecting the face (often only one side).

If you grind your teeth while you sleep, your partner may point out another problem – that you keep him or her awake!

Hypnotherapists usually treat bruxism using very direct methods such as suggesting that, as soon as your teeth touch in order to grind or clench, you stop instantly, relax the muscles of your jaw, and drift into a deeper and more refreshing sleep.

Dealing with Problems with a Psychological Basis

Although hypnosis has been around for centuries, it was the medical profession, and in particular psychiatry, that brought hypnotherapy into mainstream use, over the past 200 years. In particular, psychiatrists Sigmund Freud and Milton Erickson deserve credit for popularising hypnosis.

Currently, however, hypnotherapy is not used often to treat mental illness. Therapists in the 1960s and 1970s believed that hypnotherapy produced only temporary removal of symptoms, and that hypnosis should not be used in conjunction with counselling or psychotherapy.

Another argument against using hypnosis to treat emotional problems is the view – which is partially true – that hypnosis can make matters worse for some people with serious mental health conditions. For example, if someone is struggling with determining what is real and what is not (as is the case with schizophrenia), going into trance will certainly be destabilising. Also, a severely paranoid person probably will not allow herself to relax enough, or trust a hypnotherapist enough, to allow herself to be hypnotised.

So it's safe to say that actively mentally ill people should not be hypnotised. But does this mean that hypnosis should never be used with anyone who is mentally ill – even during periods of wellness? Much evidence suggests that hypnosis provides a useful tool in alleviating a variety of mental health problems. The following sections talk about conditions that hypnosis can benefit.

Obsessing about change: Obsessive compulsive-disorder (OCD)

The word *obsessive* is part of everyday parlance, but the psychological condition known as *obsessive-compulsive disorder (OCD)* is an anxiety disorder characterised by:

- ✔ Recurrent and persistent thoughts, ideas, images, and feelings that are perceived as intrusive and senseless.
- ✔ Repetitive, ritualised behaviours that the individual feels compelled to carry out in order to prevent the obsessional thoughts and the associated discomfort.

The obsessive thoughts, or compulsive behaviours, are severe enough to be time-consuming – occupy more than one hour per day – or may cause significant distress or impairment to the patient's normal way of life. Often the person with OCD recognises that the obsessive-compulsive behaviour is excessive and unreasonable, but is powerless to stop it. The condition is usually highly secretive and can remain hidden from even immediate members of the patient's family.

For people with OCD, attempts to resist the compulsive behaviour may cause increasing tension and anxiety, which is relieved by giving in to the compulsion.

Of the many compulsive behaviours that can be expressed with OCD, the most common are:

- ✔ **Washing:** Washing or cleaning is the most prevalent compulsion, and is characterised by a fear and avoidance of contamination, as well as elaborate washing, cleaning, or decontamination rituals.
- ✔ **Checking:** Checking behaviours – the next most common – involve elaborate and repeated checking in order to prevent a perceived disaster or dreaded event from occurring. Behaviours that may be expressed include ritual behaviours involving superstitions, and any range of other repeated, or extremely over-cautious behaviours, all intended to make

the OCD sufferer feel safer, although often causing great fear and worry instead.

✔ **Ordering:** Having to be sequential about items – for example, having specific locations for every item of food and clothing, with no variation or exceptions allowed.

Hypnosis can help with OCD issues. A hypnotherapy approach can view the basis of OCDs as the splitting off of a certain emotional part of the individual. This damaged, split-off emotional content is just out of reach of conscious thought, but is easily recognised in a dream, or in an altered state of consciousness induced by hypnosis. OCD disorders yield successfully to hypnotherapy, or any technique that seeks to reintegrate the split-off component of the personality.

The therapy approach is essentially a two-stage approach involving:

✔ **Stage one:** The split-off part is identified and treated.

✔ **Stage two:** The symptoms are removed as a separate stage of hypnosis. (Chapter 5 discusses how hypnosis helps change habits.)

Beating bulimia

Bulimia nervosa is an eating disorder characterised by:

✔ Episodes of uncontrolled eating or bingeing. During the binge, the bulimic eats enormous amounts of food (often sweet and high in calories) rapidly, until she is uncomfortably or painfully full. For example, a bulimic patient may consume a whole loaf of bread, a pot of jam, an entire cake, and a packet of biscuits in one binge episode. This bingeing provides relief from the tension experienced prior to the binge. Guilt and disgust with regard to the binge rapidly follow. These feelings promote the consequent purge or excess exercise.

✔ Extreme and inappropriate measures to control body weight, including taking diuretics and forced vomiting after meals.

✔ Distorted ideas concerning body shape. For example, a thin person who believes that they are overweight.

The two distinct subtypes of bulimia nervosa are:

✔ **Purging type:** A binge episode is followed by *purging* – self-induced vomiting, the use of laxatives, diuretics, or enemas – to control weight.

✔ **Non-purging type:** The person uses excessive exercise or fasting to prevent weight gain after a binge episode. Purging is rarely seen.

Bulimic patients are usually of normal weight. Those who are underweight tend to be diagnosed as having anorexia nervosa of the purging type. Bulimics experience a profound loss of control over their eating behaviour, and may experience *dissociation*. Dissociation experiences involve feeling cut-off from what is happening. Bulimics also cut-off when they are at their most ill and in the process of bingeing on food, or purging what they have eaten.

There may be several bouts of the binge and purge/exercise cycle within one day. The binge and purge cycle is normally secretive. Bulimic patients report complete lack of control during a binge. However, control can return, as the person stops eating if someone enters the room during the binge.

Contrary to popular belief, bulimia is not a 'women-only' condition. Although 90 per cent of all people with bulimia nervosa are female, men can experience it as well. Men who experience bulimia nervosa are more likely to have been obese prior to the onset of the condition.

Treating bulimia through hypnosis

One view of bulimia nervosa says that it's similar to obsessive-compulsive disorders. The binge behaviour is the result of a dissociated part of the individual, with the purge/exercise behaviour becoming a conditioned response to the guilt experienced after the binge.

Low self-esteem, depression, and anxiety disorders are often associated with bulimia nervosa. Hypnotherapy can help with all these conditions. One of the main approaches to helping with bulimia is to educate and address, in hypnosis, the dissociative behaviour involved when bingeing and/or purging. Bulimics are, in a sense, ideal candidates for hypnotherapy as the process of trance involves dissociating the conscious from the unconscious, and bulimics are already skilled at dissociation. Emphasising the conscious awareness of bulimic behaviour gives the patient greater conscious control and awareness over their behaviour.

The hypnotherapist may give direct suggestions, while the patient is in trance, to alter or stop the splitting off, and to become highly conscious of the hand-to-mouth behaviour that occurs during either bingeing or purging behaviour. Suggestions may be given directly to stop. That is an authoritative approach involving a powerful message to simply stop the behaviour.

Analytical approaches can also be used to deal with any of the underlying emotional issues that contributed to the behaviour. These approaches combined – dissociation awareness, direct suggestion and analytical work – can be a powerful therapeutic approach in helping people with bulimia.

Making sure hypnosis and medications mesh

When a medical condition could be part of your problem, most professional hypnotherapists will work with you only with the informed consent of your doctor. The general rule is: always go to your doctor first to ensure that all potential physical causes to your problems have been eliminated.

Be open with both your doctor and your hypnotherapist. They both want to help you. Check with your doctor that receiving hypnosis is safe for you. Likewise, always inform your hypnotherapist about medications you take that affect your mood, speech, or ability to concentrate. Other than that, medication is not usually a problem.

Hypnotherapists are often asked how hypnosis interacts with medication, at a first meeting. The question is usually something like, 'I'm on Prozac. Will it be a problem for me to receive hypnosis?' The answer is 'no'. However, it is always a good idea to discuss fully the medications you have been prescribed, and the reasons for taking them.

In general, if you feel clear-headed enough to concentrate and work on your emotional issues, it is fine to undertake hypnotherapy.

Looking at binge eating disorder

Binge eating disorder is found in approximately two per cent of the population, and is predominantly seen in women. Binge eating disorder follows a similar pattern to bulimia, except that patients do not use extreme forms of weight management. Consequently, those suffering from binge eating disorder are obese. Binge eating disorder is treated in a similar way to bulimia nervosa.

Treatment for bingeing behaviour is very similar to the treatment for bulimia: awareness of dissociative behaviour, direct suggestions to stop bingeing and, if deemed useful, analytical techniques to deal with emotional issues. Additionally, for both bulimics and binge eaters, additional lifestyle issues, such as over-exercising, poor diet, and so on, can be addressed using hypnosis.

Chapter 7

Feeling Good

. . . .

. . . .

*I*magine feeling so good that you have that 'I can't lose today' feeling. Everything is going your way for a change. Imagine that the things you want to do seem almost effortless. You begin to surprise yourself with how creative or lucky you are. You feel happy and this feeling runs throughout your body.

When you feel good, the universe provides. When you feel good, you have more energy, you feel healthier, and things just seem to fall into place. Being in a good mood often feeds on itself, meaning things that you want just seem to flow to you.

Feeling good is contagious. People relate to you more positively. It's as if your good energy is being shared in a two-way direction, from you to others and back to yourself. You become more creative and perform better in every area of your life. You may even feel sexier!

But, hey! Maybe you don't feel like this; maybe you want to, but something is blocking the way. Maybe you're asking yourself whether a hypnotherapist can help you to feel like this. Can hypnotherapy help you to feel better? Be more creative? Have more confidence? In a nutshell, the answers are: yes, yes, yes, and yes!

Your mind has awesome potential and through hypnotherapy you can enhance that potential, changing your critical thoughts into something more constructive and supportive. You have the ability to access untapped creativity, which can improve your emotional, intellectual, and physical responses. When this happens, some of the by-products are greater confidence, creativity, and an improved ability to relate to others. From this starting point, you can then combat and overcome a whole variety of problems. This chapter explores exactly how this is possible.

Conquering Performance Anxiety

Have you ever frozen with fear when giving a speech? Ever walked out on stage and dried up on the spot? Ever sat for your driving test and almost driven the car off the road because you shook so badly? If the answer is yes to any of these questions, you have experienced *performance anxiety*. The name says it all and basically means that anxiety has messed up what you are doing in front of others.

Your hypnotherapist helps you get the right amount of anxiety. 'But wait!' you say, 'Get the right amount of anxiety? Are you mad?' Actually, no. Anxiety can be your friend. A small amount can be beneficial to you; it keeps your mind alert, your adrenaline running, and your attention properly focused. In fact, without it your performance can suffer. Imagine that you are so relaxed and laid back that you can't be bothered to remember your speech. Imagine that you are so chilled out as you walk onto the football pitch that your muscles aren't toned and ready for the match. Not a good idea. An appropriate balance between relaxation and anxiety (or as we therapists like to call it, stimulation) is a positive boon to your performance.

Playing the starring role

One thing to get straight, right from the start, is what we mean by the word *performance*. The word may conjure up an image of a stage, an audience, and a performer hoping to make a good impression. This is, of course, a correct interpretation, but the definition of performance can be expanded. Just think of the stage as the world in which you live, the audience are the people with whom you interact, and you are the performer hopeful of showing yourself in a good light.

A *performance* then is any interaction you make with others in which you are likely to feel you're being evaluated. These situations can include:

✔ Work

✔ The performing arts such as playing music, dancing, acting, and so on

✔ Sport

✔ Public speaking

✔ Exam-taking

✔ Sex (oh boy, do we get evaluated on this performance! More later in the 'Touching on Sexual Problems' section.)

Feeling your star fade

You may have been performing perfectly well for some time, or maybe this is your first attempt. Whatever you're doing, it only takes one bad experience to mess up the show. The nasty thing about performance anxiety is that when it happens it just keeps repeating itself. So where does the anxiety come from? The following list offers some possibilities:

✔ **Incomplete or bad preparation:** For any performance to be effective, preparation is paramount.

✔ **A focus on your negative feelings:** For example you may believe that your audience can see that you're nervous.

✔ **Negative criticism:** This can include comments from others as well as your own self-criticism.

✔ **Memories of past bad performances:** You forget your successes and remember only your mistakes or failures. Hypnotherapy can help you to put a variety of positive spins on past bad performances in order to help you focus on raising your game.

The awful thing about anxiety is that it fuels all your fears and doubts and after it's started . . .

In fact, the more you experience performance anxiety, the worse it gets until it forms a nasty and vindictive vicious circle from which you have great difficulty breaking free. Now is the time to call in your hypnotherapist.

Acting your way to a better performance

Consider method actors. Before they perform a role, they begin to live it. They become their character before they even get onto the stage, or in front of the camera. In essence, hypnotherapy helps you use method acting techniques. Through hypnosis, you live your good performance before you have to give it. The more you live it beforehand, the more likely you are to live it when you are up on your stage.

To fully understand a film, you really need to see it from beginning to end. Come in halfway through and you may find yourself getting confused, unable to make head or tail of the plot. The same principle is at work when dealing with performance anxiety. You need to see the whole picture for therapy to be effective. That means you need to be able to view:

✔ The pre-performance period, including your preparation and the buildup to the performance.

✔ The performance itself, with you performing well.

✔ The post-performance period when you're being congratulated, feeling good, celebrating, and relaxing.

Your hypnotherapist guides you through the complete process while you're in trance so that you're able to:

✔ Prepare yourself properly. Your hypnotherapist is there to help you with the most vital part of your preparation, which is your mental attitude.

✔ See yourself performing well. Envisioning a positive outcome breaks down your negative self-image.

✔ Experience what it is like to have the appropriate, positive, and constructive feelings throughout.

✔ Change your negative self-talk into positive self talk.

By experiencing the complete process in trance, you get a good understanding of the plot and feel comfortable about how to direct your own performance.

A wise piece of advice to get in trance is to forget about yourself. By following this advice, you can focus on your audience, or your performance, instead of on your negative feelings that may sabotage what you are doing.

Actors respond to cues that prompt them to react in a certain way at the right time. And just as actors respond to cues, so your hypnotherapist helps you respond to cues. These cues are designed to give you appropriate feelings and responses at the appropriate time; before the performance, during it, and after it has been completed.

Regaining your lustre

You used to do it well, and then everything fell apart. This is a tough situation, but realise that if you've performed well in the past, you can perform well in the present and the future.

Your hypnotherapist may want to regress you to help you recapture that good past performance, and bring all those positive feelings back to the present. (Chapter 2 talks about what is called 'regression therapy', which means using your imagination, through hypnosis, to 'live through' one of your own past or future lives.) Or maybe your therapist looks for ways to transfer the feelings you had in a positive, yet unrelated, past performance to the present, merging them into your current performance in order to enhance it.

Summing up your parts

Don't forget that you are the sum of all your parts and that some of these parts can help you give that excellent performance. Some of the resources you have may be hidden from you, some hide away when you need them, some you may not even know are there! Your hypnotherapist will be able to help you get in touch with these parts – confidence, relaxation, clarity of mind, for example – and bring them into play just when you need them.

Your hypnotherapist will give plenty of suggestions that will allow your mind to slip into the method-actor mode, as you start to live your good performance.

The more you rehearse through therapy and self-hypnosis and experience a good performance, the better your performance gets. You'll soon be on your way to winning that Oscar!

Taking the Confidence Trick

Confidence is an elusive thing. You may be surprised to know that some of the people who come to hypnotherapy for confidence building are actually quite successful and are occasionally even well-known celebrities. Both of us have worked on confidence building with clients who are at the top of their professions. The point is that confidence is not something that arrives after you achieve a certain salary or status.

Confidence is extremely subjective, so the techniques your hypnotherapist uses to help you to regain it vary. However, through hypnosis your sense of self-assuredness is easily strengthened.

Feeling ten feet tall (when you're used to feeling like a midget)

Do you know anyone you really envy because they are so confident, calm and cool? If so, you can through hypnosis, 'borrow' some of their attributes and place them into your own personality! This is a really fun technique that can help you achieve your goals. It is priceless to see people rapidly become *genuinely* more confident and happy.

Try it for yourself: *Pretend* you have some positive attribute of someone you admire. Then *imagine* what differences having that attribute would make in how you feel and behave. Speculate about how different people's reactions to you would be. If you really try this exercise – even without hypnosis – you may begin to see how powerful it can be.

Changing your self-talk

If you have read the preceding section and are doubtful – perhaps even thinking to yourself 'It might work for others, but not for me . . .' – perhaps you have a strong critical sense that regularly results in putting yourself down. If you regularly rubbish yourself – think self-critical thoughts or even use humour to put yourself down – you need to work on changing your self-talk.

The common parlance is to refer to this voice as your *inner critic*. Everyone has a self-critical voice or inner critic. This is the part of you that says things like 'I'm bad', 'I'm ugly', 'I'm unlovable', 'I'm stupid', and so on.

But when you become consciously aware of your inner critic, you can bring it under control and actually change your inner critic into an inner mentor. Yes, with a bit of work, the voice that once savaged you can become your ally and coach. Imagine how good it will feel to have a voice that guides and advises you instead of criticises!

Even before you go to see a hypnotherapist about your self-confidence worries, just start noticing all the ways that you undermine yourself or put yourself down through thought, words, or behaviour. Keep a mental awareness of the broad themes that your inner critic uses against you, such as 'I'm dumb', 'I'm poor', 'I'm incompetent', and so on.

Putting your confidence into practice

So you've just been hypnotised for greater self-confidence. You're feeling more optimistic than you've felt in a long time. You go through the whole week feeling great, and for the next few days even your friends can tell you've changed somehow. But one week later, you've lost it.

The trick with sustaining any type of hypnotherapy treatment can be summed up in three words: *act as if*. I sometimes think about putting these on my therapy practice room wall. Why are they so important?

'Acting as if' for any sort of behaviour leads to the creation of habit. If you act as if you are confident for a long enough period of time, you actually *become* more confident. I also say this to people who have just stopped smoking by hypnosis – if you act as if you are a non smoker, then you remain a non smoker.

The important message here is that hypnotherapy is not a passive interaction. The hypnotherapist can provide some of the initial motivation, but the bulk of the work for *remaining* successful is your job. 'Acting as if' is the secret.

Sorting Out Your Anxieties

It has been said that the conscious mind creates most of your problems and if given half a chance, the unconscious can sort out the mess! In fact, some say that 70 per cent of what we worry about never happens and the 30 per cent that does, doesn't happen in the way we thought it would.

Anxiety is a familiar state everyone experiences now and again. It involves a combination of feelings such as fear, restlessness, and worry. It may also be accompanied by physical sensations such as palpitations, chest pain, upset stomach and shortness of breath.

Different people react differently to anxiety, both in how much anxiety they feel and in their reactions to it. If you suffer high levels of anxiety over a long period, you may develop physical ailments as a result. At the extreme end anxieties can be irrational and form a mental health problem.

Bear in mind that appropriate levels of anxiety are functional and desirable. You need a certain amount of anxiety to motivate yourself when things are urgent and have to be attended to. It's when that anxiety runs out of control that problems set in!

A variety of anxieties that people commonly experience include:

- **Panic attacks** are usually one-off experiences, involving intense, brief periods of abrupt, disabling fear. A variety of symptoms such as breathing difficulties, palpitations, and nausea may result.

  A panic disorder is an anxiety disorder involving recurrent, unexpected panic attacks, where the fear of the next anticipated attack becomes itself an anxiety.

- **Obsessive thoughts** can involve a repetitive, anxiety-provoking tendency to dwell on an idea, or series of related ideas. The thoughts can disrupt how you function and impact your quality of life.

- **Phobias** involve a powerful and constant fear of an object, a situation, or individual. Phobias can become disruptive and obsessive to the person experiencing them.

- **Stress** involves physical and emotional reactions that are the opposite of relaxation. Stress can result from either positive or negative events. *Stressors* – anxiety-provoking events – are highly subjective for individuals.

✔ **Low self-esteem** refers to a negative view a person forms of themself. Over time, low self-esteem can have detrimental effects on your physical and emotional health.

You may be relieved to know that hypnotherapy has a good track record of resolving many of these types of problems.

With the exception of severe mental health problems, hypnotherapy can help relieve your anxieties. A hypnotherapist can help your unconscious mind calm down and find new methods to cope with current and future anxiety-provoking situations in a variety of ways including:

✔ Raising your self-esteem and confidence.

✔ Identifying the themes or patterns of your worries in order to deconstruct them.

✔ Finding a healthy way to cope with a legitimate concern. For example, you may be worried about your personal safety; through hypnotherapy you can find practical ways to feel safe.

✔ Seeing yourself (in trance) in the future without the inappropriate worries, whilst teaching your conscious mind to be that way in the present.

Your hypnotherapist is not there to remove all your anxiety; He is there to help you cope more effectively with it.

Beating the Blues

Part of the human condition involves feeling a bit low from time to time. However, if you have a long-standing problem, it may be that you now have two problems: the original one as well as depression. Having a problem you can't seem to get rid of naturally makes you feel low. Hypnotherapists work with helping people beat the blues on a regular basis.

The way that you think directly affects the way you feel. If you label an experience positive, you feel good, possibly even energetic, not only about the experience but about yourself. If you view an event as bad, you feel horrible and possibly drained. Successful people often have an ability to turn a negative event into a challenge and a crisis into an opportunity.

Your hypnotherapist will work to help you understand how powerfully your evaluation of life events influences both your thoughts and your emotions.

Understanding the different types of depression

Let's clarify some terminology. What is the difference between the blues and depression? There are obviously different levels of feeling low. If you contrast the feelings at receiving a parking ticket with the death of a loved one, you get the picture. The feeling about the parking ticket isn't in the same league as the feeling of bereavement.

It is entirely natural to feel depressed over the death of someone you love or when you have a serious illness, and in similar situations. This type of depression is known as *reactive depression* because your depression is a reaction to events.

Clinical depression, on the other hand, involves a more serious and long-term condition. Psychiatrists label it as a reaction to long-standing depression not necessarily related to a specific event.

The attributes of clinical depression involve:

- ✔ Loss of appetite
- ✔ Inability to sleep
- ✔ Loss of pleasure (also known as *anhedonia*)
- ✔ In extreme forms, suicidal feelings

Clinical depression is very serious and requires urgent medical attention. Psychiatric medication is a common treatment approach, unlike reactive depression.

Working your way out of that black hole

The earlier section, 'Taking the Confidence Trick' deals with ways of making you feel good. A lot of the methods referred to involve the hypnotherapist giving suggestions to make you feel better, also known as 'ego- strengthening'. These can be straightforward suggestions such as, 'You will feel increasingly more optimistic', or 'You will feel happier and healthier than you have felt in a long time'.

Ego-strengthening is a core component with helping you to work your way out of a period of depression.

Stress Busting!

Stress, in the true sense of the word, refers to tension. Tension in itself is a neutral condition and not always negative. However, when a hypnotist meets a patient who wants to work on their stress, it is always referred to by the patient as a problem involving an overload or an unbearable tension causing fear, worry, and possibly other health problems such as headaches, or some type of emotional and/or physical problem.

You can think of *stress* simply as the opposite of relaxation. Because hypnotherapy is a marvellous way to induce relaxation, you won't be surprised to read that hypnotherapy is a marvellous stress antidote!

Because hypnosis helps you relax, it is an excellent tool in identifying new strategies for stress reductions that feel natural to you.

Cooling yourself off and hypnotherapy

Anger management has become such a buzzword recently that there is even a Hollywood movie about with that title. We haven't actually seen it, as we're too busy helping people to not be angry!

Let's say that you are coming to a hypnotherapist for anger management treatment. Most hypnotherapists begin anger management work by collecting information about how long you've had a problem with anger and how you react. They may also ask you what helps make you less angry and what winds you up the most. These questions help you to start thinking about your own patterns of anger and how you deal (or don't) with it. You may not even be hypnotised in your first session because there will be so much to uncover about you and your way of expressing anger.

Most people with anger issues feel out of control. This lack of control feeds their inner critic and makes them feel awful about themselves. So, early on, your hypnotherapist helps you to build up your confidence. You come to believe that it is possible for you to have greater self-control. At this point, the hypnotherapist can introduce any number of new coping strategies, based on your recently enhanced sense of confidence and control.

Responding with stress

If the source of an alarm hangs around for a sustained period, whether in your mind or in real life, you translate this state of constant alert into what is called a *stress response*. In short, sustaining a fight-or-flight response (which is covered in Chapter 4) leads to stress.

However, most people don't experience stress by living for long periods in immediate physical danger (unfortunately, you'd probably get the sack if you physically fought your boss for survival!). More commonly, you produce stress as a product of the way that you think about the external forces affecting you.

The physical consequences of living under stress for prolonged periods can be serious. Stress can lead to stomach ulcers, a heart attack, a stroke, or other physical ailments. Your ancestors would rest after the threat was over (after either fighting and killing a sabre-toothed tiger or fleeing to safety), giving their body biochemistry time to return to normal. Unfortunately, in today's society, many people don't experience this respite from stress; they're under constant stress – a situation that can, and often does, have adverse health effects.

Reframing your stressed-out world

Hypnotherapy can help you find strategies for changing your response to the things that stress you out. Changing your attitude toward your stressors lowers your stress and helps you avoid any detrimental health consequences.

Reframe is a therapy term that simply means viewing something in a new and more positive light. Once you can reframe a situation you view as negative, you improve your ability to cope with that situation.

You're stressed: Your life appears to be on fast forward, and you can't seem to slow down. Work and home life are no longer fun, and you just want to crawl into a hole and sleep. Worry not, becuase help is on its way in the person of your friendly neighbourhood hypnotherapist. With his expertise, your hypnotherapist can help you stand back and re-evaluate your stressors. How he does that depends on what your particular issues are.

In general, a hypnotherapist can help you to:

- Take off your blinkers and see that you do, in fact, have options.
- Look at and change your current reactions to stress.
- Reframe your feelings towards your stressors and perhaps look upon them as motivational and exciting.
- Prioritise what is important and what are unnecessary pressures.
- Ensure that you are putting appropriate effort into the necessities.
- Access your inner resources and potentials.
- Relax!

Making a molehill out of that mountain

Facing up to stress can seem overwhelming. You can think of stress as a mountain you're standing very close to and need to get by, on your journey through life. Standing so close makes the mountain seem very daunting; you can't see a way around it or through it. The only option appears to be the long, hard slog up its sheer face; a journey that is very tiring and fraught with danger. However, take some time to walk away from that mountain and you start to see it differently. For a start, it doesn't appear so challenging. You notice paths that go around it; tunnels that take you safely through. In fact, you notice that there are many easier options than taking that dangerous route up its side.

Hypnotherapy finds the molehill in your mountains. In trance you can access your unconscious mind and open up new perspectives, which allows you to find easier and safer ways to get by that stress mountain and improve your effectiveness, and your health too.

 Schedule in time for yourself. Regularly take yourself away from your stressors and do something that you enjoy. When you return, you return refreshed, invigorated, and able to deal more effectively with what you have to do.

Accessing Your Creativity

Have you ever had a dream and pleasantly surprised yourself? Maybe by telling a funny joke in your sleep and waking up laughing? Or maybe by simply having an astonishing dream that you could never have consciously devised? These simple examples are only the tip of the latent creativity within your unconscious mind. Now think how amazing it would be if you could consciously harness this sort of creativity. Well, through hypnosis you can!

Another way to understand your well of creativity is as an infinite inner oil well reserve. Imagine an oil engineer one day knocks on your door and tells you that you're living on top of an oil well of such immense reserves that it will make you rich beyond your wildest dreams. Sound good so far? You allow him to access your oil by having an oil well constructed that plunges underground and eventually (hooray!) strikes oil! Unfortunately, a few hundred barrels later, the oil well apparently dries up and stops delivering. You call back your now trusted friend, the oil engineer, who promptly identifies the blockage in your oil well and in no time flat, you are producing twice as many barrels of oil as before. You are indeed thrilled!

As if that weren't enough, your now very best friend, the oil engineer, gives you a crash course in DIY maintenance and construction of exploratory oil wells, making himself redundant and allowing you to now access all the oil you want at will! And just before he leaves, he mentions the small fact that, unlike other oil reserves, which eventually dry up, yours is different. Your oil well has infinite resources, which means you will never run out of resources. Nice fantasy, eh?

But the fantasy is real!

You really *do* possess the metaphorical equivalent of the unlimited oil well we just described. Simply substitute 'hypnotherapist' for 'oil engineer' and 'inner creativity and resources' for 'oil'. Self-hypnosis is the tool you use to access your inner resources whenever you need to. But by now, we have probably pumped this metaphor dry!

Tapping into your endless well of creativity

Your creativity is the storehouse for all your memories. This is like an immense computer that remembers everything under the broad heading of 'creativity' that you have seen, created, experienced or heard. That alone is a staggering concept! Imagine a computer that would allow you to access any of that and we are describing your unconscious mind.

How does a hypnotherapist help you access this type of unconscious creativity? The process involves:

- ✔ **Accessing** your unconscious mind in trance. This is like the computer example in the preceding section. For creative writing, click on your personal drive 'Z:', for a creative strategy to get you out of trouble, click on your personal drive 'Q:' and so forth. (Of course, the 'drives' mentioned are actually your unconscious mind. When given a task in hypnosis, you simply 'go there' without knowing how this happens, or that the info was even stored.)
- ✔ **Releasing** is the process in which your hypnotherapist helps you change your negative thoughts, views, and feelings that are causing a delay in accessing your creativity.
- ✔ **Endlessly releasing** your inner resources when needed. This means finding the previous step increasingly easy to access. The way to make this easier is to learn self-hypnosis and practise it regularly.

Some techniques your hypnotherapist may use to help you release your creative side include:

- ✔ Directly requesting your unconscious mind to convince you that you can write/paint/draw/compose easily.
- ✔ Giving your ego a boost to remind you of past successes.

- ✔ Reminding you that your unconscious has infinite ideas.

- ✔ Increasing your motivation and concentration. This can be done through simple suggestions to your unconscious mind that you will find it easier to concentrate and that you will be more motivated.

- ✔ Asking your unconscious to become an ocean of ideas, awash with creativity that flows easily from within, breaking with clarity on the shores of your conscious awareness as and when you need them. (Can't seem to shake this metaphor thing, can we?)

- ✔ Practising self-hypnosis. Your hypnotherapist will probably give you suggestions to keep the well unblocked, and this is where self-hypnosis comes in. It's a good idea to ask your hypnotherapist to teach you self-hypnosis at the beginning of your sessions. Through self-hypnosis, you can turbocharge the results of your hypnotherapy and continue to deepen and maintain the wonderful by-products of an unblocked unconscious for the rest of your life!

Relaxation is the key to unlocking your creativity. No matter what technique your therapist uses, helping you to relax mind and body plays an important role.

Don't get us wrong. We don't mean that in order to be highly creative you have to be so relaxed that you flop about all over the place! On the contrary, it's all about creating the right balance between relaxation and tension. Too relaxed and you won't get anywhere and will probably fall asleep. Too tense and you block your creativity with anxiety, and start fretting over unwanted thoughts. Just the right amount of tension and just the right amount of relaxation keeps your mind alert and focused, and your creativity flowing.

It is down to the skill of the hypnotherapist to help you achieve this balance by using, and teaching you how to use, the very thing you probably have a problem in achieving – relaxation.

Unblocking your creative flow

Whether in art, writing, or music, you may reach a state of impasse in your creative flow, particularly when faced with deadlines or overwhelming self-criticism. Suddenly concentrating becomes impossible and you are unable to supply the creative part of your nature with the necessary ideas. Your flow of creativity just dries up and with every attempt you make to clear it, the blockage just gets stronger and stronger.

The reasons for your blockage can be many and may include:

- ✔ Negative thinking about your ability
- ✔ Fear of failure
- ✔ Fear of success (oh yes, there are many out there who fear this!)

Time then to clean out your pipes and remove that blockage!

So how does this business of using hypnotherapy to access your creative resources actually work? Traditionally, once you are in trance, the hypnotherapist asks your unconscious mind to imagine its creative potential. When your subconscious mind begins to imagine being more creative, the hypnotherapist can additionally suggest that you find it easy to develop new strategies to deal with your problem.

Your hypnotherapist can choose from many techniques, depending on your specific needs. A couple of methods good for helping unblock creativity include asking your unconscious for the answers to questions about the blockage, and creating solutions. Because these solutions come without input from your conscious mind, they feel natural and intuitive. The same system operates when you have a creative impulse, or when your muse inspires you. It is an uncalculated effort and usually feels particularly imaginative and creative because the thinking, analytical part – your conscious mind – cannot take credit for the solution. It is one of the most ethereal, yet real experiences that hypnotherapy regularly produces.

Hey presto, the flow of creativity commences once more.

In many cases, conscious insight is not necessary to remove your block. Oh dear, we hear the sound of many counsellors and psychotherapists preparing the heretical bonfire! Despite what some authorities say, your conscious mind doesn't need to understand why the blockage existed after the unconscious gives permission for it to be removed.

Touching on Sexual Problems

Your sexuality is key to your identity. Freud described the sex drive as core to human personality. So if you have sexual problems, they quite literally undermine your self-esteem as well as your relationships. This double whammy can make it very difficult to seek help for sex problems (and a bit embarrassing too).

Hypnotherapy is a magnificent therapeutic tool for strengthening your ego, as well as addressing a range of sexual problems that individuals or couples may face (and remember that your hypnotherapist has heard it all before).

Although there may be physical causes to sexual problems, the majority of causes are generally psychological or emotional. A hypnotherapist will work with many of these problems only after a doctor has ruled out any physical cause, because he wants to ensure that you are getting the proper treatment.

Table 9-1 shows some of the most common sexual problems for men and women.

Table 9-1	Sexual Problems by Gender	
Men	*Women*	*Both*
Impotence and erectile dysfunction: Not being able to get and/or maintain an erection.	**Vaginismus:** Painful tensing or spasms of the muscles around the vagina at the point of, or just prior to, being penetrated (by a penis, finger, tampon, and so on).	**Anorgasmia:** Inability to achieve an orgasm.
Premature ejaculation: Inability to consistently control the timing of your orgasm.	**Frigidity:** A persistent and recurrent inability to maintain an adequate lubrication-swelling response during sexual activity.	**Lack of sexual desire or drive.**

Libido is often used as a synonym for sex drive. More correctly, it is the emotional energy associated with all biological drives, including survival. So in that sense, libido can be thought of as the source of your lust for life.

Different sexual problems require different hypnotherapeutic techniques, including many of those we talk about earlier in this chapter. Following are two examples of hypnosis working with sexual difficulties:

✔ **Lack of sexual desire:** If you have a problem with lack of sexual desire, the hypnotherapist may put you in trance and ask your unconscious to scan memories of positive sexual experiences. The concept of repeatedly reviewing memories (or fantasies) of positive sexual experiences is suggested until long forgotten feelings of arousal are again made possible. Don't worry, hypnotherapists are extremely sensitive and professional about ensuring your safety and dignity in treating sexual issues.

✔ **Vaginismus:** To help with this problem, your hypnotherapist may help you to explore the fears or anxieties you associate with penetrative sex while you're in trance. Over several sessions, your hypnotherapist would increasingly suggest that your unconscious mind associates sex with feelings of relaxation and eventually, pleasure.

Doing it for fun

Famous hypnotherapist Milton Erickson once worked with a prudish married couple experiencing difficulties having sex. The couple had an arid approach to sex and were overly intellectual, analytical, and clinical about their intercourse — or lack of. Erickson suggested to their unconscious minds that they forget the analysis of sex and just 'f**k for fun' (his words — not ours!). Very soon they reported back that they had begun normal sexual relations!

Sex is there for you (and us!) to enjoy. Learn to relax, be creative, and enjoy your performance every time. In fact, being creative and confident in your performance can lead you to being rampant in bed. Ooh! Err! Mrs!

Chapter 8

Considering the Limits
of Hypnotherapy

*Y*ou're considering sorting out a problem by paying a visit to a hypnotherapist. Before you do, we suggest that you mull over a few things about
the responsibilities of that hypnotherapist, as well as some of the realities
of hypnotherapy itself. After all, you want to go in for therapy with realistic
expectations and a clear understanding of what to expect from your therapist
and the process itself. The information in this chapter gives you just that.

Realising That Hypnotherapy Helps, It Doesn't Cure

Okay, the truth is that hypnotherapy is not magic and hypnotherapists do
not have special powers. You're not going to walk in for a hypnotherapy session and walk out an hour or so later with all your cares and woes miracu-
lously cured, hallelujah!

Many myths surround hypnotherapy (see Chapter 16 for the most unrealistic)
and many people walk into a session expecting the impossible. When you go
for therapy, enter into it with realistic expectations. That means understanding what can be done and what can't be done.

And now a word that is an anathema to hypnotherapists: *cure.* Cure is a word often misused by patients – and by some hypnotherapists. Cure implies that something is going to go away. Possibly for good. Oh, how we wish therapy were that simple. Unfortunately, it isn't, and it never will be.

No hypnotherapist worth her salt will promise a cure to her patients because she cannot guarantee that the problem you work on will go away. It may; or you may learn to live more comfortably with it; or it may go away and return at a later date; or it may be that nothing changes at all. All these possible outcomes apply to any form of therapy or medical procedure. You may be thinking 'What's the point in going for therapy then, if there's no guarantee of change?' The fact of the matter is that no therapy can guarantee change. However, hypnotherapy does have an excellent track record and the evidence shows it to be very effective at *helping* people to make changes to their lives and to achieve their goals.

Hypnotherapy helps. That means it is an aid to overcoming something, and as such, relies on the effort you are prepared to put into the therapy process. It can't do it all on its own.

Accepting Hypnotherapy's Limitations

When you go for your hypnotherapy session you need to be realistic about what it can achieve. Although hypnotherapy's effects are wide-ranging, like any other therapy approach it does have its limitations.

Setting yourself up for success

As with anything, many factors determine the outcome of hypnotherapy:

- **Your symptom:** Hypnotherapy can help resolve many different symptoms. However, it cannot help with everything. The chapters in Parts 2 and 3 of this book give you a good idea as to the type of symptoms that can and can't benefit from hypnotherapy. For example, cigarette addiction can be treated, whereas the treatment of heroin addiction should be left to the medical profession. If in doubt, ask your therapist if hypnotherapy is right for your symptom.

  Your symptom itself often determines the length of time you spend in therapy. Smoking cessation can take as little as one session to complete. However, if you are being treated for something more involved, such as bulimia, you can expect a longer course of treatment because of the deeper issues involved with this condition and its treatment.

✔ **Your expectations:** Are you expecting too much from hypnotherapy? Do you think it is a magical panacea that will get rid of your symptom at the click of a finger?

The 'I want to lose two stone by Friday' mindset is doomed to failure. Your expectations must be realistic from the outset. Hypnotherapy is therapy, not magic! Discuss your expectations with your therapist and be prepared to have the reality of the process pointed out to you.

So what can you realistically expect from hypnotherapy? You can expect to have a very good chance at relieving your symptom. However, there is also a – much smaller – chance that hypnotherapy will have little or no effect.

As with any course of treatment, medical or not, you can't have an absolute guarantee that the treatment will work. Why? Because of the factors we discuss here.

You can also expect to put some effort into your therapy process by carrying out homework assignments (see Chapter 13) that continue the therapy process, even when you are not with your therapist. You can also expect that your therapist will put in as much time and effort as is needed to help you overcome your symptom.

✔ **Your fears:** Are you at ease with your hypnotherapy session? Do you fear anything about the process you're going through, such as whether the effects of your therapy will be long-lasting, or just how effective it will be? Perhaps you're worried that you aren't going into trance in the way that you thought you would. Maybe you're concerned that being in trance now will affect you during the meeting you're chairing later in the day.

If these or any other fears spring to mind during your therapy session, discuss them with your therapist before, during – yes, you can talk in trance – or after the trance has concluded, and let her put your mind at ease. Letting such fears fester away without discussing them interferes with your chances of having a good outcome for your therapy.

✔ **The relationship you have with your therapist:** Is it a good one? Do you feel comfortable with her? Is your therapist someone you can work with?

Like any relationship, the better it is, the smoother things run. If you don't feel comfortable with, or dislike, your therapist for any reason, the all-important trust factor will not be there. If you don't trust your therapist then your mind won't trust the therapy process itself. If this is the case, then politely say 'Thanks, but no thanks' to your therapist, and find another in whose company you do feel comfortable. Remember, the therapy sessions are for you, not your therapist. For more information on how to create a good working relationship with your therapist, and what to do if it grows bad, have a look at Chapter 12.

✔ **What's going on in your life at the moment:** Life has its ups and downs and these may help or hinder your therapy. If all is hunky-dory and good things are happening in your life, you tend to feel upbeat, positive, and motivated – you have what's known as a positive mindset. These good feelings affect the way you view the course of your therapy, making you more optimistic, positive, and motivated about the whole process and its outcome. With this positive mindset you could very well find that your unconscious mind is more open to the suggestions your hypnotherapist is giving; speeding up the process of change.

On the other hand, if life at the moment is seemingly stressful or dull, then the opposite may be true. The negative mindset that these feelings create may hinder your therapy, giving you a pessimistic outlook towards it and consequently slowing the whole thing down.

No matter what's happening in your life at the moment – good or bad – your therapy is still likely to work under the guidance of a skilled therapist. In fact, let your therapist know if you are feeling negative; she can include suggestions during the session to help lift your mood – something the majority of therapists do as par for the course.

However, if these negative feelings are persistent and don't relate to the reason you are in therapy, you may want to consider booking a few sessions to help you overcome them. Have a look at Chapter 7 to see how hypnotherapy can help you with a variety of emotional issues.

Highlighting the importance of your motivation

The most important thing you can do to ensure success for your hypnotherapy sessions is to look at your motivation and make sure that it is correct. The motivations that bring people for therapy are many and varied. For some, the motivation is positive, helping them along the path to change. For others, the motivation is negative, and can actually hinder that process. A couple of examples of the negatives and why they hinder:

✔ **Because someone said you should:** So someone in your life is urging you to try hypnotherapy. Take a look at why that person is pushing you toward therapy. Is it because they have a genuine concern for your welfare, such as not wanting you to die from lung cancer because you smoke, or wanting to help you get over the turmoil you experience when public speaking – or is it because they are trying to manipulate you? Do you feel that you need to go for therapy because if you don't they are going to leave you? Do you feel that they're using emotional blackmail to get you to therapy for their own selfish ends?

If you're going for therapy only because someone else wants you to and you have no real desire to change, then your therapist can sit with you waffling on to her heart's content without making the slightest bit of difference. Even if change does happen, the likelihood is that you will be back to your old ways faster than you can say 'therapist'! Why? Because you never really wanted to change in the first place. And short of elaborate brainwashing techniques, no therapist is going to be able to make you! By the way, if someone urges therapy on you out of genuine concern, perhaps you should take a little time to listen to them. After all, if you act on their concern and go for therapy, it could very well improve your life no end – if not save it!

✔ **Because you don't want to make any effort:** This applies to the lazy amongst us! If you're trying hypnotherapy because you think it's the easy option, you aren't going to get very far. Sure, hypnotherapy can certainly speed up and ease the process of change, but this only happens if you put some effort into it too.

If you don't put any effort into the process you aren't going to get anywhere. Imagine wanting to push a stalled car. You need to put some effort into pushing, in order to get it to move. Simply rest your hands against it and you will be standing there all day getting nowhere fast!

So, in order for therapy to have the greatest chance of succeeding, you need to have the appropriate motivation. Your chances for success are much greater if your motivation:

✔ **Genuinely comes from you:** You are going for therapy because *you* want to make the change.

✔ **Is realistic:** You understand that change may take time and that hypnotherapy is not a magical panacea for all ills, and you're prepared to put some effort into the process.

Letting Go May Be Harder Than You Think

Sometimes giving up your problems isn't easy. Okay, tell us something new! Perhaps you are thinking this is a bit of an understatement. After all, you're probably reading this book because you want to get rid of a problem that's proving difficult to shift. However, some problems can be very easy to get rid of, so why is it that others prove to be difficult blighters?

Facing the fact that you may want to keep your problem

The human mind can be as fickle as the human being to which it belongs. So, even though on one level you are desperate to get rid of your problem, on another level there really might be a good reason for you to keep it. This is known as a *secondary gain*: your problem has something of benefit to give you.

Oh yes, your problems can be beneficial, even though you may not be aware of what that benefit is! That benefit may be misplaced and dysfunctional and can be achieved by other, healthier means; but the problem is still serving some important function. You may find, for example, that your problem keeps you away from a job that you don't like, or perhaps it's stopping you from having to do tasks you dread, such as shopping, ironing, or picking the kids up from school.

Of course, you may be able to resolve an issue without the need to address the secondary gain. However, you may find that you develop new and equally dysfunctional symptoms in order to provide the same benefit! In this case there would be little point in having therapy in the first place.

Uncovering secondary gains

Sometimes, uncovering the secondary gain is the key to helping a patient resolve their problem. A couple of examples:

✔ A patient who came for treatment for panic attacks arrived, accompanied by her husband, mother, father, and a neighbour. Now, it is not uncommon for patients with panic symptoms to be accompanied by someone else because it helps them to feel safe on their journey to the hypnotherapist, in case they have an attack. But being accompanied by virtually her entire family was a bit of overkill! However, as skilled therapists (well, at least we like to think we are!) this immediately suggested to us that something else was going on – a secondary gain. What was it that necessitated her bringing all these people with her? During the consultation, we asked what would happen if she no longer had the panic attacks. After a moments pause, she replied that she would no longer be getting any attention from her family. Bingo! Secondary gain uncovered! She went on to explain that she basically did everything for the family, with very little attention being paid towards her. It was nothing malicious, that's just the way the family had developed. However, when she had a panic attack, everyone crowded round her, being kind and gentle.

✔ Another patient presented for pain control. She had a bad back and wanted to be able to control her pain. She had been through every conceivable approach to getting rid of it, but to no avail! During the consultation, she was asked what she would be able to do, that she can't do now, once the pain had gone. After listing several things she gave a sheepish pause and then stated that she would once again be able to have sex with her husband. Something about the way she stated this implied that this was not something that she was looking forward to – at all! When asked how she felt about once again being able to enjoy that side of her relationship with her husband, she stated that she dreaded it. That, in fact, she no longer found her husband sexually attractive. Ta-dah! Secondary gain uncovered at last!

In both cases, the secondary gains needed to be addressed before the symptom could be dealt with appropriately – and they both were, as it happens.

Overcoming your secondary gains

It is your hypnotherapist's job to recognise, and to help you address, any issues with secondary gains. After all, if you were aware of them you would probably have done something about them already! Sometimes the secondary gains are very obvious, and sometimes they're hidden. You need to address secondary gains, because you don't want another symptom springing gleefully into your life, in order to meet the gain.

Of course, not all your problems are beset by these annoying quirks of your psyche. But that doesn't mean they don't exist.

Your therapist may want to work with you in several ways when helping you to overcome a secondary gain:

- ✓ **Discussing:** Where the secondary gain is obvious, you can discuss what is happening with your therapist and develop a strategy from there. Your therapist can develop suggestions to give you in trance to help.

- ✓ **Dissociating:** If the secondary gain is not obvious, your therapist may wish to use dissociation techniques that allow you to safely isolate the part of your mind responsible for your problem and to have a conversation with it to help uncover what is going on. Once the secondary gain is uncovered then something can be done to alleviate it. (See Chapter 2 for a complete discussion of dissociation.)

- ✓ **Allowing your unconscious mind to sort things out appropriately:** Maybe you don't know how to address the secondary gain at a conscious level. However, your unconscious mind knows what's needed, and can collaborate with your skilful hypnotherapist to come up with a new behaviour or response that addresses the secondary gain in a much more appropriate way.

- ✓ **Referring you to another agency:** Maybe the secondary gain cannot be addressed through hypnotherapy alone. For example, if couples counselling is needed, your therapist may want to refer you to a relationship counsellor in order to get the matter sorted.

Whatever the secondary gain, you can find ways to address the issues that it brings forth. After you address those issues, your symptom will probably be much more amenable to therapy.

Sabotaging your own therapy

As we said before, your mind can be a fickle creature. On the one hand, you're desperate to get rid of a symptom, and on the other, your mind seems to pull out all the stops in an attempt to retain it. It's as though the mind has put up a barrier to change. You can agitate your inner saboteur without real-ising it. For example:

- ✔ **Unconscious defiance:** Some people have a natural resistance to author-ity figures. That means offering up some measure of defiance to anyone they perceive as being in a position of authority. These people may look upon their hypnotherapist as being in such a position (even without knowing it) and unconsciously block or do the opposite to whatever the therapist says or does.

  If you fall into this category, be prepared to discuss this part of your personality with your therapist. There are ways around this. But just remember that you are in the therapy session as an equal and that the work you are doing is a team endeavour.

- ✔ **An unconscious need to prove superiority:** Some people seem to have the mindset that no matter what their therapist does they always try to go one better, or try to prove her wrong. This is certainly the case with some hypnotherapy patients. The therapist suggests X and they do Y. Not only is this frustrating for the therapist (though once they are aware of it they can rework their strategy), but it could end up with the patient having to spend much longer in therapy than is strictly necessary.

- ✔ **'Forgetting' to tell your therapist some important piece of informa-tion:** We are all forgetful to some degree. However, some hypnotherapy patients have selective memories, omitting to tell their therapist some piece of vital information that is relevant to their symptom – despite the in-depth questioning they underwent during the taking of the case his-tory. Not being in possession of that snippet of wisdom, their therapist goes ahead with therapy only to find that things aren't working the way they should.

  A way round this is to begin to write down, well in advance of your first session, every piece of information you feel may be relevant to your visit to the hypnotherapist. In this way, if your mind begins to play tricks during your session, the information will hopefully be at hand on that piece of paper – as long as you remember to bring it with you!

Don't worry. If any of these gremlins of sabotage begin to rear their ugly head, your hypnotherapist will be able to plan a strategy to foil their little game!

Resistance is a conscious or unconscious attempt by a patient to avoid going into trance or to avoid accepting the therapeutic suggestions given by the therapist. Despite seeking out hypnotherapy in the first place, you may resist attempts to change. Your hypnotherapist may explore the reason for this resistance because it may be central to resolving your problem.

Examining Your Hypnotherapist's Ethical Responsibilities

Any reputable, professional hypnotherapist holds an ethical responsibility towards every person she treats. But what does this term mean and how does it apply to you? In therapy terms, *ethics* refers to a code of conduct based on *morals* – the ability to distinguish between right and wrong – that govern the professional conduct of your therapist.

So, your therapist's ethical responsibility is to ensure that her professional conduct is appropriate when working with you. That means:

✔ Telling you about their fees and availability in advance.

✔ Explaining the therapeutic process to you.

✔ Answering your questions honestly.

✔ Not prolonging therapy unnecessarily.

✔ Ensuring that you are as comfortable as possible during the therapy process.

✔ Showing a professional regard towards other therapists and therapies (for example, not criticising them!)

✔ Working within their own level of competence.

✔ Ensuring the confidentiality of anything that you may tell them.

On top of this, your therapist should show you what is known as *unconditional positive regard*, which means not being judgemental and accepting you as you are – a complete human being with the normal human problems that affect us all. After all, your therapist is only mortal and is subject to the same pitfalls in life as the rest of us. If you ever have the misfortune of meeting a hypnotherapist who says that they aren't, then walk away quickly, as you have just met a very deluded person. Unfortunately, one or two of them are out there!

Your therapist's professional ethics come from a variety of sources:

✔ **Personal ethics:** Derived from her own belief systems and moral values.

✔ **Workplace ethics:** Laid down by the powers that be, at any institution from which your therapist works.

✔ **A professional code of conduct:** Mandated by any professional society your therapist belongs to. As a condition of membership, your therapist is required to comply with rules governing her conduct in therapy.

Maintaining a therapeutic relationship

When you visit your hypnotherapist, you are going to see a professional, and as such they should treat you in a professional manner. That means that they maintain a professional working relationship with you. In other words, if any other relationship develops between you both, the therapeutic relationship should cease.

The dynamics of a professional relationship are very different to those of a friendship or love relationship. In a professional relationship, the therapist can provide impartial help; in other associations, impartiality is compromised by the close emotions that accompany more personal relationships. As nice as these feelings are, they won't necessarily lead you to a successful outcome for therapy.

If you want to know what your therapist's code of ethics is, just ask her. As a member of a professional body that governs her professional conduct, she should be able to show you the code of ethical conduct she agreed to abide by. Check the Appendix for an extract taken from the British Society of Clinical Hypnosis Code of Ethics to see what such a code may include.

Make sure that your hypnotherapist is a member of a bona fide professional organisation. Such a membership means that she's bound to act in a professional way during therapy. It also means that you can use the society's complaints procedure should you have any concerns about your therapist's conduct – which we certainly hope you won't!

Looking at Your Hypnotherapist's Legal Responsibilities

Okay, now for the legal bits. Your hypnotherapist is bound by whatever laws are applicable to your particular country of residence. State laws (in the US), national laws, and international laws (in the European Union) apply to determining who can practise hypnotherapy, how they can advertise, what they can advertise, and so on.

The extent to which hypnotherapy is regulated depends on the individual laws in each country. For example, in the UK and certain other European countries, no laws directly govern the training and practice of hypnotherapy. (A disgusting state of affairs, we know. Thankfully, moves are afoot to rectify this!). In the US, some states have very stringent laws, whilst others have virtually none.

On top of all this, every hypnotherapist should have professional indemnity insurance, that covers for malpractice, should a case be brought against them. To check whether your therapist is insured you can, of course, ask her; or better still, make sure that she belongs to a professional body that insists on professional indemnity insurance as a requirement of membership. How do you do that? Find out which professional body your therapist belongs to and phone them up and ask.

Incidentally, if you're worried whether your therapist has had any lawsuits for malpractice brought against her in the past, the professional body will also hold that information.

Part III

Expanding the Reach of Hypnotherapy

In this part . . .

This part looks at some of the lesser-known hypnother-apy applications. Past-life regression is a fascinating way of visiting the past – and even future – lives. Could you have been a cook in the court of Henry VIII? We examine the evidence and give you the no-nonsense, plain speak-ing facts.

This part discusses working with children as hypnotherapy subjects to help solve problems such as bed-wetting and anxiety. We also look at removing phobias, using many dif-ferent hypnotherapy technicques.

Chapter 9

Your Kids and Hypnotherapy

. . . .

. . . .

*I*f you're considering taking your child to a hypnotherapist, you can play a crucial role in assuring successful treatment by reading this chapter. We describe how safe hypnosis is for your child, and how you as a parent (and in this chapter we use the word *parent* to refer to the primary guardian of the child) can feel comfortable about their hypnotherapy experience.

Children live in a fantasy world for much of their waking hours. Their play and their involvement with television and books require deep imaginative participation.

Watch children at play. When they are deeply engaged and unselfconscious, they are transported to another world! They literally hypnotise themselves into the role they're playing – be that a warrior, a mother whose doll has become their 'baby', or some famous celebrity or sports figure. When my (Mike's) children are watching the *Dora the Explorer* cartoon, they are right there beside Dora and her monkey friend Boots, sharing their adventures in the jungle!

This same state of self-hypnosis would require some work from a hypnotherapist to create in an adult. But children enter this state regularly and with ease. This imaginative sense is exactly the quality of trance that can lead to effective hypnotherapy.

Kids – and as an American, I (Mike) use this term affectionately to include children and adolescents – are much easier to hypnotise than adults because they readily access their unconscious mind. As you become an adult, you lose some of this ability as society encourages you to become more focused and realistic.

Considering Ethical Issues

As you can imagine, working with children is an extremely serious business that requires the highest levels of professionalism and sensitivity. There are strict rules that hypnotherapists must adhere to when working with adults, but particularly when working with children.

The word *ethics* pertains to the principles of conduct governing an individual or a profession. Any qualified clinical hypnotherapist belongs to some professional hypnotherapy organisation that has a written document explaining the professional do's-and-don'ts. Usually called something like a 'Code of Conduct' or a 'Code of Ethics', this list is available for anyone interested to read before an initial session. Simply contact one of the national hypnotherapy organisations listed in the Appendix of this book.

An ethical hypnotherapist will allow you, as the parent, to be with your child throughout treatment sessions in order to ensure you and your child's confidence. However, the therapist may insist that the child answer some questions him or herself, so that the hypnotherapist can engage with your child directly. Also, your view of the problem may be completely different from your child's.

If your presence in the room is absolutely forbidden, you have every right to question why, and if not satisfied with the response, to seek help elsewhere.

You're welcome to be present in any part of the session, as long as your child agrees. Your absence may be necessary at times to allow your child to speak freely.

Alternatively, you may be happy to leave your child alone with a therapist you have confidence in. However, in our experience, by far the majority of parents want to be present in sessions and that is usually all right.

The hypnotherapist makes clear his reasons for his decision whether to have you involved in the session, and negotiates the outcome of treatment accordingly. However, he won't make you (the parent) feel that you have been doing things in the wrong way. He may however, occasionally suggest a different strategy to your approach to your child's problem to ensure success.

Some hypnotherapists may act as brokers between parent and child by asking the child what they would like their parents to do differently in order to help them feel better, or solve their problem. The hypnotherapist can then feed this information back to the parent(s) privately.

Noting the Differences in Hypnotising Children

Working with children is great fun because it's more like play than work. In fact, it is play. Children don't require the same sort of explanations of trance or even the same sort of trance inductions used on adults. So a hypnotherapist has to be good at imaginative play to work well with children.

Children are already in a state of hypnosis most of the time. Their world revolves around them. Until they develop their *critical factor*, a level of maturity that enables them to more objectively analyse information, children tend to believe that anything is possible and that what adults and authority figures say is true.

An ethical hypnotherapist, skilled at imaginative play, can work well with a child to bring about the desired results. To the observer, the interaction between hypnotherapist and child may seem like mere play. But the hypnotherapist understands the heightened state of suggestibility of a child, and is watching for opportune moments to offer therapeutic suggestions when the child is most receptive.

When I (Mike) first hypnotised children, I was often not sure if they were really hypnotised. They would appear wide awake, fidgeting sometimes and still speaking to me. Hypnotised adults are easier to spot because their eyes are usually closed, their face and body muscles are very relaxed, and they may even occasionally drool! But because children may not close their eyes, their response to trance is very different. This situation requires a more subtle detection on the part of the hypnotherapist.

Of course, children don't directly tell you that 'I am now in trance', so knowing when this occurs is more likely to happen with someone who has been trained to observe the physiological signs of trance – like a qualified hypnotherapist!

Two of the biggest differences in hypnotising children and adolescents, as opposed to adults, are:

✔ Kids don't need to close their eyes to go into trance. They may still fidget while in trance, but in a subtly different way – more slowed down.

✔ Children and adolescents are more trusting, and go more easily and deeper into trance early in therapy. They are particularly suggestible to ideas while in trance.

With eyes wide open

Children – and to a lesser extent, adolescents – have such powerful imaginations that unlike most adults, they don't need to close their eyes to go into a hypnotic trance.

You can probably recall vivid childhood imaginings – perhaps something as simple as becoming really involved with playing with dolls, or dreaming of being a superhero. Sporty children may also pretend to be their favourite athlete, and recreate the scenes of prowess and skill they view in sporting events.

Children put themselves into imaginary situations quite easily and naturally. Adults don't do this without a degree of effort in hypnosis. Adults have to be highly suggestible or in a very deep trance, with previous experiences of hypnosis, before trance is possible with their eyes open.

Similarly, when hypnotising a child, not only is eye closure unnecessary, insisting a young child close his eyes may make him feel unsafe, or at the very least, too suspicious to maintain trance.

Adults tend to think that trance requires that you remain physically still. This does not apply to children in hypnotherapy. Children can be in trance and receive hypnotherapeutic suggestions while they are fidgeting in their chair. In fact, movement can be used as part of inducing a hypnotic trance – if done skilfully.

Trance through imagination

Because of children's strong imaginative sense, hypnotherapists don't have to induce trance the same way as they do with adults. Trance with children is a normal, natural state. It can also be gained, or deepened, through play and by invoking the child's favourite fantasies or images. This is very different from adults, with whom it is necessary to answer questions about hypnosis and gain a great deal of trust first.

For a child or adolescent, the main hypnotherapeutic goal is to engage them in their favourite imaginative scenario. The hypnotherapist does this by simply talking and playfully encouraging them into making this scenario as all-encompassing as possible.

For example, if you were asked to imagine one of your favourite holidays and what you specifically enjoyed about it, you might be encouraged to elaborate at great length by someone who was genuinely interested in your experience. Chances are that your recall of the events would become increasingly vivid. These memories would be the beginnings of trance.

Trancing through talking

Steve, 15, is an adolescent who came into my (Mike's) clinic for a problem with nail-biting. Steve's dad brought him, and asked me a few questions in my office initially. After talking to me about Steve's problem, asking me standard hypnosis questions and generally checking me out, Steve's dad volunteered – unprompted – to return to the waiting room. This was great, because Steve had remained quiet with his father around. Steve was a shy 15-year-old who had begun to experience problems with nail-biting after his parents divorced. He'd had to move to a new school, as a result of the downsizing of the family home. Rather than talk to him in-depth about these changes, I just chatted to Steve to find out what his interests were and what excited him. He began to talk about music and his love of 'grindcore' bands – an extreme form of heavy and death metal rock music.

He talked about how he had been playing guitar for a while. After moving to his new school, Steve couldn't believe his luck when he met two boys who played bass and drums, and who were looking for a guitarist. They liked the same style of music and immediately formed a band. Steve began to go into a light trance as he described how they 'totally rocked' at a recent party. This led him into even greater fantasies about the band's plans to record a demo of three songs he'd written. (He sang a couple of verses which perfectly reflected his own teenage angst. His songs were an appropriate therapeutic outlet for his recent upheavals. They also reflected his feelings of powerlessness in his parent's break up.)

The more Steve talked about his music ambitions, the deeper his trance became. I encouraged him to talk more about his dreams of success and shifted this into an encouragement of how any success could lead to other, possibly unrelated, successes in his life. The old 'success breeds success' aphorism. I increasingly talked more generally about success, with the intention of pleasantly relaxing him, and soon he was in a medium-deep level trance. I then gradually introduced suggestions of success in alleviating his nail-biting. *'And you will be pleased at how successfully and easily you can stop any unwanted habits and have smooth fingernails. See those healthy fingernails as you play guitar. You can also see those healthy nails as indicating your ability to have other successes in the future . . .'* and so on.

I also gave Steve a lot of suggestions for feeling better and happier. (I only hoped that becoming happier would not get him in trouble with his grindcore band members!) When we ended our first session, Steve found it difficult to believe that he had gone into trance, but he was aware that somehow he had. We scheduled one final session for the following week.

Interestingly, before our second session Steve's father rang me excitedly to tell me that Steve had stopped nail-biting for the first time in several years! We still met for one final session to ensure that Steve could learn self-hypnosis to maintain his success.

The same is even truer with children and adolescents; they are likely to go even further in their imaginations than adults. This means that an excellent level of trance can be reached as their recollection deepens.

Helping Your Child with Therapy

As a parent you play a crucial role in how effectively hypnosis can help your child's problems.

It is natural for parents bringing their children to hypnosis to be apprehensive. However, the better informed you are (say, from reading information like this), the more relaxed you can be when you come to a hypnotherapist with your child. If you convey confidence, your child feels safe and can benefit from their session. Your child picks up on how you feel about his upcoming hypnotherapy. If you are anxious and uncertain, your child will be more so. Showing confidence that the experience will be a good one has a positive effect on your child's participation, and on the results.

As a parent you want to know what you can do to help your child overcome their problem before you make a decision to seek help from a hypnotherapist. Some general things you can do to help your child are:

✔ Don't force them to talk about the problem if they feel uncomfortable.

✔ If they *do* want to talk about it, become a better listener by

- Checking with them that you understand what they say.

- Repeating back some of the words they said to you.

✔ Avoid blaming, shaming, or teasing them.

✔ Avoid offering unwanted, unhelpful advice.

✔ Let them know that you love them, and will support them through their problem.

✔ Gently suggest that they have more control over the problem than they may realise, and that they can solve this problem and not be a victim of it.

✔ Encourage them to have hope that the problem will be solved.

The general idea is to give your child support, and really try to restrain from commenting, criticising, or giving advice. Make it your main goal to say less than you would normally and convey a supportive attitude.

Making the decision to seek therapy

Try gently suggesting getting help from a hypnotherapist to your adolescent, so that he thinks it's his own idea. With the increased popularity and success of hypnosis as a therapeutic tool, an adolescent may well recommend it to resolve a personal problem or issue, and have a more vested interest in achieving that goal.

As a caring parent, you can talk about a hypnotherapist to a younger child as a professional who can help with a particular concern, the same way other professionals help with other concerns.

In either case, the parent will accompany the child and ensure the child's comfort and wellbeing with the hypnotherapist, before and possibly during the first session.

Never pressure your child (or an adult) into seeking help. It may only cause resistance to therapy. This can even lead to the child sabotaging their own chances for success, out of resentment towards the parent and hypnotherapist.

So one of the best things you can do is to decide together that seeking help is a good idea.

Listening to your child's hypnotherapist

Every hypnotherapist works with parents differently. Be guided by your child's hypnotherapist and remember the importance of not undermining your child, or the hypnotherapist. Listen to your child's hypnotherapist about how to handle your own anxieties.

Ask your child's hypnotherapist, when you first make an appointment, how much information they need from you. Find out whether he wants you to be present during the session, or for part of the session, or just during the 'get acquainted' phase. Your child may ask you to be there initially, but discuss with the hypnotherapist whether you should excuse yourself from the room at some point. When the time is right will vary, of course, depending on the age of your child.

As a concerned parent, you may certainly tell the hypnotherapist what you perceive the problem to be with your child, but do it privately. However, be open about how the course of therapy may proceed. Let your child explain their problem to the hypnotherapist in their own words. You may be surprised that your child's perception of the problem is not necessarily the same as yours!

It is important that your child feels that he is in the driver's seat, so that his unconscious mind can prepare to go to work, and not have to depend on your authority as his parent. Remember that it is your child's mind that needs to be activated through hypnosis.

Understanding Some Common Childhood Issues

What are some of the problems that hypnotherapists see children for?

- ✔ Anxiety
- ✔ Bed-wetting

We explain in detail how hypnotherapists remove habits in Chapter 5.

A range of other issues may exist. Speak to a hypnotherapist before arranging an initial appointment, to see if hypnotherapy can help your child.

Hiding behind sofas: Dealing with your anxious child

Arguably, children are under more emotional pressure today than ever before. Societal, academic, and parental pressures often lead children to anxiety issues that show up in a multitude of ways, including shyness, stuttering, bed-wetting, insomnia, and appetite problems (including both food avoidance and overeating).

If your child is experiencing anxiety related problems, hypnotherapy may be ideal for them. Remember, hypnotherapy can help to relax the body, which is at the root of treating anxiety. Please do not hesitate to speak to a hypnotherapist to see if they can help your child.

Solving bed-wetting

Bed-wetting – enuresis in medical terms – is one of the most common childhood problems hypnotherapists address.

Enuresis is the repeated, involuntary voiding of urine, after an age at which continence (staying dry) is usual – about 3 years of age. This is assuming of course, that there are no other possible medical or physical causes. In other words, the inability of the child to avoid wetting himself or herself. Enuresis is a term most used in conjunction with children, but on rare occasions, it applies to adults.

Housing Cathy's nightmares

Five-year-old Cathy's favourite cartoon character is Bob the Builder. Her parents brought her to hypnotherapy because of her recurring, and extremely disturbing, nightmares. When her parents asked her to describe the nightmares, Cathy could never recall their content.

Cathy could not describe the nightmares to me either, so we played Bob the Builder instead. I asked her to pretend to be Bob and build something. She became very physically involved with building, and during this physical activity I spoke to her about the details of the house.

Cathy told me that she was building an imaginary toy doll's house for the doll she had brought. When she completed it we both stood back and admired it. Then I asked her if she could build another house. This time I asked her to build a larger house – one which would be big enough for her to go inside. She agreed.

By now she was in trance, and I suggested that she build a *safe house* made of bricks, like the one that the Three Little Pigs hid in to escape from the Big Bad Wolf. She smiled and became physically very active in building her safe house. She told me when it was completed and we commented on her fantastic handiwork. She enjoyed the praise immensely and added a few more details to her safe house.

I then suggested to her that she could take this house back home and put it in her bedroom. I suggested that she could use that same safe house each night before she went to sleep, and that no one but her could enter it. I said that she would feel very, very happy and safe each night inside the house that she had just built. I asked her to promise me that she would pretend to go inside her safe house each night, before she fell asleep. She agreed.

Her parents reported back to me that her nightmares had stopped soon after our first meeting.

It is common for children to wet their beds during the first two to three years of life. At this age hypnosis is inappropriate as bed-wetting is natural. Even continued bed-wetting after the age of 3 years, does not necessarily indicate a problem. However, bed-wetting is considered a problem after the age of 6 years.

Children who bed-wet after the age of 6 years may not have yet developed strong enough bladder muscles to retain large amounts of urine. This is why it is so important to seek your doctor's help to receive medical tests to confirm if this is the case for your child. Expect the hypnotherapist to ask if your child has been thoroughly tested medically before starting any hypnosis.

There are two types of enuresis:

- **Diurnal enuresis:** Wetting occurs during the daytime. This is more common in females.

- **Nocturnal enuresis:** This is what is more commonly called bed-wetting, and is more common in males.

Nocturnal enuresis is more common than diurnal enuresis. It can obviously cause unhappiness and distress to the child who experiences it. Parents and siblings may inadvertently cause additional shame by chastising or teasing the child. If punished for bed-wetting, the distress is even further enhanced for the child. Further unhappiness may occur because of the limitations nocturnal enuresis imposes on social activities and holidays.

The good news is that hypnosis is a very powerful tool in relieving bed-wetting. The hypnotherapist speaks to the child's subconscious, suggesting that they avoid drinks before bed, wake up if they need to urinate, have greater bladder/muscular control, and most importantly, to imagine waking up to a dry bed. (The word *wet* is avoided in treating enuresis – the desired state is dryness – so any words involving wet are counter-productive.)

Chapter 10

Visiting Your Former Selves

In This Chapter

▶ Defining past-life regression

▶ Finding out how to get back to the past before you were born

▶ Getting back to the present

*A*nd now you seemingly enter the world of the mystical to find out how to travel back in time to visit yourself before you were even born. We are, of course, talking about past-life regression (PLR), a therapy technique that many find baffling and many more find exceptionally fascinating. PLR is an approach to helping you overcome your problem, based on the concept of *reincarnation*; a belief that your soul is reborn into different bodies and that you have lived a life (or lives) before your current one.

For many in the Western world, the idea that we have lived other lives before this one is frankly laughable. We have one life and once it's over, that's your lot. End of story. But many millions of people throughout the world, both Western and Eastern, are just as convinced in their belief in the concept of having lived many lives in the past. And it is from this belief that the very powerful hypnotherapy technique of past-life regression has been developed.

Examining Past-Life Regression

Past-life regression (PLR) is one of the techniques that people often associate with hypnotherapy. PLR is a technique used in hypnotherapy that works with a person's belief in reincarnation. PLR takes you back in time, in your mind, to visit a life, or lives, you lived before. PLR has wonderful esoteric connotations of the mystical hypnotist with staring eyes, lulling his subjects into a trance and then parting the curtains of the mists of time as they travel back to some major historical event. All very nice, and it looks wonderful in those low-budget movies; however the reality of PLR is actually quite mundane.

Hypnotherapists are not taught to tear apart the fabric of the space-time continuum – nor do they have the power! If you believe in reincarnation, then your hypnotherapist may consider using PLR.

Many people who believe in reincarnation think that traumatic or upsetting events that occurred in a life they lived before are the root cause of problems they're experiencing in the life they're leading now; especially if they feel that they didn't have the opportunity to resolve those events before the end of that particular past life. PLR gives you the opportunity to resolve those events and by extension, resolve those issues in your current life that stem from them.

So, do you need to believe in reincarnation for PLR to be effective? The answer is no. To understand why this may be, have a look at the next section, 'Beliefs about PLR'.

In general, however, if you don't believe in reincarnation, your therapist won't touch PLR with a bargepole.

Beware of a therapist who pushes her belief system onto you. It doesn't matter whether your therapist believes in past lives or not. Any therapist worth her salt works with your belief systems, not hers. Your hypnotherapist should not try to influence you either way with regard to your beliefs in reincarnation – or hers.

Beliefs about PLR

Okay. So is PLR real? Who knows? As yet there is no absolute proof one way or the other. Remember, we are dealing with belief systems here and that means, if you truly believe you have lived before, then it is very real . . . for you!

Many people and therapists believe in the powerful therapeutic results of PLR, but don't necessarily believe in reincarnation. So what do they believe PLR is? Here are some of the most popular theories:

- ✔ **PLR accesses genetic memory.** One school of thought believes that certain memories are encoded in our genetic make-up. In other words, somehow memories are stored in our genes. When you experience PLR, these memories are dragged up out of your DNA and once again experienced.

- ✔ **PLR accesses the collective unconscious.** This idea comes from Jungian psychology. Carl Jung was around at the same time as Sigmund Freud. One of the many psychological theories he developed is that of the *collective unconscious*. Jung believed that we all store in our unconscious a whole host of memories that are shared by everyone , and which are passed down to us from our ancestors. PLR provides a means of accessing the collective unconscious and experiencing these memories.

✔ **PLR is a dissociative experience.** This theory says that a person experiencing a PLR is creating a new existence in their mind from various pieces of their existing memory. Basically, you create a person and an existence through which you can 'observe' your problem, and its solution, in a metaphorical way – so that you're split off, or dissociated, from the problem. The distance provides a safe way to deal with the problem and the unconscious means to apply the solution.

✔ **PLR accesses memories from past lives.** Okay, we're back where we started. In this model, you believe that you've lived before and can access these past lives through hypnosis. As you access past lives, you can also influence them by helping your past self to resolve the unresolved issues that occurred in the life.

Whatever the truth of the matter about what PLR is, when it boils down to it it's *your* belief that is most important. So, if you truly believe that your problem stems from something that happened to you in a past life – and who's to say you are wrong? – then discuss this with your therapist. If she judges that it is right for you to explore this idea, then she will be happy to take you back into your past existence.

Reasons to revisit past lives

So, why do you want to go back and visit your past lives? Usually for one of two main reasons:

✔ You're simply curious and want to find out about who and what you were before you came into this life.

✔ You believe that the problems you're having stem from events that occurred in a life, or lives, you experienced prior to this one.

Many therapists happily help you explore your past lives for no other reason than you're interested in who you were. But it is the second reason that explains PLR's most common use in the therapy room.

As you go through life, you have many conflicts and experiences that you need to work through and resolve. However, there are also many that you don't. Obvious so far, but this is where past-life theory kicks in. Past-life theory has it that some unresolved issues may well be so significant, that when you pass into your next life they continue to affect you, creating some of the problems that you may now be experiencing.

That doesn't mean to say that the unresolved issue you had in a past life will manifest itself in exactly the same way in your current life. Far from it, what you're likely to experience is something that is almost a metaphor for the past problem. For example:

✔ **Weight issues:** It may be that you were starving in a past life, and your weight problem is an attempt to prevent that from occurring in this life.

✔ **Psychosomatic pain:** It may be that you had a violent accident in a past life where a part of your body was seriously injured. In your current life you experience a pain for which there is no demonstrable cause, in a similar area of your body.

Psychosomatic pain refers to pain that is purely in the mind. In other words, you are feeling pain somewhere in your body, but there is absolutely no physical cause for that pain.

✔ **Phobias:** Maybe you were locked in a dark room, or cell, in a previous existence. That experience then filters through to your current life where you have an irrational fear of the dark.

✔ **Personality issues:** Perhaps you were an oppressed peasant in a past life, always having to hold onto your emotions and feelings. In your current life you vent these feelings by being overly aggressive or emotional.

These are only a few examples of an almost endless list. In order to resolve these problems, you may need to go back to the life where they first occurred. If you can resolve the issue in the past, the likelihood is that the problem in the present fades away too. Of course, after your past-life issues are resolved, you may have work to do on your current life, helping you to adjust to the positive changes that PLR has brought about.

Often, your current problem is an accumulation of unresolved issues from a whole variety of past lives, each needing to be dealt with and resolved.

Journeying to Your Past Life

Okay, you and your therapist agree that it's a good idea for you to go back and sort out those unresolved issues experienced by a past you.

The PLR session, or sessions, will be very similar in nature to any other hypnotherapy session, with just a few differences.

Revealing any past-life memories

Along with taking a normal case history, your therapist may also ask you about the following:

✔ **Your belief in reincarnation.** Your therapist wants to know what your understanding of PLR and reincarnation is. After all, she'll be working with your beliefs. She also needs to know of any past experiences you had visiting former lives, either through a therapist or spontaneously. (On rare occasions, some people spontaneously slip back into a past life when they are dozing, just about to fall asleep, or as a dream experience.)

✔ **Why you think that a past life experience may be responsible for your current symptom.** What tells you that your solution lies in a past life? When you think about your symptom, what indicates that its cause lies way back, before you were born?

Just because you believe that your problem comes from a past life, that doesn't mean that your hypnotherapist will automatically take you there. She will consider many factors before taking you down that route.

✔ **Whether you're aware of the particular life responsible.** Some people are very aware of the life responsible for their current problem long before they go for therapy. If you know, let your hypnotherapist know too.

Keep in mind that this may be only one of several lives contributing to your problem (then again, it may be the only one!). You may need to visit other lives before your problem is solved.

✔ **Any relevant dreams you've had.** When you dream, you allow your unconscious to roam freely, and your unconscious may well access a past life. When you awaken, you may be aware that this particular dream holds something of significance.

✔ **Any spontaneous thoughts you have been having about past lives.** Is your unconscious trying to tell you something? Do you have spontaneous thoughts about events from a past that doesn't seem to belong to you? Could this be your unconscious saying 'Hey, this is where the seat of your problem lies!'?

Let your hypnotherapist know about any experiences on this list, because your awareness of your past lives may be pointing you in the right direction.

When many people think of reincarnation they often make the erroneous assumption that they were someone famous in a past life. In actual fact, it is extremely rare to come across well-known characters from history. On the contrary, by far the most common manifestation of a past life is that of a very ordinary person. Is it likely that you were Henry VIII? No! A cook in the court of Henry VIII? Yes!

Choosing a route

There are many approaches to taking you back to a past life, none of which require magic or any special powers, so let's leave that idea to the fantasists!

What route will you travel on through the centuries? Well, the path you take depends on the creativity of both you and your hypnotherapist. Your hypnotherapist may ask you to imagine one of several scenarios:

✔ You're walking down a long and comfortable corridor. On either side of you are doors, with each one leading to a specific past life. Your therapist may invite you to find a door that is particularly attractive to you, for whatever reason, and to imagine walking through that door into the relevant past life.

✔ You're walking up a safe and well-lit tunnel. When you reach the end, you step out into your past life.

✔ You're climbing a gentle hill and when you reach its summit, you step out into another past life.

Or maybe you step into a time machine, or through the pages of a book, or through a mirror, or . . . the possibilities are endless.

Even though you think you know which life you need to visit at a conscious level, your hypnotherapist may want to be unspecific when she takes you back. She may use a phrase along the lines of 'And you can step through that door into the life that is most relevant to the reason you are with me today'. She isn't ignoring you, she just knows that your unconscious mind will recognise the most important life you need to visit. Consciously you may think you know, but your unconscious often knows best in these cases. Let it be your guide!

Reaching a dead end

You step through the door with excited anticipation of entering into and exploring that past life and . . . nothing! Zilch! Not a sausage! Nothing except a big sense of disappointment.

So what's going on? Why aren't you getting anywhere on this journey? Well, there can be several reasons, the main ones being:

✔ **You're not ready to go back.** Perhaps it was too early to try a PLR. Maybe you need to do some more work in the present before you attempt to go back into the past. Yes, you believe in past lives, but maybe you have fears about going there. Perhaps you don't fully trust your therapist yet, as that all-important rapport (see Chapter 13) hasn't been sufficiently built up yet.

You can address whatever issues are putting up the roadblock with your hypnotherapist, and try PLR once they are resolved.

✔ **The route back was not right for you.** If you don't like the method of transportation (maybe the enclosed space of the tunnel makes you nervous, or the height of the hill seems too steep), the likelihood of reaching your past life destination is minimised. Why? Because if you feel a little uptight and tense, your unconscious mind protects you from taking a path that is not right for you.

To resolve this, discuss your feelings with your hypnotherapist and agree on a route that is more acceptable to you.

✔ **Something in your current life needs to be resolved before you can go back.** Maybe an issue in your current life is demanding attention. Sometimes these issues can be very selfish and won't let you go back despite your strong desire.

Your therapist can use techniques such as dissociation, or a regression, to the event in this life (Chapter 2 talks about these techniques), to help clear the current life roadblock (which, by the very fact it's demanding attention like this, needs to be addressed), and therefore re-opening up your path into time.

✔ **The problem doesn't stem from a past life.** If the genesis of your problem is not in a past life, you can't go back to resolve it.

Of course, after you resolve your current life problem, your therapist can take you back through the portals of time just simply to have the experience, if you wish.

Whatever the reasons for not getting back to a past life, they can be cleared up. With a little perseverance from both you and your hypnotherapist, your past lives will open up like the pages of a wonderful history book.

What to Expect during Your PLR Session

Ready to go back in time, but are a little unsure as to what to expect? Well, read on, because these sections cover what you may find happening during your PLR session.

But wait! Before you go back to a past life, we need to point out one thing. One of the experiences that often take people unawares during a PLR session is that when they get back to their past life they may well find that they are the opposite sex. That means a man may well have been a woman in a past life and vice versa. Let us just point out here and now that this is not a reflection of your sexual orientation, nor does it mean that you have a deep-seated desire for a sex change! It just means that the quirks of time travel do not recognise the gender boundary, and it is entirely possible that you were a member of the opposite sex in many of your past lives.

Setting the scene

During your PLR session, you are not necessarily going to step out of your current life and straight into a full, technicolor awareness of your past life. Your mind may need a little help orientating to this new experience and your therapist helps you get settled in through a process of questioning. She wants to find out from you:

> ✔ **Who you are.** No, she won't just ask 'Who are you?' Your therapist needs to help you build up your awareness and may ask you:
>
> - What you're wearing
>
> - How old you are
>
> - Your name
>
> ✔ **Where you are.** Your therapist may ask you to tell her:
>
> - What you see around you
>
> - The name of the place you're in
>
> - The date
>
> - The time of day
>
> ✔ **What you're doing.** Your therapist may ask you to:
>
> - Describe what you are doing (obviously)
>
> - Explain why you're doing it
>
> - Share how you feel about doing it
>
> ✔ **If anyone is with you.** Your therapist may ask you:
>
> - If anyone is with you (er, again, obviously!)
>
> - If so, who that person (or persons) is and why they're with you
>
> - How you feel about having that person (or people) with you

This may seem to be quite an interrogation, but it is very important in helping you really get into the character and experience of your past life. Once you are fully there, you can get on with exploring all that it contains. Who knows, you could be an ancient Greek standing on a cliff top, or a Victorian gardener going about his business, or even a proud Mayan mother tending to her children.

If you step into your past life and see nothing or hear nothing, bear in mind that you may be blind or deaf in that life, or perhaps you are in a dark or very quiet room! I (Peter) once carried out a PLR with a patient who reported that they could neither hear nor see anything when we were trying to set the scene. In a moment of inspiration I asked that they reach out and tell me if they could feel anything. A moment later they reported that they could feel a wall. It turned out that in the life they were visiting they were both deaf and blind.

In most cases, you experience the past life as if you are there, so don't be surprised if your voice changes a bit and you feel the emotions you felt back then.

Visiting those important times

You're in a past life, so now what? Is this the part of the life you need to visit? Not necessarily. This may only be your entry point to that life; a quite mundane period that allows you to adjust gently. On the other hand, you may step out into the thick of things; right into the heart of the matter, at the point in that life where the problems you're experiencing in this one began.

Wherever you start off, your therapist will ask you to visit the important times in that life relevant to your problem. Keep in mind that there may be more than one event in more than one life. This is an insight gaining exercise, helping both you and your therapist understand how your problem got started. As you visit these times, your therapist may ask you what's happening, how you're feeling, and what you feel you need to do in this situation.

You may find that all your hypnotherapist does is ask you to experience these times. At times, you may feel the need to let out some emotion. If you do, go ahead and let it out. It may be that this pent up emotion has been festering away inside you in your current life, contributing to your problem.

By the way, if the thought of crying or laughing, or even shouting in front of your hypnotherapist is embarrassing, let us reassure you. Your therapist is very used to seeing displays of strong emotion and welcomes them as a healthy release for you. If you don't feel any of these emotions, don't worry – there may be none for you to feel at this time.

Being present at your death

Right, put on your black armband and bring in the doom and gloom brigade, because this is where it gets a little morbid – but for a very good reason. How you meet your end in the life you are visiting, may have a very strong relevance as to why you are experiencing your problem. For example:

> ✔ **Was your death violent?** If it was, it could very well be a contributing factor to your problem. The way in which you shuffled off this mortal coil may be representative of the reason you're seeing your therapist. Maybe you drowned and now have a phobia of water. Maybe you

starved to death and now have a weight problem. Maybe you were poisoned and you now have irritable bowel syndrome.

If your death was peaceful, it may not be a contributing factor to your problem. However, what happened to your body after your death may be, so read on.

✔ **What happened to your body after your death?** In many cases, this can influence a current life problem. Maybe your body wasn't discovered and you have an unexplained sense of being lost in your current life. Or perhaps your body was unceremoniously cremated and you now have a phobia of fire. It could be that your body was misidentified and you were buried under the wrong name, and you now lack a sense of who you are.

✔ **Was anything left unfinished at your death?** Were there things you needed to do, but couldn't as your life was cut short? Were there people you needed to say something to, but didn't get the opportunity to do so? Any unfinished business can follow through and cause havoc in your current life. Maybe you had unpaid debts in your past life and are too frivolous with your money in this one. If you didn't show enough affection to a loved one you may find that you are now too emotional in relationships. It is possible that you were harsh with someone without getting the chance to apologise and now find that you carry a sense of guilt with you wherever you go.

Healing past hurts

You've been through it all; lived and died, and now have an understanding of why your problem started. Is that it? Is your problem resolved? Maybe. For some, the very act of gaining understanding is enough to kick a problem out of their lives forever. However, that isn't true for every person or every problem. Not to worry. There is another step to take in your PLR session to help ensure that your problem is truly dead and buried.

To round off your session, your hypnotherapist gives you the opportunity to 'heal' that past life. In other words, to go through it and make amends, to change what needs to be changed, to say what needs to be said and so on. How can she help you do this? A very popular way is to visit the point of death (here we go with the morbidity again!), and as your spirit leaves your body, allow it to go through the life and to heal whatever it is that needs to be healed.

Resolving past-life problems

The problems of past lives manifest in many ways. Often, just going back and seeing the cause becomes the cure. Check out these examples:

✔ A patient came for therapy with a severe pain in her right shoulder. The medical community could not find anything wrong with her, nor could they provide her with any lasting relief from the pain. Eventually, a friend of hers suggested that the pain may be present as a result of something that happened to her in a past life. Desperate to get the pain sorted out, she came for PLR hypnotherapy.

She entered into a life in which she was a Native American. Her village was attacked by a rival tribe, and during the onslaught, she was shot in her right shoulder by an arrow. She didn't die from the arrow but from an infection that set in afterwards. She carried the pain of the wound and the infection into her current life.

During a PLR session, she floated out of her body and laid her spirit hands over the wound in her shoulder. When she removed them, the wound had healed. When she came out of trance she reported that the pain she had been experiencing in her shoulder had finally gone.

✔ A man came to see us because he didn't feel 'grounded' (his words) in his life. He had a strong belief in reincarnation and sensed that his feelings came from an event in a past life.

When he visited the relevant life in Tibet, he found that he had met a violent end and that his body had been left unburied. He immediately made the connection between his not feeling 'grounded', and the fact that his body had not been put into the 'ground' after his death.

In his spirit form, this unburied Tibetan found his sister from that life, and guided her to his body. She picked it up (she was very strong!) and carried it up a mountain and buried it beneath a tree near their village.

Several days after this session he called to say that he felt so much better, more grounded and able to concentrate on the important things in his life.

✔ A patient came for therapy who had very strong feelings of frustration that she couldn't pin to anything specific. She visited a past life where she was a wealthy landowner in Edwardian England (and very surprised to find that she was male). She'd had a good life and had died very peacefully, but unexpectedly, in her sleep. Unfortunately, prior to her death, she had a very nasty and prolonged argument with her best friend that resulted in their not talking to each other anymore. She recognised that she was to blame for the argument and decided to make amends and apologise. Unfortunately, she came to this decision on the night the Grim Reaper came a-calling and she never got the opportunity. She expressed an incredible sense of frustration over the fact that she had died with all that bad feeling between them.

In her spirit form, she was able to visit her friend as he dreamt and, after several lengthy dream conversations, was able to give her apology and have it accepted. She then left that life with a sense of freedom and lightness. She subsequently went on to leave her boyfriend and her job, go on the holiday of a lifetime, and returned to enter a career she had always wanted to be in, but had been afraid to try. Who says hypnotherapy doesn't change your life for the better?

Completing the journey and returning to the present

So that's it, the life is healed and there is nothing left to do. Just wake me up and I'll be on my way then. Wrong! There is plenty more to do. After all, you don't mend the hole in a tyre, but not put it back on the bike. You need to put your past life back where it belongs, and then make sure that nothing else needs fixing:

- ✔ **Sever the tie to the past life.** After you heal a past life, many therapists suggest that you sever the tie you have to that life, so that you can be sure that it will no longer influence you or encourage your problem to return. How they do this depends on the therapist. Some have you imagine cutting a silver thread that attaches you to the life. Some have you imagine that that you are permanently shutting and locking the door to that life. Others may be less specific and have you cut the connection in whatever way you feel is right for you.

    Your therapist should suggest that before you sever any tie, you bring with you all the positive learning that the life gave you into your current existence.

- ✔ **Come out of the past life.** It is important that you are formally brought out of the past life. If you simply emerge from it, you may be somewhat disorientated. Don't worry; the disorientation will pass in time. But to avoid this, the general rule of thumb is that you're brought out of a past life the same way you were taken into it. If you stepped through a door, you step back through a door. If you walked down a tunnel, you walk back up a tunnel, and so on.

- ✔ **Check that there are no other lives you need to visit.** Before you are fully re-oriented back into your current life, your therapist should help you to check that there are no other lives that need to be visited. After all, more than one life may be contributing to your problem, and you want to clear the lot out in order to really ensure that it has been dealt with.

    You may find that you can do this in one session, or it may need to be done over several sessions, depending on how much needs to be worked through in each life.

Whether you are doing it for fun, or using it to solve a problem, you will find that every hypnotherapist will have their own particular approach to carrying out PLR. Whatever your reason is, you will find that a visit to your past selves can be a very interesting, rewarding, and ultimately problem releasing experience for you.

Past lives are not the only ones you can visit. Some therapists will work with you to find out what happens during your inter-life experience. In other words, exploring what happens between each of your lives. Yet other therapists will have you experience future lives – those that you have yet to live after you kick the bucket in this one.

Chapter 11

Removing Your Phobias

In This Chapter

▶ Looking at what a phobia is

▶ Understanding that phobias can be about anything

▶ Getting rid of your phobia with hypnotherapy

▶ Contracting to face up to your phobia

*A*re you scared of the dark? Do you freeze with fear whenever a cat saunters nonchalantly across the road in front of you? Do you go apoplectic at the very thought of visiting the dentist? Does the idea of taking a flight to some sunny holiday destination send ice-cold tingles of dread down your spine? If the answer to any of these questions is yes, then you have a phobia!

Phobias are one of the most common reasons people seek hypnotherapy. Many millions of people in this world have phobias. Most manage to get along in life without the phobia interfering too much in their day-to-day existence; in other words, the phobia is mild. However, a significant number of people have phobias that greatly restrict their life in one way or another, and when these phobias get really bad, people seek out therapy.

Rationalising the Irrational: Defining Phobias

Phobias are not something you are born with. They are something you learn. You learn to fear an object or situation of some kind, and that fear is accompanied by many irrational thoughts and behaviours.

Explaining phobias

A *phobia* is an abnormal fear of an object or situation, experienced immediately when confronted by the object or situation, directly or indirectly, through seeing it on television, or in a magazine or book, for example. In general, fear makes you avoid whatever it is that triggers your phobia. So, a phobia involves fear and avoidance, but what else makes a phobia a phobia? Well, you may have a phobia if you experience any of the following:

- **Excessive or unreasonable fear:** Some situations may induce just a mild fear response considered normal or non-phobic, something most people would experience in that situation. Your fear is excessive or unreasonable if you find yourself frozen in place, perhaps wanting to escape, possibly trembling or sweating in that situation.

    A fear of heights is a phobia if you are paralysed by fear on the third rung of a ladder, or if simply watching someone standing on the edge of the Grand Canyon on television makes you break out in a sweat.

- **You recognise that the fear is excessive or unreasonable:** You know that what you are experiencing is out of proportion to what you should be feeling. You know, for example, that going to visit your dentist should only give you a mild anxiety, not that 'running down the street shrieking your head off' anxiety you experience when you walk in through the surgery door.

- **The trigger of phobic response always causes anxiety:** You either have the response, or not. You can't be scared of mice one moment and think that they're cute the next.

- **You avoid whatever causes your phobic response:** All phobics avoid whatever it is that they are afraid of, which is a logical response, really. If you can't avoid it, then you suffer the experience with intense anxiety or stress. For example, imagine that you have avoided flying for years, travelling wherever you needed to go by car, bus or train. However, for one reason or another, you find that you need to travel by plane somewhere. Getting you on the wretched thing may mean that you have to be dragged kicking and screaming, or else you have to be pumped full of enough tranquilisers to stop a rampaging bull elephant in its tracks!

Phobic fear most often causes physical and emotional reactions, including any, or all, the following:

- Your breathing may become shallow and your heart race, with just the thought of the *possibility* of encountering the object of your fear.

- You feel tense and anxious, altering your life to avoid any encounter.

✔ You feel a sense of shame or embarrassment at harbouring an obsessive fear, which may, in turn, cause you to withdraw from people who don't understand your terror.

As your fear looms large in your mind and in your life, you spend a great deal of your time, energy, and thought on it, which actually fans the flame of your phobia.

Oh, and just so you know, phobias can sometimes be accompanied by a *panic attack*, too. During these nasty episodes, your fear rockets through the roof and rational thought flies out the window, causing your breathing to become very rapid and shallow, which is known as *hyperventilating*. Hyperventilating increases the amount of oxygen in your blood and brain. You may think that more oxygen is a good thing, but too much oxygen in your system increases the symptoms you experience during a panic attack, resulting in more fear, trembling, sweating, weakness and tingling sensations in your limbs, and irrational thoughts that you are going to die.

To stop hyperventilating, put a paper bag over your nose and mouth, and breathe into it. This causes you to breathe in carbon dioxide and subsequently brings down the level of oxygen in your system.

Comparing phobias to plain old fear

Phobias involve fear. But does that mean that all fear is really a phobia? The answer is no. One or two things about the fear you experience when you have a phobic response make that fear very particular to a phobia.

Fear is a natural survival mechanism. In the ancient past, when humans lived in caves, the fear response kept us away from things that could harm us. If we didn't have it, you probably wouldn't be reading this book today, because the human race wouldn't exist. Imagine for a moment, that we didn't develop a fear response. You have just left your cave for a nice stroll around your Palaeolithic neighbourhood. On your way you notice a rather large and cuddly looking pussycat, fast asleep under a tree. You go up to it (remember, no fear) and start stroking it. The next thing you know: snap! You're a sabre-toothed tiger's hors d'oeuvre! Apply that to the rest of the human race and it wouldn't last for very long.

Put fear into the equation and things are different. You're having your little caveman stroll and see a bundle of fur curled up under a tree. From past experience, you know that similar bundles of fur tend to attack you. As this registers in your brain you begin to feel fear. The fear that you feel makes you become very wary, you back off and return to your cave.

Many feelings of fear stem from a rational sense of survival; you fear what may physically harm you. You may also fear what others around you fear, or fear the unknown, or fear what may happen to others close to you.

The fear you experience with a phobic response is an *irrational fear*. Basically, it is a fear of an outcome that statistically won't happen. For example, air travel continues to be far safer than any other form of transportation, so being afraid of dying in a plane crash is an irrational fear. Likewise, phobias are born of fears of an improbable result you believe will happen when you encounter the object or situation. For example, it's highly unlikely that you will actually have a heart attack if a spider comes near you.

You may be thinking 'So what about a phobia of snakes? They can hurt you, so that must be a rational fear!'. Yes and no (you probably knew we were going to say that). If you walk down the street and come face to face with a boa constrictor slithering along then yes, the fear you experience would be a rational fear. If you were flicking through a magazine and came across a picture of a snake and let out a shriek of fear, then that would be an irrational fear – a phobic fear. After all, the wretched thing won't leap out of the page at you, will it? Therefore there is no threat to your survival.

Pointing out triggers

So where do phobias come from in the first place? How do you develop them? After all, no one sets out to deliberately become scared of something. Unfortunately, we don't have a simple answer. The causes of phobias are as varied as phobias themselves.

Starting with stress

When you experience severe stress, such as being stuck on a crowded bus in a traffic jam, or having a project deadline looming at work, your objectivity and ability to rationally analyse the situation may be compromised. The feelings you have as a result of the stress – such as anxiety or fear – can attach themselves to whatever you are stressed about.

Even though this is not always the case, when it does happen that means that if you enter into a similar situation, or come across a similar object, then you experience anxiety or fear. Remember, a phobia can occur to anything, so any situation in which you find yourself stressed has the potential to turn into a phobia.

Going through an extremely rough patch with your significant other obviously causes a lot of stress. This feeling can become attached to any confrontational situation and therefore result in you developing a phobia of confrontation.

However, your mind is a fickle thing and sometimes the fear is attached to something unrelated; you become scared of that and not of whatever it was that frightened you in the first place.

A patient came for therapy with a phobia of buttons (quite a common phobia, as it happens). He felt okay when confronted by buttons attached to clothes, but experienced an incredible sense of dread and anxiety when faced with a loose button lying around; convinced that it would suddenly lodge itself in his windpipe. He experienced the fear to such an extent that he couldn't enter a room if he knew there was a loose button somewhere inside. On top of wanting to get rid of his phobia, he also wanted to understand where it came from. Using a regression technique (see Chapter 2), he was taken back to a time in his early teens when he had been summoned into his headmaster's office in order to atone for some transgression or other. This was in the days when headmasters were still given free rein to take out their sadistic frustrations on their pupils, and our patient ended up being given the cane! What came to light during the regression was that as he was bent over the headmaster's desk receiving six of the best, he caught sight of a loose button. The stress and anxiety he felt by being given the cane transferred to the button, and from that moment on he began to fear loose buttons in general.

Picking up a phobia from another person

A classic way to assume a phobia is to inherit it from someone who serves as a role model for you. Through witnessing that person's phobic response, you learn to be afraid of whatever it is that they are afraid of.

A mother who is afraid of mice passes on that fear to her daughter. A son picks up his father's fear of spiders. When you witness your role model being scared, you believe that the object that he is afraid of is something that you need to be scared of too. Obvious really, if he is scared of it, then there must be something terrible about it. Unfortunately, this is not necessarily true!

However, you don't pick up phobias only from family members. Anyone you are in close contact with – be it a friend, neighbour, or complete stranger – can transmit their phobia to you. Even witnessing a phobic response on film or television can do the trick!

Building up to a phobia

A single experience of something mildly anxiety provoking may not necessarily end up with you developing a phobia of it. However, if you're repeatedly exposed to the same, or similar, experiences then the anxiety can become cumulative, reinforcing each experience with more and more fear until, wham! – you're slapped in the face with a full-blown phobia. It's as though you didn't see it coming.

Take for example flight crew members who frequently experience varying degrees of turbulence during the flights they make. They appear to cope (and in most cases they do so very well), but for a few members there is an underlying feeling of anxiety that gets reinforced with each bout of turbulence, accumulating away in the back of their mind until it springs forth in the form of a full-blown flying phobia.

Creating a phobia from past trauma

A *trauma* is an event that produces a severely painful physical or emotional experience – and could realistically lead to your death or injury. A trauma can lead to the development of a phobia of whatever it was that caused you that pain. Even witnessing such an event is traumatic and can result in the development of a phobia.

You're driving along in your car and some idiot swerves in front of you. Unfortunately, they misjudge the distance and – crash, tinkle! You both end up with a trip to the garage to get the major dents in the bodywork of your vehicles beaten out. A car crash comes under the heading of a trauma and is a very frightening experience for all concerned. The next time you think about getting behind the wheel to drive, you may very well begin to experience anxiety. Perhaps you begin to avoid driving. Unfortunately, the more you avoid driving because of the anxiety, the more the anxiety builds. The more the anxiety builds, the more likely you are to end up with a full-blown driving phobia!

Examining the Various Types of Phobia

Each individual phobia has its own particular characteristics. To be helpful, medical science has divided phobias into the following categories:

✔ **Animal and insect phobias:** The heading says it all. Any type of animal can be included in this category, from cats and dogs, through to cows and wombats! Insects are traditionally objects of fear, and any of the thousands of species that survive on this planet can become a phobic's worst nightmare.

✔ **Natural environment phobias:** These are phobias about some aspect of your environment. For example it may be that you are afraid of the dark – typical in children, but also afflicting many adults too. Or maybe you are scared of heights, or water, and so on.

✔ **Blood, injection, and injury phobias:** It's never pleasant having an injection. However, for some this can prove to be the object of a very severe phobia. In fact, any medical procedure that is invasive can come under this category. The sight of blood too, is often the trigger for a complete freak-out!

✔ **Situation phobias:** All phobias that are the result of having to do something, or of having to be in a specific place, come under this heading. If you have a fear of flying you belong under this category, for example. Fear being in a lift or elevator? You're here too. Shake and tremble before going to school? This is your category. Get the picture?

Perhaps the two most famous situation phobias are *claustrophobia*, a fear of enclosed spaces, and *agoraphobia*, a fear of open spaces.

✔ **Miscellaneous phobias:** A bit of a cop out, this heading! Anything that doesn't come under the other headings in this list belongs here. For example, a fear of clowns (honest!), a fear of falling down when standing away from a wall (honest, too!), or a fear of getting ill (now that one you've heard of!), are all included in this category.

You can develop a phobia to anything. So don't worry if you have a phobia you think is strange. It's a dead cert that someone else has had it before you.

Table 11-1 offers a very incomplete list of the variety of phobias out there. (We can't list everything on the planet!) Don't worry if yours isn't there. It doesn't mean that it doesn't really exist, or that you are unique; all it means is that for whatever reason (not enough space, for one thing) we didn't include it.

No matter how strange some of these phobias seem to be, they are very real fears for the people who experience them.

Before we get to the table, one phobia deserves special mention, if only for the sheer audacity of its name. And that is the phobia of long words, ironically known as hippopotomonstrosesquippedaliophobia. Who says scientists don't have a sense of humour!

Table 11-1	Phobias A to Z
What the scientists call it	*What it actually means*
Acrophobia	A fear of heights
Agoraphobia	A fear of open spaces or crowded places. It can also mean a fear of leaving somewhere you feel safe
Apiphobia	A fear of bees
Bromidrophobia	A fear of body smells
Cardiophobia	A fear of the heart or heart disease
Claustrophobia	A fear of confined spaces
Coprophobia	A fear of faeces
Dendrophobia	A fear of trees
Dental phobia	A fear of dentists or dentistry
Emetophobia	A fear of vomiting
Erythrophobia	A fear of blushing or of the colour red
Frigophobia	A fear of the cold or of cold things
Gerontophobia	A fear of elderly people or of growing old
Hippophobia	A fear of horses
Ichthyophobia	A fear of fish
Isolophobia	A fear of being alone
Kainophobia	A fear of new things
Koniophobia	A fear of dust
Ligyrophobia	A fear of loud noises
Lygophobia	A fear of darkness
Mechanophobia	A fear of mechanical things
Molysmophobia	A fear of being contaminated
Necrophobia	A fear of death or dead things
Ornithophobia	A fear of birds

What the scientists call it	What it actually means
Social phobia	A fear of negative evaluation in social situations
Spheksophobia	A fear of wasps
Technophobia	A fear of technology
Zoophobia	A fear of animals

Specific phobias

If you're phobic about only one thing, you have a specific phobia. This used to be called *simple phobia*, but as any phobic will tell you, there's nothing simple about a phobia. Perhaps in recognition of this, science changed its name.

A *specific phobia* means your irrational fear is attached to one thing, and one thing only. You're scared of heights and nothing else, for example. And it is only when you are in the presence of the actual phobic stimulus, or when you think about it, that you feel the fear.

More complex phobias

A *complex phobia* develops when the specific phobia you started off with spreads into other areas of your life. For example, you have a fear of snakes. You only felt scared when you thought about them, or when you were confronted with one in the zoo or on television. But now, your fear is starting to spread. You see a rubber snake in a toyshop and go apoplectic. The hosepipe lying on the ground fills you with fear and dread – after all, it looks like a snake!

Unfortunately, your phobia is generalising out and you are starting to fear other objects. This can lead to you becoming multi-phobic. In other words, you begin to develop phobias for other things. If this continues, your life can become more and more restricted. In the end, you may end up with *agoraphobia* – fear of open or crowded spaces – and become increasingly confined to your home. Being out, in the outside world, becomes an object of fear itself.

Some people are naturally *multi-phobic*, meaning they may well have more than one specific phobia, each one contained in its own little phobia world, bearing no relation to the others. A multi-phobic person may have a fear of flying. And a fear of wasps. And a fear of cats. And so on.

Removing Your Phobia through Hypnotherapy

One thing about phobias is that you can avoid dealing with them for only so long. Eventually you have to face up to the fact that you must sort out your phobia. Why? Because your phobia is making your life unbearable and increasingly interferes with your family, social, and work life. Have no fear (get it? Have no fear?); your hypnotherapist is there to help.

A hypnotherapist can take several approaches to helping you get rid of your phobia. What all approaches have in common is that they bring your fear under control. In fact, hypnotherapy allows you to confront the thing that freaks you out, with a sense of calmness and appropriate relaxation. You no longer avoid whatever it is; in fact, you look it straight in the eye and thumb your nose at it! You put your fear into proper perspective.

This doesn't mean to say that you go from being unable to climb up a ladder to standing on the very edge of the Empire State Building, looking down on New York City below. It simply means that you're able to deal calmly with those everyday occurrences of whatever it was that you were phobic about.

Your therapist won't spring surprises on you. Many phobics come to hypnotherapy fearing that their therapist will suddenly produce whatever it is that they fear. That approach went out with the Ark! You won't suddenly have a spider dumped in your lap, nor will your therapist shut you in a room with his pet canary to cure your bird phobia. Of course, if this is what you want, it can be arranged. However, by far the majority of hypnotherapists don't work this way. If you are at all concerned about unpleasant surprises, ask your hypnotherapist, in advance, about the approach they plan to use. If they intend to do something you don't agree with, say 'Thanks, but no thanks', and find someone else.

Starting with the basics

You've done it. You turned up for your appointment and are about to undergo hypnotherapy. So what can you expect? Well, for a start, your hypnotherapist is going to take a good case history (see Chapter 13 for complete info on giving a case history). As part of that case history, your therapist wants to know as much about your phobia as possible. Be prepared to tell your therapist

✔ **When your phobia first started:** This gives an indication of how your phobia came about in the first place, and may provide a pointer as to the therapy technique your hypnotherapist will use.

✔ **When your phobia first became a problem for you:** Could you cope with the fear to begin with? What was it that eventually turned your fear into a full-blown phobia?

✔ **Your worst phobic experience:** This can be important as it may be a major contributing factor to the continuing build-up of your phobia.

✔ **Your last phobic experience:** How long is it since your last experience? How did that affect you?

✔ **Whether anyone close to you has the same phobia:** This may indicate whether you picked up the phobia from someone else. If you didn't get it from the person who shares your phobia, perhaps that person could be reinforcing your phobia, because they talk about their own phobic responses in front of you.

✔ **Specific information about your phobia:** The specifics are important, and your therapist will want to find out as much as possible about how you experience your phobia.

For a fear of heights, your therapist may want to ask you about the heights you can cope with, whether you cope if there is a barrier between you and the drop, how you feel if you see someone else standing in a high place, and so on.

For a fear of cats, your therapist may want to know if you cope more effectively with black cats or ginger cats, if a sleeping cat is less scary than a moving cat, how you feel when you see pictures of cats, and so on.

✔ **How you want to be after your phobia is gone:** It's no good just focusing on the negatives, your therapist also wants to help you focus on the reason you are sitting in their therapy room. And that means finding out from you just how you want to be when you encounter that phobic stimulus. Remember, you can't make things perfect – you must be realistic. Most spider phobics don't want to have one of their nemeses crawling around on their hand. Rather, they want to feel okay about picking one up out of the bath, on the end of a piece of newspaper, and flicking it out the window.

We'll let you into a little secret. Even though you probably assume that the therapy occurs only when you are hypnotised, the truth is that the taking of the case history information is very therapeutic in its own right. Being able to talk about your problem to a sympathetic pair of ears is a great set-up for the formal hypnotherapy to come. And don't worry; your therapist has heard it all before. No matter how strange you think your phobia is, your hypnotherapist has, more than likely, encountered it at some point. Oh, and he won't laugh, either!

Approaching the trance

So, what can you expect to happen in the trance? Your hypnotherapist may use several different approaches, alone or in combination with each other.

It may take more than one session to help you get rid of your phobia. Be prepared to carry out any homework assignments your therapist gives you to do between sessions – such as self-hypnosis – because these help the therapy process along no end.

Being hypno-desensitised

A very popular approach based on a behaviour therapy technique, created by behaviourist Joseph Wolpe, has the rather posh title of *reciprocal inhibition*. What that means is you can use one feeling to override another. The feeling you get when you experience your phobia is anxiety. Your therapist uses relaxation to override the anxiety. After all, you can't be relaxed and anxious at the same time!

Several approaches to hypno-desensitisation exist. A very common one is for your therapist to help you create something known as an anxiety hierarchy. Simply put, an *anxiety hierarchy* is a series of events you come up with regarding your phobia, ranked according to how much anxiety they produce. You rank these events from 0, which means that you feel no anxiety, to 100, which means that you feel the worst anxiety you can imagine. In hypnosis, your therapist gently takes you through the hierarchy, starting with the events ranked at 0, whilst giving you suggestions that you are calm, relaxed, and in control. He will then question you to find out whether you are indeed calm and relaxed. If you are, he then moves onto the next scene on your hierarchy. If at any point you feel anxious, your therapist will emphasise suggestions for relaxation so that you begin to feel relaxed again.

This is where the reciprocal inhibition really comes in – letting the relaxation wash away the anxiety. Don't worry, your therapist won't force you up the hierarchy too quickly, nor will he take you beyond the point at which you feel comfortable. By creating the association of relaxation with the various images from your hierarchy, you change the way your mind thinks about your phobia. When you encounter it in real life, you find that you cope very well indeed.

Going back to regression

This approach is sometimes used by analytical hypnotherapists who believe that to get rid of a phobia you need to understand and deal with its origin. Your therapist basically takes you back into your past, to the time when the phobia began.

Your hypnotherapist asks you to witness what happened, and perhaps to 'alter' the event in your mind, so that you experience yourself coping well in that situation.

Of course, you won't alter the real event but rather your perception of it. By doing this, you create a domino effect that tumbles into the present, wiping out that irrational fear. For more on regression, see Chapter 2.

Accessing positive resources

This approach also uses regression, but this time to get resources from your past. These resources are positive feelings that allowed you to cope and feel good before; feelings such as relaxation, confidence, an inner sense of self-control, humour, and so on.

While in trance, you're asked to create an image that represents your phobia. You're then asked to drift back in time and pick up wonderful, positive feelings that help you cope, and bring them forward to the present. You then are guided to fuse your positive resources to the image you created of your phobia.

By doing this, the resources overlay the anxiety the image produces (good old reciprocal inhibition!), and helps to alter the way you think about whatever it is you were scared of. When you are out and about and eventually encounter your phobia; you're fine – calm and relaxed and wondering what all the fuss was about.

Trying the fast phobia cure

This one is worth a brief mention as many hypnotherapists use it. It comes from a school of therapy called Neuro-linguistic Programming (NLP), which hypnotherapists have adapted so that it can be carried out in trance.

The fast phobia cure essentially disrupts the way you maintain the thoughts and images you hold in your mind about your phobia. For more on this, and NLP in general, turn to Chapter 15.

Following EMDR

Not strictly hypnosis this one, though many hypnotherapists are trained in its use. Eye Movement Desensitisation and Reprocessing (EMDR) is a very powerful technique originally developed as a treatment for trauma. However, it has also been shown to be very effective in the treatment of phobias.

In EMDR, you are asked to follow your therapist's fingers with your eyes as you hold certain images or thoughts in your mind. The idea is that this speeds up the way your mind processes upsetting events, allowing you to get rid of that phobic fear. Chapter 15 has more on EMDR and how it works.

Picturing your life without your phobia

The images, feelings, thoughts and pictures you had in your mind with regard to your phobia are what encourage and egg on the phobia in the first place. After the main part of your therapy is complete, your therapist will take you forward in time, in your mind, so that you experience yourself coping effectively and thinking and feeling in a more positive way about whatever it was that used to cause your phobic response. This technique is called *pseudo orientation in time* and is explained in Chapter 2.

The idea is to reinforce those changes made during therapy to the images, associated thoughts, and so on, which have been causing your anxiety. This allows you to view your phobia differently; to no longer view it as something that strikes terror into your heart, rather to view it as something you know you can cope with very effectively. It is the icing on top of the proverbial therapy cake.

Confronting Your Phobia: A Contract for Action

If the icing on the cake is pseudo orientation in time (see the previous section), then the cherry that tops it off is the *contract for action*. No, this doesn't mean getting your lawyer in to look over some complicated legal contract. Far from it; *the contract for action* is simply an agreement between you and your hypnotherapist that, after you complete therapy, you will go out and confront your phobia. Some hypnotherapists may even write down what they want you to do in the form of a contract and ask you to sign it (remember it's only symbolic, and definitely not legally binding!).

You may be thinking that this sounds very daunting. And, yes, it may seem daunting to you now, but remember that you're asked to do this only *after* your therapy is complete. So, you should be feeling fine about your phobic object or situation. Also, as it's you who is making the choice to go out and confront your phobia, you are in complete control of the situation.

So, why would your hypnotherapist ask you to do this? Well, simply to find out if your therapy worked. You can lie back in trance imagining whatever your therapist wants you to imagine, listening to his suggestions to your heart's content, but unless this translates into your real life, you still have your phobia. And after all, you went to see your hypnotherapist in the first place so that you can face up to your phobia.

Part of what makes a phobia a phobia is avoidance, so don't avoid going to see your hypnotherapist. Don't let that anxiety build and your phobia get worse. Pick up the telephone now and book your appointment.

Part IV
The Practical Stuff

The 5th Wave   By Rich Tennant

"Here's a tip – if you hear yourself snoring,
you're hypnotised too deeply."

In this part . . .

This part helps you to get ready for experiencing hypnotherapy yourself by discussing topics such as choosing a hypnotherapist, and how to best practice self-hypnosis.

You can find lots of new therapies related to hypnotherapy, which we go into in Chapter 15. Interested in finding out more about neuro-linguistic programming or Thought Field Therapy? This is the part for you.

Chapter 12

Finding a Hypnotherapist

. . . .

. . . .

*F*inding someone you trust to help you repair anything you value can be difficult. How do you find the right person? How do you avoid being ripped off by a charlatan? Even if you meet someone who seems pleasant, honest and qualified, how do you know that they will do a satisfactory job?

These questions are even more relevant when you are looking for someone to work on personal issues, particularly hypnosis. This chapter helps you become an informed consumer where selecting a qualified hypnotherapist is concerned.

Looking Out for a Hero

It's always ideal to have a strong recommendation from someone you know and trust when looking for a hypnotherapist. But this is not often possible. So we help you to cut through the confusion surrounding exactly how to choose an excellent hypnotherapist for you.

The hypnotherapy resources in the Appendix of this book includes a list of professional organisations of hypnotherapists throughout Europe, the US, Canada, and Australia. If you have access to a library or the Internet, you can contact these organisations to ask for a list of qualified hypnotherapists near you.

Knowing what to look for

Do not be impressed by a string of letters after someone's name – particularly if you don't know what the letters mean! These letters may reflect a recognised, quality hypnotherapy training over a number of years – or they may be letters gained from a few training weekends.

There are broadly two streams of practising hypnotherapists:

✔ Those with professional training, linked to a creditable hypnotherapy organisation: A professional undergoes a very lengthy, involved training. This training, which can take from anywhere from two to four years, depending on national requirements, includes many lectures, supervisions, practical sessions, and examinations to ensure that the trainee understands and can demonstrate a certain level of expertise.

✔ Those who took the fast track: Fast-trackers have only minimal training – often just a couple of weekends, perhaps less than a month – often with no quality control.

It's safe to say that a lengthy training (a minimum of two years) is more likely to represent a quality training.

Training length

How exactly do you know whether your hypnotherapist's training is a quality one or a non-quality one? Length of training is one of the first things to look at. If the training programme is not about two years long as a rule, it may be an indication of a less than reputable training.

Keep in mind that requirements vary from country to country. For example, the United States requires PhD-level training to become a qualified hypnotherapist in certain states, whereas this level of training is not required for professional status in the United Kingdom.

This is not to say that UK hypnotherapy training is less rigorous than in the US. For example, the London College of Clinical Hypnosis (LCCH), which runs training centres across the UK and Europe, provides an extremely thorough training for medical and non-medical practitioners. Its training programme is approved by a variety of national professional organisations. So, similar to US trainings, the LCCH trains doctors, dentists, and lay practitioners to become hypnotherapists.

However, the UK places less of an emphasis on obtaining the research component/dissertation associated with earning a PhD in the US, hence European trainings tend to be around two years duration rather than four.

You can try a couple of methods to find out about your potential hypnotherapist's training:

- ✔ Ask the hypnotherapist directly
- ✔ Look at the qualifications after their name on their brochure or Web site, and do either an Internet or a library search on these qualifications. The qualifications will be associated with a hypnotherapy training organisation, which will provide you with training information regarding that qualification.

Training organisations

It is important to determine which organisations are the quality ones and which are the 'fast-tracking' ones. Check the Appendix for reputable hypnotherapy organisations. These national hypnotherapy organisations can help guide you to a qualified therapist.

Believing adverts – or not

We strongly recommend that you identify practitioners through a professional hypnotherapy organisation, as opposed to random adverts you may come across.

This is not to imply that legitimate, professionally qualified hypnotherapists don't distribute leaflets, or advertise in creative ways – sometimes they do. However, mixed in with the legitimate adverts are significantly less qualified practitioners whom you probably wouldn't want to work on your worst enemy. . . or, perhaps you would!

Some therapists make special offers at different times throughout the year, such as special prices for stopping smoking in the New Year, or summer holiday discounts.

Check with the main professional hypnotherapy organisations – listed in the Appendix – to ensure that the advert you are looking at is from a respectable practitioner.

Cruising the information superhighway

The Internet is a fabulous way to find out about hypnotherapists, hypnosis, and its many possible applications. We list the main accrediting hypnotherapy organisations, in both America and Europe, in the Appendix. Use their Web sites not only to find a hypnotherapist registered with them, but also to discover more about the various areas of hypnotherapy.

The Internet makes it so easy to find anything you want, you may be attempted to bypass these organisations and just search on a phrase like `hypnotherapist + your city name`. We strongly advise against this approach to finding a hypnotherapist. Why? Because you want to ensure that you get a well trained, professional, qualified hypnotherapist.

Try looking for hypnotherapy training organisations and compare the type of training they offer. Most of these organisations have a section on their Web site to help you find a therapist whose trained with them.

For example, you could start your Internet search by searching on a phrase such as `hypnotherapy training` on a popular search engine. As you link to the organisations that result from your search, you'll quickly get a feel for the type of organisations that appeal to you. You can then find a hypnotherapist from one of those organisations or societies. Happy shopping!

Even if you don't have Internet access, you probably have a friend or relative who does. Failing that, most local libraries now have Internet terminals and will be glad to help you on your search.

Relying on word-of-mouth

If possible, get a recommendation from someone you know who has had a positive experience with a hypnotherapist. This is by far the best possible means of finding a good hypnotherapist.

You can casually mention to people that you read an article about hypnosis and are interested in experiencing it for yourself. You don't have to share your specific problem. (In fact, please avoid telling your work colleagues about deeply personal problems – they may say things that are unhelpful based on their own discomfort.)

You may be surprised at how many people around you have seen a hypnotherapist. Many times you hear straightforward success stories of people who have stopped smoking, had their phobias removed, and achieved other goals through hypnosis.

Don't be too quick to judge if you hear a report that someone tried hypnosis but it didn't take away their problem. Admittedly, sometimes the hypnotherapist is at fault, but people often sabotage their own therapy or otherwise make choices to continue, or resume, the habits they went to a hypnotherapist to be cured of. A hypnotherapist can help you sort out your problems; it's your responsibility to help that process along.

If, for any reason, you don't feel comfortable asking friends or colleagues for referrals, you have a couple of alternatives:

- ✔ **Ask a medical doctor:** Your family doctor or GP may know of a hypnotherapist who has helped their own patients. Many hypnotherapists receive referrals from local GPs and you can be sure that your doctor won't recommend anyone that they don't have a good relationship with.

- ✔ **Ring a clinic** *where hypnotherapists practice:* You can often find where hypnotherapists practice by looking up 'hypnotherapist' in the Yellow Pages. The listings you find there may range from individual private practices, to psychology departments based in colleges and universities, to health clinics.

    For example, I (Mike) work sessionally in a clinic in South London, along with a couple of other hypnotherapists. We often receive new clients from people who have seen the Web site and just rung the office. If you talk to the clinic receptionist or office manager, they may even be able to help you to determine which particular practitioner may be best suited to help you, if you can broadly describe your objective. But again, if you don't want them to know the nature of your visit, you don't have to.

Looking Into Your Hero

Now that you have names of a hypnotherapist, or perhaps a couple, what next? The enthusiasm of a friend does not necessarily mean that their hypnotherapist is the right one for you. At this stage, you're in a position similar to when one friend says to another, 'You really must meet my friend – you two will have *so* much in common.' Then when you actually *do* meet said friend, both of you find that you don't exactly click. You may even feel awkward around each other after your mutual friend has told each of you about each other so enthusiastically. You definitely want to avoid this type of experience when shopping for a hypnotherapist, but how do you do this? The following subsections tell you how.

Researching by word-of-mouth

If you received a referral from a friend, ask the friend questions about the hypnotherapist they told you so fondly about. Find out how their hypnotherapist made them feel, what background the hypnotherapist has, and even their physical appearance (you wouldn't want to go to an obese hypnotherapist to help you to lose weight would you?).

You can also ask your friend about the hypnotherapist's background. Your friend may not have a lot of information, but it can be useful if you decide to meet with their hypnotherapist. Knowing how someone came into the work they're doing, particularly someone in a helping profession like hypnotherapy, can tell you a lot about that person.

You have a greater chance of success in your own hypnotherapy if you feel positively about your practitioner. Knowing a bit about their background can be a great help in that way. If you feel positively before you even meet them, it can only be an aid to your therapy.

Making sure your hypnotherapist is professionally trained

You can ask the hypnotherapist directly where they trained, how long the course was, and what qualification they hold. Sometimes therapists put this information on their brochures. You can also find out about their training from the Internet (see the preceding 'Cruising the information superhighway' section for tips on how to research), or through professional hypnotherapy organisations.

Keep in mind that different countries have different standards of training. Make sure that you understand the standards for the area you're in. Don't assume the qualifications are the same as in the country you're familiar with. Don't forget that you can ask directly.

Just to repeat, the training is a really crucial factor. The rule of thumb is, the longer the training, the higher the chances are that you will find someone who is a more proficient hypnotherapist.

Talking to a few therapists

By contacting professional hypnotherapy organisations and/or their Web sites, you can usually find a list of local hypnotherapists.

You can then call each practitioner and speak with them – briefly – about how they work, whether they're experienced with your problem, and what their rates are.

Most practitioners will appreciate your asking considered questions, because your way of being serious about ensuring being successful in your therapy.

Asking the right questions

Most hypnotherapists do an initial assessment the first time you meet. The point of this meeting is to let both of you get to know each other, in order to determine whether you're comfortable working with each other.

Little or no therapy may occur during this first meeting, but you can expect to be asked lots of questions about your background in terms of how as it relates to your problem (more on this in the next section), and you can take the opportunity to ask questions of your own. (Chapter 13 has details on what to expect during an initial assessment.)

Using your instinct is key here. Some questions you may want to ask include:

- How long have you been working as a hypnotherapist? You want someone who has a few years of experience at least.

- What's your professional background? Earlier sections in this chapter discuss the need for a substantial training. Added bonuses may be if the hypnotherapist has other qualifications such as medical training, or is also a counsellor, or psychotherapist.

- How did you choose to become a hypnotherapist? The answer to this question can tell you a lot about the person's motivation. If you get any answers about the decision being based on making money, ring another therapist!

- Have you treated clients with my problem before? Hopefully, yes!

- What approach would you take in working with me to achieve my goal? The hypnotherapist should be able to briefly outline the process, but if they say that they will need to see you again before discussing treatment, this is also legitimate.

- How many sessions will the treatment involve? You should be wary of any quick answers, with the possible exception of one-session stop smoking.

   If therapy needs several sessions due to working on serious psychological issues, ask whether the session fees remain the same, or whether the therapist would consider a discount.

You can probably find other questions to ask, but hopefully this list will get you on your way.

Try not to overdo the questions, but make sure that you find out all you need to know without being unduly fussy. You're aiming to find someone you trust, so it is important to get your questions answered.

Selecting Your Therapist

Any hypnotherapy session is a collaboration between you and your hypnotherapist. That means you work together towards a common goal. You can think of it this way: both you and your therapist are travelling in a car. You are the driver and your therapist is the navigator. You know where your journey's end is, but you're not sure how to get there. Your navigator – the hypnotherapist – is there to give suggestions as to which route to take. In order to get to your final destination, the pair of you have to collaborate as you travel along on that journey. Choosing the right navigator for your journey is an important part of reaching your destination.

Don't feel pressured into choosing a hypnotherapist before you're ready, but once you make a decision, it's courteous to inform any other hypnotherapists you met with that you will not be working with them. You can do this via their answering service, or by a postcard, if you don't want to speak to them.

Weigh up the information you gathered from telephone interviews about each therapist's qualifications, experience, and personality. (Give extra marks for a sense of humour, which isn't essential, but it sure helps!)

You may have more specific criteria as well. For example, if your issues are related to gender, choosing someone of the same gender may be relevant to you. Likewise, choosing a therapist of the same race, nationality, sexual orientation, and so on may be a priority for you. But be flexible on these issues, if possible. There is much to be said for choosing someone who is *not* from your exact background. Sometimes a different perspective is invaluable.

Sift through all the information you gathered, then choose the person who made you feel most comfortable and had the attitude you most appreciate. Let that person be your hypnotherapist.

Trusting your gut instinct in choosing a therapist is a good step to take in your hypnotherapy because ultimately, hypnotherapy gives you the tools and encouragement to trust that your unconscious can heal you.

Good luck!

Chapter 13

Your First Hypnotherapy Session Step by Step

● ●

In This Chapter

▶ Meeting your hypnotherapist

▶ Relaxing your way to clarity

▶ Going deeper into your session

▶ Making positive suggestions

▶ Following up on your session

● ●

*Y*our very first hypnotherapy session can be an exciting or an intimidating experience. Exciting if you're prepared and know what to expect. Intimidating if you have fears about hypnosis and are worried about how the session will go. (Check out Chapter 3 for tips on preparing for your first session.)

So what should you expect when you arrive? While specific techniques differ from therapist to therapist, most sessions follow the same general course. In this chapter, we take you through all of the stages of a typical hypnotherapy session, from the first getting-to-know-you questions to the follow-up activities.

A hypnotherapy session really is one of the few things in life that's truly about you. And other than a few common sense items, you don't have to do a great deal of preparation. So relax. Armed with the knowledge in this chapter, you can achieve the best possible results from your hypnosis sessions.

Entering the Office

One of the most empowering things to do when you go to your hypnotherapy session, is to arrive just a bit early. The reason for this is simple: You have a fixed amount of appointment time. Arriving early ensures that you don't waste your money by being late. Besides, being early allows you to relax, compose yourself, and focus on your goals for the session.

Hypnosis is most effective on patients who are able to relax. So find your inner calm and be prepared to see what a difference hypnotherapy can make in your life!

Caring enough to pay your own way

Money and session payment are two very interesting subjects for us hypnotherapists. Not only because we pay our mortgage and grocery bills through the fees we collect, but from a motivation perspective. Consider two hypothetical clients:

> Joan saved her money for a quit smoking session.

> Musa was given the money by his father for a quit smoking session.

Who do you think has the greater chance of success?

It may be unscientific, but it's safe to say that Joan probably has the better shot at quitting smoking than Musa does. In general, self-paying clients tend to be more motivated. This may simply be due to the fact that when you use your own money, you're more highly motivated to get value for it.

When we meet a patient who is not paying for their own therapy, we ask additional questions to determine whether they're motivated. We want to ensure that they aren't being sent to therapy against their own wishes. Because, if that is the case, hypnotherapy is much less likely to be effective for them.

Budgeting for your hypnotherapy sessions

The cost of hypnotherapy varies so much that even stating a ballpark figure would lead to misrepresentation, confusion, and inaccuracy.

Hypnotherapists with expensive premises in city centres will charge more than suburban or ruralbased therapists. Hypnotherapists who are medically qualified charge differently. There are many possible permutations on fees.

Your hypnotherapist will be happy to tell you his fees, whether you're having a one-off session of a couple of hours, or several sessions over a number of weeks.

Knowing how many sessions it may take

Every hypnotherapist is different, but hypnotherapy is very solution focused. It generally achieves results rapidly compared to most talking therapies. One reason may be that counselling and psychotherapy are concerned with gaining insight, and understanding *why* you have a problem and what its origins are. Hypnotherapy, on the other hand, is more concerned with obtaining rapid and lasting change than in finding a cause. Gaining insight is a bonus in hypnotherapy, not the goal. Rapid change is the goal, and in our experience, what most clients want.

You may wonder how rapid this rapid change is. Well, for example, many hypnotherapists conduct a stop-smoking treatment in a single session. Granted, the session may involve an extended, slightly longer period – 90 minutes being a common time duration for a stop-smoking session, as opposed to the normal 50 minutes for all other treatments. The reason for a single stop-smoking session is to give the message that once you're hypnotised to be a non-smoker, subsequent sessions are redundant and actually undermine that message.

However, if you're coming to hypnotherapy with a fairly serious problem – something like an eating disorder, or a problem that is profoundly affecting your quality of life – expect anywhere from two to half a dozen sessions and possibly more, depending on the seriousness of the problem.

Starting Your Hypnotherapy Session

So are you ready? You booked your first session. What's next?

A hypnotherapy session, rather like most stage presentations, follows a familiar sequence of events with a beginning, a middle, and an end. To be sure, some stage presentations mix the sequence up a bit, like *Phantom of the Opera*, where the curtain rises on a scene years after the masked man finished playing the organ. A bit odd, that. Of course, if the phantom had undergone hypnotherapy, maybe he wouldn't have had quite so many personal issues . . .

A hypnotherapy session begins, well, at the beginning, probably with introductions and a little small talk to put you at ease. This gentle start not only helps the hypnotherapist establish a good rapport with you, it helps you relax – and relaxation is the key to allowing hypnosis to happen.

After the small talk, the hypnotherapist asks you on what issue you want to work. Tell him. Don't be surprised if he tells you that it's an issue he has worked on successfully with other patients. In our experience, most patients do a bit of homework and are familiar with some of the basic areas that hypnotists can work with. After reading this book, you will also be familiar with lesser-known issues hypnosis is effective with.

After that, although therapists may differ slightly in their approach, a single hypnotherapy session typically has specific stages. The rest of this chapter goes into each in detail. No mask or organ music required.

Many hypnotherapists avoid doing any hypnosis during the first session. They may prefer to take a detailed personal history during the initial session. Then again, other hypnotherapists may treat you during your initial session. There really aren't any clear-cut rules about this.

Getting acquainted with your hypnotherapist

Hypnotherapists are skilled at helping people to relax, so feel free to have a chat with yours. He no doubt already realises that you may be a bit nervous, or even sceptical of hypnosis. Feel free to tell him exactly how you're feeling and what concerns you have, even if it's that you see hypnotists as strange beings – a cross between a mystic with mind-reading powers and a stage performer. Your honesty helps to get the session underway and helps the hypnotherapist to learn a bit about you and what helps you.

The aim is to ensure that you feel comfortable about working with this person.

This whole getting acquainted stage should only take a few minutes. In other words, 4 to 5 minutes out of your (most likely) 50-minute session.

Creating a working relationship

Relationships are a big deal to hypnotherapists. Remember that your hypnotherapist is like other helping professionals in that he's genuinely interested in working with you to help you to achieve your goals.

The basis for any effective therapeutic relationship is trust. It is important to feel that you can trust your hypnotherapist – always trust your instincts.

By establishing trust, you build rapport with your hypnotherapist. *Rapport* is a mutual trust and confidence between two people. Yes, rapport is a two-way street – not only do you need to have trust and confidence in your hypnotherapist, but your hypnotherapist needs to feel the same way. The hypnotherapist must feel confident that you're there for the right reasons, that you really want to achieve your goals, and that you can be honest in discussions about your problem. And that you won't do a runner and leave him with an unpaid fee!

Think of rapport as an emotional bridge between you and your hypnotherapist. Effective hypnotherapy begins with building a rapport and making the patient feel respected, welcomed, and reassured that their therapy will be effective. When you have rapport, you have empathy and understanding of how someone's problem may affect their life. This is as important for the hypnotherapist as for the client.

Establishing rapport in any type of personal development work is a crucial part of the therapy. Ample research evidence explains that establishing positive rapport enhances treatment efficacy.

Teaming up with your hypnotherapist

If you can approach the work that you are about to do as a joint effort with your hypnotherapist, you have a greater chance of achieving your goals.

Some patients expect the hypnotherapist to do all the work without putting in any effort themselves. It just don't work like that folks!

In fact, you can liken you and your therapist to a sports team. You are the excited player, eager to win the game, which may mean overcoming a phobia, or being able to stop smoking. Your hypnotherapist is like a powerful coach, enabling you to unleash inner resources you may have been unaware you possessed. Together, you combine into a powerful unit, ready and able to tackle the toughest opponent.

All hypnosis is a joint effort. This is why we emphasise the need to consider you and your hypnotherapist as a team.

Supplying a Case History

Your hypnotherapist wants to know how best to help you, so logically he needs to know a little about you before he begins. During your initial session he'll probably ask you a few questions in order to obtain information relevant to your stated problem or goal. This helps him to formulate a treatment plan to determine how best to use hypnosis for you. Some of the questions you're asked are similar to those that other professionals ask at a first meeting. They include:

- ✔ Your full name
- ✔ Your contact details
- ✔ Your date of birth, medical history, and current employment
- ✔ How long you've had the problem
- ✔ In what ways you've tried to solve the problem, and the results of these attempts

Taking a case history involves asking about the whole of your life. This may include asking who the members of your immediate family are, getting an overview of your medical history, relationship patterns, your current relationship situation, and discovering whether you have children. Your hypnotherapist may also be interested in any other therapies you've engaged in – counselling, psychotherapy, alternative or complementary treatments, and earlier attempts at hypnotherapy. Your hypnotherapist may not ask about all of these, but he will try to touch on anything he deems relevant to your current problem.

During the course of this portion, the therapist may ask permission to take notes. First check that his notes remain confidential, and then give him that permission. Notes help the therapist recall important information that enable him to make your sessions more productive.

Is your hypnotherapist just being nosey?

Why does your hypnotherapist need to know about your recent messy divorce? Or how many brothers and sisters you have? Or what your hobbies are? Those questions have nothing to do with your problem . . . do they? Isn't the hypnotherapist just being nosey?

Not at all. You can be assured that the information being sought is relevant to developing a fuller picture of you and your problem. The hypnotherapist is not in this line of work for titillation. He is asking you these questions in order to discover how best to help you.

You can assume that information you give is treated as confidential and not shared with any other parties. (The only exception is if any incidents of violence towards children arise. In most cases, a confession of violence towards children has to be reported to social services or the police, by law.)

Going Into a Trance

In Chapter 1 we define *trance* as the altered state of consciousness you enter into naturally, many times, daily. In this section, we describe what being in trance may feel like, and talk about how the hypnotherapist ensures that your trance is deep enough to be effective.

Basically, being in trance is a pleasant, relaxed feeling. Hypnotherapy is generally very enjoyable.

Inducing a trance

Induction is the technique used to establish a hypnotic trance state. Inductions are wonderful. They help you to relax and go deeply into trance.

Inductions can be done in as many different ways as there are hypnotherapists and patients, though they don't usually involve the corny expressions you see in TV shows or movies. You won't, for example, be induced into a trance state by someone waving their hands in front of your eyes and shouting 'You are getting sleepy . . . sleepy . . . SLEEPY!!!'. Not unless your hypnotherapist turns out to be Vincent Price.

Hypnotherapists use a variety of ways to induce a trance, including asking you to give your attention to one particular idea, such as:

- Fixating your eyes on your hands.
- Listening to your therapist count down from ten to one, with each number helping you to become more deeply relaxed.
- Evoking images in your imagination that bring up feelings of safety or relaxation.

Induction involves speaking to you in some way that both relaxes you and gets you to focus on a single thing that is somehow relevant to your problem – for example, staring at your hands to eliminate fingernail biting.

The hypnotic induction process consists of fixating your attention internally. The hypnotherapist gradually gets you to remove your awareness from the outside world (the room you are in, the ticking of the clock, street sounds, and so on), and to focus your attention on your thoughts and feelings. Focussing your attention in this way, has the double effect of slowing down your conscious mind and bringing to the fore your unconscious mind – the abstract part of you that dreams and holds your unlimited memory and inner resources for healing. The feeling is a bit reminiscent of pleasantly daydreaming during your school maths class.

The hypnotherapist may aim at getting you so relaxed that your eyes close. Alternatively, you may be asked directly to close your eyes while you are spoken to about becoming more relaxed.

Homing in on what a trance feels like

Trance is a common state of mind that you experience many times daily. You're in a trance state – without hypnosis – whenever you focus your attention onto a single thought or feeling for an extended time.

Entering a trance state through the guidance of a hypnotherapist is a no less pleasant experience, and one in which you feel you're contacting a very deep, resourceful part of yourself.

Examples of trance states include a range of emotions and experiences such as:

- **Reading:** Have you ever 'lost yourself' in a good book? This is a form of trance that can be very pleasant.

- **Exercising:** Look at people immersed in exercise and you can see trance in action. These people may be very much 'in the zone' and imagining competing, or even imagining a scene unrelated to the physical exercise they are doing, to spur them on.

- **Daydreaming:** This type of trance can produce vivid, real life feelings.

- **Studying:** This can be like mental exercising, in that the focus excludes what is happening around you.

- **Anger:** Being in a blind rage can lead people to act while they're in a 'dream like' state. After an outburst of rage, people may struggle to accept the actions they committed during their anger induced trance state.

✔ **Anxiety and panic:** Depending on the level of anxiety, you may even change your heart rate and other physical symptoms while you're entranced by fear or stress.

✔ **Obsessive or compulsive behaviour:** People with obsessive or compulsive behaviours may easily enter a trance state as they repeat behaviours and envision what these behaviours are doing for them, such as helping them to feel safe, avoid illness, and so on.

We list these to give you the idea that trance is *not* simply a pleasant, dreamy state of mind. The character of a trance is influenced by what you focus on. Your hypnotherapist encourages you to focus on pleasant sensations that help you to feel safe and relaxed. This enables you to comfortably receive the suggestions for therapeutic change that come later.

Taking you in and taking you deeper

Once you are in a state of hypnotic trance, the hypnotherapist proceeds to deepen your trance state. *Deepeners* are the words or techniques used to keep you relaxed, and help you go even deeper into trance.

Why do you need to go deeper if you are already in trance? Because the deeper the trance state, the more successfully you can absorb the therapy. Also, the deeper the trance state, the more easily you can bypass your critical conscious thoughts that may try to sabotage the therapy. Remember, change is very scary to the conscious mind, whereas the unconscious mind is quite mutable and receptive to change.

Experiencing the Actual Therapy

Now for the part that you've been waiting for – the magic! You're relaxed and in a very deep and relaxed trance. What happens next?

This is the stage of the session when the actual therapy begins. By *therapy*, we mean the process in which suggestions given by the hypnotherapist are transformed by your unconscious mind. 'Transformed' because your mind finds its own way to implement the suggestions that you're given.

The therapist doesn't necessarily tell you what to do, but he is more likely to make suggestions so that it is possible to achieve the change or goal you're seeking. New possibilities are suggested, changing your negative beliefs and counterproductive thoughts – the ones that are causing you to feel stuck with your problem – into positive and productive feelings. In this way, you become unstuck.

Choosing the best approach for you

Does a hypnotherapist use the same suggestions for all problems, regardless of the individual? No way! Your hypnotherapist designs the therapeutic suggestions so that the words spoken while you are in deep trance have the maximum chance of success.

'How does he do this?' you may ask. Well, during the initial meeting (see the 'Starting Your Hypnotherapy Session' earlier in this chapter) the hypnotherapist subtly assesses you and the language you use. This evaluation shouldn't make you self-conscious – it's part of his job! Your hypnotherapist does all this to understand your perspective on your problem and your life. The vocabulary you use, the emotions you express – or don't express – are all noted in order to tune into your wavelength. Then, when it is time to do hypnosis, the therapist can speak to you in your language, which makes you feel that he understands you. In this way the rapport between you and him is increased.

If you think about this approach you realise that you do the same thing all the time. You unconsciously speak differently to different people. Think about the different voices you use when you speak to

- ✔ Your mother or father
- ✔ Your boss at work
- ✔ Your partner
- ✔ Someone you find attractive (partners included!)
- ✔ A child
- ✔ A policeman about to give you a speeding ticket
- ✔ Your best friend
- ✔ Your worst enemy

I'm sure you get the idea. You don't use the same voice, or even vocabulary, with different people. Likewise, a hypnotherapist tailors his approach with different patients, to give each the best possible chance of success.

Receiving post-hypnotic suggestions

After you're deeply hypnotised, the therapist helps you by making post-hypnotic suggestions. Post-hypnotic suggestions are the therapeutic part of hypnotherapy; they're what you come to hypnotherapy for; they're what alters your way of dealing with the problem, and leads you to achieving your goal.

Specifically, a *post-hypnotic suggestion* is a therapeutic suggestion given when you're at a sufficiently deep of trance. The *post* part merely signifies that the suggestion is given after you're hypnotised.

Post-hypnotic suggestions deal directly with your problem. The style of the suggestion varies depending on your specific issue and your personality. For example, if you are a person who respects strong authority, your hypnotherapist will speak more directly to you in the suggestion offered. If you are more of a rebel, who resists authority, the post-hypnotic suggestions offered to you will be more gentle and indirect.

Language is critical at this stage. Effective post-hypnotic suggestions involve a sort of logic that you would agree with even if you were not in trance. Skilful hypnotherapists use suggestions in ways that agree with your mindset, suggestions such as:

- ✔ The more relaxed you are, the more confident you become.

- ✔ Your unconscious mind is more resourceful than you realise.

- ✔ With each breath your unconscious searches for answers.

- ✔ You may be pleasantly surprised how easily you make the changes.

Strengthening Your Ego

After the main therapeutic suggestions are given to you, your hypnotherapist may well add some ego-strengthening suggestions to make you feel more optimistic and confident. The term *ego-strengthening* is simply technical speak for a pat on the back.

Ego-strengthening is a powerful tool hypnotherapists use in promoting your aims. How exactly does feeling better about yourself help to achieve your goals? Why should you stop smoking, for example, just because you feel better? The answer is simple: when you feel defeated, you find it more difficult to struggle against adversity or challenges. Conversely, when you feel confident and energised, you are more likely to take on board the sort of challenges that you want to overcome. Ego-strengthening is a bit like getting extra emotional energy to become more resourceful.

Adding the feel good factor

Most problems can benefit from additional ego-strengthening suggestions. However, you need to imprint these suggestions permanently in your subconscious. By receiving a carefully worded ego-strengthening statement while in trance, your unconscious absorbs the positive suggestion and begins to believe deeply in it which, in turn, gives a boost to your self-esteem and your ability to succeed.

Some possible ego-strengthening suggestions include:

- ✔ You begin to feel increasingly optimistic.
- ✔ You are better able to cope with challenges.
- ✔ You feel more energetic than you have felt for a long time.
- ✔ You are able to obtain your goals easily.

Ego-strengthening suggestions are usually spoken after the crucial therapeutic suggestions. However, they may be the main focus of the therapy if, for example, your main issue is linked to low self-esteem. Low self-esteem problems are taken seriously. If the problems worsen, they can lead to a range of psychological problems from loneliness, panic disorders, social phobias, and even alcohol or drug dependency.

Ego-strengthening techniques are most effective with people who are very critical of themselves. People who tend to think negatively about themselves and view life in a negative way are prime candidates for ego-strengthening suggestions.

There are groups of people for whom ego-strengthening may *not* be beneficial. This group includes people having problems with hostility or *narcissism* (obsession with one's self to the exclusion of others), and those who have distorted, grandiose views of themselves. Even though some of these problems may actually involve low self-esteem, ironically enough, ego-strengthening is not be the best therapeutic approach to use initially, as it may make the problem worse.

Bolstering a weak ego

To understand how ego-strengthening helps you to achieve your goals, answer this question: What's the opposite of a strengthened ego? If your answer is 'a weak ego', congratulations! But what exactly is a weak ego? Check out these examples of characteristics of a weak ego:

- A victim attitude: 'I can't win no matter what I do.'

- Dependency on substances and/or external props: alcohol, drugs, money, social status, and so on.

- Highly critical and damaging self-thoughts: 'I'm a loser,' 'I'm disgusting,' 'I'm a sinner.'

- A tendency to belittle others in order to feel better about yourself.

These and similar behaviours and modes of thinking are counterproductive to understanding your true self-worth. In fact, if these weak ego states worsen over time, they can lead to some form of self-destructive behaviour.

People who think negatively about themselves generally benefit from some education about how their negative attitude links to difficulties achieving their goals. Hypnotherapists are used to helping patients change their world view from negative to positive, and then witnessing how they meet their goals a short time after.

Working toward a more healthy, strengthened ego can reverse a fatalistic world view.

When you feel good about who you are, the world and the people in it suddenly seem more benign. You're able to meet challenges with a good chance of success, people respond positively to you, and life is more likely to give you what you need, when you need it.

Do not underestimate the power of ego-strengthening techniques.

After successful ego-strengthening sessions, patients often find happy 'coincidences' begin to happen, where the world starts to give them an opportunity. These 'coincidences' are, of course, not coincidences at all but a demonstration of how our view of the world directly influences our reality.

Waking Up

After the therapeutic and ego-strengthening suggestions are delivered, the next critical step for your hypnotherapist is waking you from the trance state.

The awakening process usually involves two elements:

- ✔ **A gradual awakening:** Your hypnotherapist may count up from one to ten, with the suggestion that with each number you become more awake. So, for example, with each ascending number from one to ten, your hypnotherapist may suggest that you begin to feel more optimistic, more energetic, and happier than you have felt for a long while.

- ✔ **A full awakening:** Your hypnotherapist tries to ensure that you feel fully awake and present – that you feel completely normal. If you have been in a particularly deep trance during your session, the hypnotherapist will ensure that you are given ample time to feel alert and clear, before the session ends.

The way that you're awakened is directly related to both the induction method used and, if relevant, the type of therapy conducted. For example, if you were induced into trance by methods involving feeling heavier and deeply relaxed, your therapist would remove this suggestion when waking you up. The hypnotherapist may do this by suggesting that 'When you awake, you will feel wide awake and all parts of you will feel normal'.

If the type of therapy applied involved changing your perception of time, such as age regression (going backwards in time), age progression (going forwards in time), or past-life regression, your hypnotherapist will also return your perception of time back to the present, as it was before you were hypnotised.

Jarring you awake

If your hypnotherapist says something upsetting to you while you're in trance, you are most likely to simply reject or ignore the idea. If you feel very strongly about the comment, you may come out of the trance.

Most hypnotherapists are very skilled at listening to your phrases and using language that you are comfortable with, to ensure that the therapy is effective. Only an inexperienced hypnotist would ever say something so jarring that it takes you out of trance.

Be assured that this is a vary rare situation that you are unlikely to encounter if you seek help from a qualified hypnotherapist.

Coming completely out of trance

If you've ever seen someone sleepwalk, this is not dissimilar to what you'd be like if you weren't carefully emerged from a hypnotic trance. This somnambulant state wears off eventually, but a good hypnotherapist wants to ensure that your trance is completely terminated before the end of the session.

As a matter of routine, clinical hypnotherapists look after their patients carefully when awakening them. Another reason we stress for making sure that you visit a qualified hypnotherapist. There are many unqualified practitioners around who may not be careful in this sense. In particular, stage hypnotists don't take a lot of time carefully awakening and talking with hypnotic subjects.

Do not leave the therapist's office if you are still in a trance state! The feeling is the equivalent of sleepwalking. Take your time when leaving and be sure that you're clear-headed. Most hypnotherapists check with you for this, but it's also good for you to make sure that you are completely alert and out of trance when you leave your session. The easiest way to test this is from your physical sensations – during hypnotherapy, your body may feel numb, but when you emerge from trance all normal sensations should return.

Continuing therapy while you're coming out of trance

When you're emerging from the trance state, you are still highly suggestible. This state is not dissimilar to the state you're in every day of your life, just before you go to sleep and just after you wake up.

Most hypnotherapists are very skilled at using these final moments of awakening as it's a good time to give you some of the most powerful post-hypnotic suggestions, as a sort of therapeutic seal on the main work you're doing together.

Your hypnotherapist may seize the opportunity to give you a final ego-strengthening suggestion, or repeat what was said while you were in the deepest level of trance. He may repeat or rephrase key points as you emerge from trance, or even in the first few minutes after you come fully out of trance.

Doing Your Homework

Don't worry – no equations are involved!

Some – though not all – therapists give their patients some work to do after the session ends. The homework is meant to keep you involved in the work until the next session. Think of homework like reinforcing glue between hypnotherapy sessions.

Someone being treated for a phobia, and who has had a few sessions, may be given a task related to facing their phobia in some way that isn't too threatening, to see how it goes before the next session.

Homework tasks can involve a range of activities that you're responsible for practising. These tasks can include just about anything relevant to the work you're doing with your therapist, although you won't be expected to do deep therapy on yourself!

Something simple is the norm. You may be asked to visualise your goals, or, if you've been taught self-hypnosis, doing some really simple trance inductions on yourself.

The most common type of homework is practising self-hypnosis – if this is appropriate and your hypnotherapist has told you how to do it. Chapter 14 explores self-hypnosis in detail.

Your hypnotherapist may use the beginning of subsequent sessions to follow up the homework he asked you to do. A tiny review may take place, to discuss what worked well and what you found difficult. In this way new tasks can be set that ensure that your therapy is successful.

Chapter 14

Practising Self-Hypnosis

. . . .

In This Chapter

▶ Making your goal concise

▶ Discovering how to hypnotise yourself

▶ Determining when self-hypnosis is appropriate

▶ Writing your own hypnotherapy scripts

▶ Practising self-hypnosis

. . . .

There's something absolutely fascinating about the first time you success-fully hypnotise yourself. You feel that you've done something that you thought previously impossible. Then there's the satisfaction of achieving your goal. I'll never forget the first time that I (Mike) successfully hypnotised myself. I had had writer's block on a project for several weeks, and desper-ately needed to overcome it because a deadline was imminent. I was alone in a hotel room and after ten minutes of self-hypnosis, I immediately began writing – pages and pages!

Most people who learn self-hypnosis from books start by reading generalised scripts. You may have already read some scripts elsewhere in this book. After reading this chapter, you will know how to customise scripts, and even create your own, so that you can specially address your needs.

So, get ready for a step by step explanation of what you need to do to hypno-tise yourself.

Connecting to Your Unconscious

Self-hypnosis is a relatively quick and marvellous way to access your uncon-scious mind, which is where the actual changes take hold in your life.

Your unconscious is the non-emotional part of your mind, which is simply about the business of preserving and protecting you. The intention of your unconscious mind is always to make your life better in some way. It is literally open to suggestion!

But to get there from here, so to speak, and enter self-hypnosis, you must bypass the critical factor of your analytical conscious mind. This simple process, a skill actually, becomes very easy with practise. The moment the critical factor is pushed aside, voila! You're in direct communication with your unconscious mind.

Setting Your Goal

The first step in self-hypnosis involves forming a clear understanding of your goal. Though you may have many goals, it is best to address them one at a time. So make a list if you want to, but focus on only one at a time. Give each goal the exclusive time and attention it deserves.

Think about what you want to achieve or change and state your goal in a single sentence. Making your goal concise and to the point lets you repeat it and remember it easily. That means that your unconscious mind can then absorb the goal and begin to help you seek your own ways of achieving the outcome you want. Stating your goal in a single, simple sentence also helps your unconscious form ways of achieving your goal.

Keep your goals positive and use the present tense.

Some examples of single sentence goals:

- ✔ I am calm and peaceful when I lie down at night, and drift to sleep easily.
- ✔ I remember all I've studied when I take an exam, and can recall the information at will.
- ✔ I have greater public speaking confidence because I am knowledgeable, and the audience wants to hear what I have to say.
- ✔ I honour my health and vitality by selecting foods that are nutritious.

One method helps to clarify goals brilliantly – the *magic wand question*. It goes like this:

> If you had a magic wand and could change one thing about yourself, and one thing about your immediate world, what would be different after you used your wand?

This question immediately forces:

- ✔ A concise focus on the problem.

- ✔ An awareness of the connection between how your perception affects your reality.

- ✔ An ability to focus and visualise the change you want to make.

When I ask clients the magic wand question, I can see a slight physical change that indicates they are entering a light trance state.

Use the magic wand question to formulate your goal for self-hypnosis.

Hypnotising Yourself

If you understand the concept of trance, which we explain in Chapter 1, you already have a firm grasp on self-hypnosis. And, after you know what trance *feels* like, you can easily hypnotise yourself.

The basic steps for self-hypnosis are similar to those you undergo in a normal session with a hypnotherapist, except that you are the hypnotherapist! (Chapter 13 goes stepbystep through an initial hypnotherapy session.) The following sections cover what you go through when you experience self-hypnosis.

A couple of tips that can help you establish your self-hypnosis practise include:

- ✔ **Establish a place to practise:** Choose a place where you can be completely comfortable, whether sitting in a chair or lying down. The environment you choose should be free of distractions and potential interruptions. Your skin becomes sensitive when you are in trance, so be sure that the room temperature is just right (better to be a little warm than too cool). Though not necessary, some people prefer soft lighting, soothing music, or even a scented candle. Self-hypnosis is your gift to you. Whenever possible, indulge yourself in total comfort!

- ✔ **Set a time limit:** Mentally give yourself the following suggestion: *'Exactly 10 (or 15) minutes from now, my eyelids open automatically and I feel calm, rested, and refreshed. I am ready to take on the rest of the day, or I am ready to drift off to sleep'* (whichever you prefer). Don't worry about looking at a clock. Your unconscious mind knows how to measure time and will, with practise, reliably disengage you from hypnosis in the precise time that you allotted.

Dealing with distracting thoughts

Don't be discouraged if distracting or unwelcome thoughts float into your mind during your first few self-hypnosis sessions. Your thoughts are accustomed to bombarding you throughout the day in a rather undisciplined, sometimes chaotic, way. With self-hypnosis, you're retraining your mind so that you can choose which thoughts to attend to and which thoughts to discard.

A helpful technique is to create a mental inbox and outbox. If the thought that crosses your mind is truly important, simply put it into your mental inbox to attend to later. Don't worry, you won't forget about it. If the thought is frivolous, mentally put it in your outbox where you don't have to consider it again.

Inducing your own trance

An *induction* is the method used to put yourself into trance. In self-hypnosis you induce yourself into trance.

You can choose from a variety of induction techniques, many of which you can easily teach yourself. The next subsections offer some induction methods you can try.

As you read more about hypnosis, you may come across induction scripts that use generic phrases that sound harmless, but in certain cases are to be avoided, such as:

- ✔ If you're obese or worried about your weight, avoid the word 'heavy'. Don't think to yourself 'I am feeling heavy and tired', just 'I am feeling tired'.

- ✔ If you are depressed, avoid the word 'down'. Don't say 'I will sink down into trance', but 'I will go into a pleasant trance'.

Progressive relaxation

Using the *progressive relaxation* induction technique, you focus on gradually relaxing muscles over every part of your body. This relaxation helps you to go into trance.

1. **Begin by simply closing your eyes and taking a few deep breaths.**

   Imagine that with each breath you are exhaling bodily tension, which will help you to increasingly relax.

2. **Start progressively relaxing all your muscles, from head to toe, or toe to head, whichever you prefer.**

   Give yourself repeated suggestions to relax all your muscle groups.

   Keep in mind that it is not an anatomy test. Forgetting to relax a specific body part – your knees, or elbows, or toes, or whatever – isn't crucial. Your unconscious will fill in any parts you forget, if you think of your whole body being relaxed, after taking yourself through this script.

   You can use phrases such as 'Let them relax' and 'Let them go limp and slack'. Deliver these quite neutral phrases in a very permissive tone.

   The nearby sidebar, 'Sampling progressive relaxation', offers a script to follow.

The goal of progressive relaxation is to create an overall feeling of comfort from head to toe.

Sampling progressive relaxation

This sidebar contains an example of a progressive relaxation script. You don't have to use it word for word – feel free to adapt it in any way that works well for you.

'I'm now letting go of all unnecessary tension in my body . . . relaxing all my muscles from the top of my head to the bottom of my feet . . . letting them go nice and relaxed . . . my head and face are now going nice and slack . . . my forehead and eyes and eyelids . . . my cheeks, mouth and jaw muscles . . . it's a wonderful feeling as I let my face totally relax . . . I can actually feel the skin settling, smoothing out . . . I'm just letting it happen . . . unclenching my teeth and relaxing my tongue . . . the more I physically relax, the more I can mentally relax . . . my neck and shoulder muscles now . . . becoming completely relaxed . . . the tops of my arms . . . letting all tensions drain away . . . down through my elbows . . . into my forearms . . . down through my wrists and into my hands . . . right the way down into the very tips of my fingers and thumbs . . . just letting all those muscles go nice and relaxed . . . even my breathing is becoming slower as I relax . . . more and more . . . all tension in my chest area is leaving my body . . . relaxing my stomach muscles . . . relaxing my back muscles . . . down to my waist . . . my abdomen . . . down to my buttocks and my thigh muscles . . . becoming nice and relaxed . . . so are my knees . . . down through to my shins and calves . . . all becoming nice and loose . . . allowing all those areas to relax and let go . . . down on through to my ankles, my feet . . . into the very tips of my toes . . . all the muscles of my body beautifully relaxed and easy . . .'

Eye fixation technique

Possibly the simplest of all self-hypnosis methods is to simply choose a spot ahead of you – a picture on a nearby wall, for example – and simply stare at it until your eyes tire. When your eyes tire, relax them by closing them and let your whole body also relax. Then allow yourself to slow your breathing down, and go into a nice relaxed trance state.

Deepening your trance

Once you achieve a light trance state, you need to deepen and maintain the trance. Following is a very easy deepener you can use:

The ten-to-one countdown is probably one of the simplest ways of deepening trance for beginners once a light trance has begun. Basically, you count down from ten to one and tell yourself that with each number you'll become more relaxed, both physically and mentally, and go deeper into trance. The nearby sidebar, 'Counting down' has a sample script.

Counting down

This is a sample script for counting down to deepen your trance:

'In a few moments time . . . I will count down from ten to one . . . with each descending number . . . between ten and one . . . I'll become one-tenth more relaxed . . . ten per cent more relaxed . . . with each descending number . . . and each descending number . . . will help me to go . . . one-tenth deeper . . . into a wonderful hypnotic state of relaxation . . . a light trance state . . . this will become deeper and deeper . . . as I count on . . . and if, while I am counting . . . I will begin to experience a very pleasant . . . physical sensation . . . as if floating down . . . into an ever-deepening state . . . of physical and mental relaxation . . . that will become deeper . . . and deeper . . . as I count on . . . Ready . . . 10 . . . 9 . . . deeper, deeper . . . 8 . . . 7 . . . 6 . . . drifting down . . . ever more deeper relaxed . . . 5 . . . 4 . . . 3 . . . deeper and deeper still . . . 2 . . . 1 . . . and all the way, deep down relaxed . . . '

Alternative deepeners may involve

- ✔ Imagining yourself in a relaxing scene.
- ✔ Imagining walking down steps, and at the bottom is a comfortable place to rest.
- ✔ Making a fist, and as you release the fist, imagining a soothing feeling being released throughout your entire body.

You may now even begin to invent your own deepeners!

Trusting your unconscious mind to carry out your suggestion

When you're in a deepened trance state, you start using the goal statement you devised for your self-hypnosis session. (See the 'Setting Your Goal' section at the start of this chapter.) Now you realise why we tell you to state the goal in a single sentence. When in the trance state, you want to minimise words to allow your unconscious – the non-verbal part of you – to work its magic.

At this stage, just remember your single sentence goal statement. Then simply let go. Let the goal statement pass from your conscious mind, just say it a few times before starting the trance, allowing it to sink into your mind, then trust that you have handed it over to your unconscious mind, and that this wise part of you will now solve the problem.

This is the focal point of self-hypnosis. Don't just think your goal statement – imagine hearing it, seeing it, and experiencing the change actually occurring. Use as many of your senses as possible to incorporate your goal into your trance state. If you can visualise yourself having made the changes, that's even better. The point is to ruminate over your goal and make it as vivid as possible in your imagination. Your unconscious mind will do the work you have given it, if you are clear, focused, and concise on what you want.

Strengthening your ego

Ego strengthening is the icing on the cake after the main therapy. This is where you encourage yourself to feel happier, more confident, and all the other 'feel good' statements. Add these after you've repeated and imagined your goal statement. It can be a very powerful thing to give your unconscious mind positive messages for a change!

Waking yourself from trance

Although you may not feel it necessary, it is a good idea to count yourself awake, and tell yourself that you're no longer in trance. This helps you to disconnect from the self-hypnosis experience and return to a fully alert state.

Try counting *up* from one to ten. Counting up essentially reverses the ten-to-one countdown you use to deepen your trance. Your mind responds to it as it is the opposite of how you entered trance.

You can tell yourself:

> 'As with each ascending number from one to ten, I will become more awake, and confident that my unconscious mind is already seeking new ways to obtain my goal.'

Using awaking scripts helps to come out of trance and back into your normal conscious state. These scripts also give you confidence of success.

A few minutes after awakening from self-hypnosis, you are still in a highly suggestible state. Use that time to reinforce how relaxed and calm you feel, and how pleased you are that your unconscious mind is helping you reach your goal.

Examining the Pros and Cons of Self-Hypnosis

One main difference between this book and others is that although we acknowledge the power of self-hypnosis, we still advocate that serious problems are best dealt with in conjunction with a professional clinical hypnotherapist. In the following sections, we describe when self-hypnosis is and isn't appropriate.

When self-hypnosis is appropriate

We want to encourage you to enjoy the amazing benefits of self-hypnosis. Even though you may not have access to a professional hypnotherapist, it doesn't mean that hypnotherapy is out of the question. Self-hypnosis can be an extremely beneficial tool when used appropriately.

Some appropriate goals for self-hypnosis are:

✔ Doing homework assigned by your hypnotherapist.

✔ Boosting your confidence.

✔ Encouraging healthier living and eating choices.

✔ Enhancing your creativity.

✔ Controlling pain.

✔ Lifting your performance in sports, school, the arts, and so on.

Of course you can use self-hypnosis in many other ways, but you may find these suggestions helpful in choosing a goal for your own self-hypnosis.

When self-hypnosis isn't appropriate

It is important to know the limits of self-hypnosis. You should not attempt to hypnotise yourself in certain situations, and it's important to be clear on those occasions.

Following are examples of when not to attempt self-hypnosis:

✔ If you have a serious mental illness (for example, schizophrenia).

✔ If you have issues relating to serious trauma (for example, rape, violence, childhood abuse).

✔ If your problems involve relations between you and other people.

✔ If you have serious phobias.

In any of these situations, we encourage you to work with a professional hypnotherapist. Why? Because with serious problems, it is very difficult indeed to resolve them alone. A professional hypnotherapist has the expertise to help you to achieve your goals and overcome problems that may have roots outside of your conscious awareness.

Developing Your Own Scripts

Hypnotherapy scripts must be individually tailored to be effective.

One of the most exciting things you can do at this stage is to choose a script and rewrite it so the words and message feel natural to you. We present several sample scripts throughout this book that help you understand how hypnotic suggestions are phrased to help you achieve your therapeutic goals.

Take any script in this book that interests you and re-write it in the language that you use when you think or speak to a close friend. Using your own language and phrasing makes it more likely that your unconscious will absorb the suggestions and start searching for change.

Follow these general guidelines for script writing:

- ✔ Phrase sentences like you breathe – don't be too wordy, and use short phrases.
- ✔ Aim for the simplest language possible.
- ✔ Avoid using negatives such as 'no', 'never', 'not', and 'won't' – state goals in the positive.
- ✔ Avoid being too specific about how to achieve your goal. Trust your unconscious to find its own solution.
- ✔ Avoid setting deadlines for achieving your goal. Again, trust your internal clock.
- ✔ Be realistic about your goals.

Believe that you will succeed and you will.

Ongoing Self-Hypnosis

How can you best reach your goals? By being true to yourself and discovering the best way that you absorb new information. Hypnosis is a lot like going to school. The difference is that with hypnosis, you are learning a new behaviour.

We are all different, and what works well for one person won't work as well for another. The following subsections offer tips that may be helpful for you to think about when deciding what works best for you.

A great deal of material on self-hypnosis is available, some of it contradictory. The old saying 'be true to yourself' applies here strongly. It is really important to be true to yourself when trying different self-hypnosis scripts and techniques. Don't try a script that doesn't feel right to you. It just won't be as effective as one that you really believe in.

Making your hypnosis work

If you want to be really successful, you should:

- ✔ Try to be hypnotised by a hypnotherapist before trying self-hypnosis.
- ✔ Practise self-hypnosis regularly.
- ✔ Set realistic and simple goals.

As with any newly acquired or desired skill, it is very important to persevere with your practise. Praise yourself for practising regularly, and don't punish yourself if you miss a practise session; just keep persevering!

Establishing a routine

If your hypnotist teaches you self-hypnosis, she will give you direct advice about how often to practise, and tips for how to get the most with your practise.

As a beginner, you first need to prove that you can induce trance. At this beginning stage, you can keep the hypnosis brief – maybe two or three times a day for 10 to 15 minutes at a time.

Just before bed, and after waking up, are excellent times to practise self-hypnosis.

As you get better at hypnosis, you will get quicker and be able to hypnotise yourself in seconds. But be patient, this takes a good deal of practise.

At the risk of sounding obvious, the secret is to practise as much as you can without overdoing things. If you practise too often you don't give your unconscious enough time to process your previous self-hypnosis session. You must trust that even if you don't get instant results, your unconscious self is working on your goal on its own timetable.

Regular practise, over a period of time, is more effective than huge gaps of time with no practise and then overdoing it in a single day to compensate.

Improving your effectiveness

The main way to deepen your trance is to read scripts, and to see a variety of approaches to the problem, or goal, that you are trying to work on. The Appendix can point you to books and other resources that offer a broad range of techniques.

A technique called *pseudo orientation in time* helps you visualise yourself in the near future, having achieved your goal. Using an hypnotic trance to see yourself in the future without the problem greatly increases your chances for success.

To use the pseudo orientation in time technique, you hypnotise yourself to go into the near future, with the change having been made sometime ago. Then you simply experience the feelings and changes made after achieving your goal. You then return to the present with these feelings of change embedded in your unconscious. (This technique is the bedrock of much hypnotherapy, and was one of the most frequent components of the work of Milton Erickson.)

Practising seeing your problem in the past under hypnosis activates your unconscious to move you towards the solutions and goals you want to achieve. This is one of the most tangible proofs that your hypnosis is working – when you find that you have suddenly solved your problem, without actually mapping out a conscious strategy to do so!

Chapter 15

Meeting the Family: Some Cousins of Hypnotherapy

. . . .

In This Chapter

▶ Understanding why your hypnotherapist may not use hypnotherapy

▶ Reading into eye movements

▶ Finding out about emotional freedom

▶ Explaining Neuro-linguistic Programming

. . . .

*E*very family is composed of a wide variety of relatives. Some get along very well, some not so well, and some are in complete disagreement over one thing or another. Therapy is very similar to such a family, with many branches and many differing points of view. When you come for therapy yourself, you generally expect to see one member of that family. But don't be surprised if you turn up on the doorstep to find that one or more cousins have turned up too.

Your hypnotherapist is a very skilled person who has gone through several years of training and skill building by the time you book your appointment to see him. Much of that training and skill building has obviously been in hypnotherapy; after all, he is a hypnotherapist! However, you may also find that your therapist is trained in other powerful therapy techniques too, and may wish to use them with you during your therapy consultation.

Always seek out a properly trained therapist. After all, you want to put yourself into qualified hands when sorting out your issues. That means that you want to ensure that your therapist has been properly trained not only in hypnotherapy, but also in any other therapy technique that he uses. See Chapter 12 for complete advice on finding a hypnotherapist.

There is more to all these techniques than what is covered in this chapter. This chapter only gives you an idea of what to expect, but fortunately there are many good books available if you want to find out more.

Looking at Reasons to Use Something Other Than Hypnotherapy

Being curious people, many hypnotherapists are drawn towards other therapies, wanting to find out more about them, and possibly seeking out training in their methods. Even though we are hypnotherapists, we acknowledge that there are other powerful therapy techniques that can help our patients to resolve their particular problems. From our point of view, some of these techniques are closely associated with hypnotherapy, although purists within those fields may argue otherwise!

So, does that mean your hypnotherapist is Jack-of-all-trades and master of none? No, absolutely not. Just as a doctor or architect has a range of skills – some relating directly to medicine or architecture, and others not so closely related – so too does your hypnotherapist. That doesn't mean that if your therapist only practices hypnotherapy, he isn't any good. Far from it; it just means that he has chosen to focus solely on the use of hypnotherapy as his therapeutic tool.

You may be thinking that hypnotherapy may not be as good as it's cracked out to be, if hypnotherapists use other therapies. Rest assured, it doesn't quite go like that. Hypnotherapy is just as good, and can do just about anything that these other techniques can do, too. So, why use them? Well, there can be many reasons, including:

✔ **You are not responding to hypnotherapy.** For some reason or other, hypnotherapy is not working for you, and your therapist may suggest that you try a different technique.

✔ **Your therapist wants to give you something to take away with you.** The ability to bring on a positive feeling at will is very useful, so your therapist may want to include *anchoring* from Neuro-linguistic Programming (NLP), or *tapping* from Emotional Freedom Technique (EFT), as part of your therapy (both therapies have their own section later in the chapter).

✔ **The technique may help to enhance your hypnotherapy.** If, for example, you are working through a trauma, your therapist may want to include something like the great trauma-buster technique Eye Movement Desensitisation and Reprocessing (EMDR), at some point.

✔ **Your therapist's personal preference.** Hypnotherapists are only human, and we all have techniques that we favour, or find exciting to use. Your therapist may choose to use a technique just for this reason. Don't worry; he only uses it if he knows that it is of direct benefit to you!

✔ **Your personal belief system.** You may have Eastern beliefs and your therapist may want to help your therapy along by linking into those beliefs, especially if he is trained in techniques such as Emotional Freedom Technique (EFT) or Thought Field Therapy (TFT), that use concepts derived from the Chinese acupuncture system.

The main core of your therapy is hypnotherapy. The cousins are brought in to supplement or enhance whatever you are doing in order to help you towards a full resolution of your problem.

Asking why your hypnotherapist isn't using hypnotherapy

Your therapist always makes sure that you consent to the use of any technique he may consider using.

If you are at all concerned that he may be using a different method without you realising it, then simply ask your therapist what is going on. Ask him what technique he is using, and why he is using it. Any reputable therapist should be quite up front about the whole thing, and give you a simple explanation as to what he is doing and why.

Making sure that you understand what your hypnotherapist is doing

Whenever you go for hypnotherapy it is important that you have an understanding of what is happening, as well as of the process being used. The same proviso applies when your hypnotherapist uses a technique other than hypnotherapy.

For a start, it's just common courtesy on behalf of your therapist to keep you informed. But further to this, there may be a good reason why you don't want a technique used. For example, you may have eye problems, and the eyetracking movements of EMDR may cause you discomfort. Or perhaps you don't like being touched, and you would find the tapping of the meridian points on your body during TFT or EFT annoying. Or you may have fallen foul of some annoying door-to-door salesman and find the language patterns of NLP irritating!

Just remember, the basic rule of thumb for any therapy is that you find it acceptable. If you feel pressured into doing it, then it just isn't going to work! Your mind puts up a barrier to it; you feel frustrated or annoyed, and in the end you're wasting your hard-earned money.

On the other hand, when you have an understanding of what is going on and have consented, then your mind is open to the technique and you should find it a marvellous addition to your hypnotherapy.

Gazing at Eye Movement Desensitisation and Reprocessing (EMDR)

Oh boy, is this a powerful and impressive technique! EMDR is very useful in helping people overcome the wide variety of effects that trauma can leave.

Trauma is the psychological effects of having been through or witnessed some terrible event. The effects of trauma can be long lasting, disrupting a person's life for many years, and in many different ways.

In a nutshell, *EMDR* is a technique that allows you to confront and work through disturbing memories using eye movements. No surprise there, considering the full name of EMDR: Eye Movement Desensitisation and Reprocessing.

Walking into EMDR

EMDR was developed in the late 1980s, by psychologist Francine Shapiro who, as the story goes, was wandering through a park one day pondering some nasty thoughts. She noticed that as she was thinking them through, they began to disappear. When she again retrieved those thoughts, she also noticed that they didn't seem to have the same power as they did previously. Being the psychologist that she is, she started to examine what was happening, and noticed that as the disturbing thoughts came

into her mind, her eyes started to move rapidly from left to right. This appeared to cause a shift in the way she related to the thought, stripping it of its power to disturb her.

Ever the scientist, she went off to her laboratory and began to experiment with this concept; that eye movements could alter the way we relate to our memories. Over several years she developed the technique we now know as Eye Movement Desensitisation and Reprocessing, or EMDR for short.

To understand what this technique involves, take a closer look at what that name means. The eye movement bit comes from you following your therapist's fingers with your eyes. The desensitisation and reprocessing happens as you do this. Your therapist asks you to follow his fingers with your eyes, and at the same time, asks you to think of the worst part of the disturbing memory (called the *node*), for example. He may also tell you to focus on a positive belief you want to have that you don't hold at the moment because of the incident you are thinking about, or on the feelings you have in your body as you think of that incident. By doing so, the process of working through and resolving how you feel about the memory begins, eventually allowing you to come to terms with whatever it is you are working on.

EMDR is not just about resolving traumas. It can also help you overcome a phobia in a very similar way.

Now, don't be surprised if you find that your therapist doesn't use eye movements. In her researches, Francine Shapiro, the psychologist who developed EMDR, found that rhythmical tapping on the left and right hands works too. She even found that rhythmical sounds in your left and right ears also do the job. It's still EMDR (Finger Clicking in the Ears Desensitisation and Reprocessing doesn't seem to have the same ring to it). And if your therapist is a technophile, you may find that he uses a snazzy machine that does the finger movements, or hand tapping, or even makes the sounds for him too (not that we think he is lazy . . .).

Eyeing EMDR's theories

How EMDR works is steeped in many theories, and to help in your understanding of we set out the main ones in the following subsections.

Information processing

This theory springs from the idea that there is a natural system within the brain that can process information about traumatic or upsetting events. When we experience one of these, our brain effectively separates the event from the rest of our mind. Certain memories, feelings, and thoughts are corralled away, helping us to deal effectively with what is happening. Over a period of time this material is slowly and safely allowed to join the rest of the mind through a process of talking about the event, dreaming about it, thinking about it; allowing us to eventually come to terms with what happened.

You have a nasty row with your partner. You are furious with them. As the days go by, you mull things over in your mind, perhaps bending the ear of a good friend over a drink, dreaming about what happened when you sleep at night. After some time (and perhaps a romantic make-up meal for two), the row doesn't seem to affect you in quite the same way as it used to. In effect, your information processing system has allowed your mind to heal from the upset.

Okay, so what happens when it all goes wrong? What if, for whatever reason, the information processing system doesn't come into play, and the corralled material remains penned in? Well, some serious problems can occur. That trapped material is certainly not happy sitting there and tries to get the rest of the mind to take notice of it. Unfortunately, it won't be too subtle with the way it goes about it. You may find yourself experiencing panic attacks, flashbacks, or a whole variety of other psychological nasties that continue until the material is safely allowed to join the rest of your mind.

The corralled material needs to be let out safely, and EMDR does this by a form of accelerated information processing. In other words, it kick-starts the mind's natural process of assimilating the material, and then allows it to do so very rapidly and safely.

Memory channels

The idea of memory channels is central to EMDR. This theory has it that the mind stores information in a series of related memory channels, a bit like a filing system.

So, a memory channel may contain an image of a particular event from your past. Associated with this memory channel are others that contain related thoughts, feelings, and images. In order to be comfortable with a particular memory, all its associated memory channels need to be flowing freely. When your mind corrals information, it causes the associated memory channels to block, resulting in a back pressure of problems.

EMDR is a bit like a psychological plumber. It comes in and clears out the blockages in the memory networks, allowing the information to again be associated, accelerating the natural information processing system.

Wagging a finger: EMDR in action

Enough of theories! What happens if you agree to have EMDR? Well, to start with, there's a lot of finger wagging! Intrigued? Then read on.

There are several approaches to working with EMDR, and which one is used depends on whether your trauma was recent, or occurred several years ago. Specific methods are used to help you work through a phobia as well. But, whichever method is used, it has the same basic components as all the others. These components are holding your trauma or upset in place, and your therapist helps you to safely work through each of them, using the eye movements:

- ✔ **Node:** This is the picture you're asked to bring up in your mind, which represents the worst part of the traumatic incident you are working through. For example, if your trauma is a car accident, your node may be the image of your car crashing into a tree.

- ✔ **Negative belief:** This is the image you have about yourself in the present, as you think of that incident. For example, as you think about that crash, you may believe that you are a useless person.

- ✔ **Positive belief:** This is the belief you want to have – a positive belief to replace the negative one. For example, I am a worthwhile person.

- ✔ **A scale of your feelings:** As you think of the node and the negative belief together, your therapist asks you to rate the level of the feelings that bother you on a scale of 0 to 10, where 0 is no disturbance and 10 is the worst disturbance you can imagine.

- ✔ **A scale of how much you believe in your positive belief:** Your therapist asks you to rate how much you believe in your positive belief, on a scale of 0 to 10, where 0 is 'I don't believe it', and 10 is 'I completely believe it.'

- ✔ **The sensations in your body as you think about the incident:** Your therapist asks you to notice if you have any sensations in your body as you think of the node and the negative belief. For example, you may feel tension in your stomach.

Tuning into Thought Field Therapy (TFT)

Before looking towards the East in order to understand a little about the next cousin, a visit to the good old US of A is first necessary.

Developed during the late 1970s and early 1980s by the California cognitive psychologist Roger Callahan, Thought Field Therapy is a technique primarily used to treat anxiety conditions such as trauma, fears, and phobias.

At the basis of its approach is the intriguing idea, borrowed from Chinese medicine, that we all have energy flowing through us along pathways called *meridians*. Chinese medicine claims that these meridians, along with various points scattered along them, known as meridian points (around about 365 of them in all!), are very important in the maintenance of both physical and psychological health. Get a blockage or disruption in the flow of energy along one of these pathways, and ill health or psychological disturbance is the result. Dr Callahan theorised that blockages could occur in the energy flow as a result of disturbing thought patterns, such as feeling anxious or being traumatised.

In acupuncture (a branch of Chinese medicine), the practitioner inserts needles into various meridian points and gives them a little twiddle in order to free up the blockage. Not being keen on skewering his patients, Dr Callahan discovered that gently tapping on certain meridian points frees up the flow of energy, as well as wiping out the unpleasant feeling associated with your trauma, fear, or phobia.

A few definitions can help in understanding TFT:

✔ **Thought field:** An invisible field created by thought. If you're a bit sceptical about the concept of fields, remember that there are such things as invisible magnetic fields and gravity fields, so why shouldn't there be thought fields?

TFT theorists believe that each thought has its own particular thought field, created by the energy zooming round your body along the meridians. The thought field reproduces the biological and psychological responses that occurred when the event we are thinking about actually happened.

If you have a phobia of spiders, you react with fright when you see a spider. Various things happen to your body, such as your nervous system releasing adrenaline and your mind creating statements such as 'Oh my gosh! That thing is HORRIBLE!' When you subsequently think about that event, a thought field is created that causes your body and mind to respond as if the spider were actually there.

✔ **Perturbation:** To put it simply, this weird word refers to the power that generates the changes made by a thought field. If you can remove a perturbation, then you can think about something without those nasty feelings occurring. You thereby lessen the impact of the trauma, fear, or phobia.

If you remove the perturbations that cause you to react with fear when you think about spiders, then you are able to think about them calmly. When you see a spider, the perturbations are no longer active, so you react calmly and hey presto, your phobia is gone!

✔ **Algorithms:** The very precise tapping patterns carried out on a variety of meridian points to eliminate perturbations and free up the flow of energy along the meridians to alleviate your symptom.

What can you expect if your hypnotherapist uses TFT with you? The first thing to point out is that it doesn't hurt! The tapping is gentle, and normally you're the one doing the tapping.

Your therapist asks you to think about whatever it is that is disturbing you; spiders for example. You are then asked to rate your level of anxiety on a scale of 0 to 10, where 0 is no anxiety and 10 is AAARRRGGHH! You're then asked to tap on a variety of specific meridian points, as determined by an algorithm, and every so often to rate how you feel on the 0 to 10 scale. The idea is that, as you tap and eliminate the perturbations, you gently slide down the scale until you reach 0; no anxiety!

You may be reading this with some scepticism, but remember you are probably reading this with a Westerners point of view. In the East, these ideas have been around for a very long time, helping to keep the population very healthy indeed. So suspend your scepticism and give TFT a try if it's offered. Who knows, it may just work for you!

Feeling Out the Emotional Freedom Technique (EFT)

The younger sibling of TFT (see the preceding section), Emotional Freedom Technique (EFT), was developed by personal development coach Gary Craig, who was trained in the use of TFT by its founder, Dr Callahan.

Craig took the concepts of TFT and revised them. Instead of tapping on the 365 or so meridian points, Craig's method focuses on the more manageable number of 11. Dispensing with TFT's scale of anxiety, he added the use of the patient voicing positive affirmations, as they tapped away to relieve blockages in the meridians.

There are several variations to the type of affirmation used in EFT, but an affirmation goes something along the lines of 'Even though I have this phobia of spiders, I deeply and completely accept myself.' Sound a bit happy-clappy, daffy-sappy? Try it out. It never hurts to say something positive to yourself, with or without the tapping!

Talking about Neuro-linguistic Programming (NLP)

Probably hypnotherapy's closest cousin, NLP was developed during the 1970s by two people: Richard Bandler, who had a background in psychology, and John Grinder, who had a background in linguistics. They studied other therapists' work (see the nearby sidebar, 'Looking to others for NLP's beginning') to develop their own method. NLP helps you challenge negative thoughts and beliefs about yourself and the world around you whilst helping to create positive attitudes that free you from problems that beset you as you journey through life.

Apart from being used in therapy, NLP is also used in:

- ✔ **Education** to help people develop strategies that allow them to learn more efficiently.

- ✔ **Business** to build rapport and communication skills. You know those annoying door-to-door salespeople? Well they've probably been trained in the communications aspects of NLP.

- ✔ **Law** to develop persuasive language patterns, and to understand the verbal and behavioural responses of judge, jury, accused, and so on.

A book we recommend on all things NLP is *Neuro-linguistic Programming For Dummies* by Romilla Ready and Kate Burton (Wiley).

Looking to others for NLP's beginning

The founders of NLP, Richard Bandler and John Grinder, originally set out to understand the patterns of therapy used by three famous therapists who consistently had good results with their patients. Their intention was to study these patterns, and to eventually be able to teach them to other therapists. The three therapists they scrutinised are:

- ✔ **Fritz Pearls,** the founder of a school of psychotherapy known as Gestalt.

- ✔ **Virginia Satir,** a very successful family therapist.

- ✔ **Milton Erickson,** a hypnotherapist around whose techniques the school of hypnotherapy, known as Ericksonian hypnosis, was built.

Bandler and Grinder were also influenced by the ideas of Gregory Bateson, an anthropologist who wrote extensively on subjects such as systems theory and psychotherapy.

Digging into the name

The two colleagues gave their work the rather laborious title of Neuro-linguistic Programming, which was not surprisingly shortened to NLP. Apart from looking impressive (and perhaps a little scary), this rather cumbersome title does have a meaning:

- ✔ **Neuro:** Refers to the mind, but particularly to the use of the senses of sight, hearing, smell, taste, and touch, to explore the world.
- ✔ **Linguistic:** Refers to the use of language to communicate externally with the world, and internally to sort out thoughts and behaviours.
- ✔ **Programming:** The communications that humans use internally create programmes that in turn organise thoughts, ideas, and behaviours, into something that produces outcomes and results.

Phew! To put it even more simply, *NLP is a way of making changes to your experience of life by examining and altering your own self communication, as well as the communications you have with others.*

Looking at NLP in practice

Of the plethora of techniques that NLP has to offer, your hypnotherapist may use any, or all, of those we outline in the following subsections.

Making meta modelling clear

Meta modelling, to put it simply, uses language to clarify language. In other words, this technique helps you to be more precise when talking to your hypnotherapist.

Normal communication tends to cut down on long-winded explanations. You use words and phrases that have a general meaning and convey a sense of what you are experiencing.

This is fine for day-to-day interactions, but when it comes to therapy, such generalities just won't do. Your therapist needs to have as complete an understanding of what you are experiencing as possible, in order to design an approach to your therapy personalised for you. Saying something like 'I feel bad' may mean a lot to you, but it doesn't convey very much to your therapist. Your view of 'bad' may be very different from your therapist's. He wants to know precisely what you mean by 'bad', and will ask you to define your experience of 'bad', so that he doesn't have to make his own interpretation.

Tying down anchoring

Anchoring is a very useful technique that, amongst other things, helps you to get in contact with positive feelings almost instantly, whenever you want them.

Your therapist helps you to associate (or *anchor*) the positive feelings you're seeking to a specific action, such as squeezing your thumb and index finger together – something that you can do easily and unobtrusively, whenever you want to call up that changed feeling.

The association is made by your therapist asking you to fully remember the feelings you had at a time when, for example, you felt really positive and happy. When you are experiencing these feelings at their peak, your therapist asks you to squeeze your thumb and index finger together. By repeating this procedure several times, you begin to develop a conditioned response (or set an anchor as they call it in NLP speak), which allows you to achieve this specific feeling each and every time you squeeze those fingers together.

After the anchor is set, the next time you are feeling negative about some situation, you give a little squeeze and enjoy that wonderful glow of positive feelings spreading through your mind and body.

Watching for eye accessing cues

This interesting technique helps your therapist to understand how you are thinking at any one moment in time. No, we don't mean that he is reading your mind; rather that through observing you, he understands how you represent things in your mind. By watching you, your therapist can determine whether you are remembering something and seeing it as a picture in your mind, or are constructing sounds in your mind, or remembering feelings. How does he do this? As we said, by observation, specifically by watching the position of your eyes as you think.

It is thought that the position of the eyes at any one moment is an indication of how you're thinking about, or processing, information. Robert Dilts (a well-known figure in NLP circles) conducted research that showed that there are recognisable eye movement patterns associated with the way people process information. Table 15-1 lists eye movements and their associations.

Table 15-1	Eye Cues
Eye movement	*Meaning*
Up and to the left	Remembering images
Up and to the right	Constructing images
Looking straight ahead	Remembering or constructing images
Horizontally to the left	Remembering sounds
Horizontally to the right	Constructing sounds
Down and to the left	Mentally talking to yourself
Down and to the right	Experiencing feelings

So if you catch your therapist looking with interest into your eyes, he is doing nothing more than observing your eye accessing cues!

Going for the fast phobia cure

A famous one, this one, and one that often comes up when people talk about NLP. The *fast phobia cure* is a dissociation technique (Chapter 2 talks about the technique) that helps you rapidly eliminate your phobia.

The fast phobia cure works by having you take your mental representation of the phobia and to play around with it as you run the events backwards and forwards in your mind. By doing so, you disrupt the way your mind holds on to your phobia, and the fear evaporates away. The technique follows these steps:

1. **Your therapist asks you to imagine that you are sitting in the projection booth of a cinema, looking down into the auditorium, watching yourself sitting in a seat looking at the cinema screen.**

   (We said it was dissociation!).

2. **You're told that on the cinema screen is a projected image of yourself, just before you experience whatever you're phobic about.**

3. **Your therapist asks you to run the film forward, perhaps in blackand white, as you watch yourself in that phobic situation.**

4. **At the end of the situation, your hypnotherapist asks you to freeze the film and jump into it.**

   (Remember, it's dissociation.)

5. **You're then told to run the film backwards, very rapidly, in colour.**

6. **You repeat this process a few times.**

By the end of the process, you are, hopefully, free of your phobia.

Cuing up the swish technique

This powerful little technique is very useful if you want to eliminate bad habits, or unwanted behaviours. Your therapist uses the following steps:

1. **You're asked to create a picture in your mind of whatever it is that triggers the habit or behaviour.**

   This is known as the *cue picture*.

2. **You're asked to create a picture in your mind of what you would like to have instead of the habit or behaviour.**

   Known as the *outcome picture*, it may be healthy nails for nail-biters, or clean lungs for smokers, for example.

3. **You're asked to make the outcome picture very small, and to place it into the corner of the cue picture.**

4. **You're told that when your therapist says 'Swish', you are to, very quickly, expand the outcome picture so that it covers the cue picture.**

   You repeat this step several times.

By the end, having smashed through the cue picture with the outcome picture, you find that your habit or behaviour has significantly changed for the better.

Part V
The Part of Tens

The 5th Wave   By Rich Tennant

"I don't mean to appear unenlightened, Mr. Grove, but I don't think this is the time to explore alternative forms of treatment."

In this part . . .

The Part of Tens provides helpful lists of useful information under themed topics. Read this part to put to rest any misconceptions you may have about hypnotherapy; and find out more about the founders and history of hypnotherapy. We also advise you on qualities to look for in a professional hypnotherapist. Finally, you'll discover ten tips for finding a good training programme in case this book has inspired you to become a hypnotherapist yourself.

Chapter 16

Ten Common Misconceptions about Hypnotherapy

. . . .

In This Chapter

▶ Debunking the magical, mystical illusions

▶ Realising that hypnosis is safe and easy

▶ Understanding that you're in control

. . . .

*O*ur experience as hypnotherapists and trainers tells us that people often have similar types of misconceptions about hypnosis. Some may sense that their beliefs about hypnosis are inaccurate, but a small part of them still believes in the misconceptions. Typically, we hear something like, 'I know it sounds ridiculous but . . . (fill in your misconception here)'.

These inaccurate beliefs may prevent people who could actually benefit from hypnotherapy from seeking help. Perhaps some of these misunderstandings play a part in holding you back from seeking hypnotherapy.

Understanding misconceptions about hypnosis can alleviate your fears about being hypnotised, so in this chapter we list the misconceptions that we have come across most frequently, in no particular order.

Hypnosis Is Magical and Mystical

Throughout history, hypnosis has often been connected with the occult. The concept of hypnosis having an occult connection has often been the image perpetuated by some of the earliest known practitioners, the Egyptian priest-hood, who entranced religious followers.

Magic and hypnotism were often linked by people who wanted to invoke a fearful sense of power and control over others. Hollywood movies and low-brow fiction also contributed to the idea of the hypnotic bogeyman. Often the underlying implication is that the public should be afraid – be very afraid – of anyone who wielded the evil 'hypnotic eye'.

Consequently, even today people erroneously believe that hypnotherapists have a power that allows them to manipulate others, but this is simply not true!

The reality is that trance is a natural state of mind. Hypnosis is any technique that brings about trance. In actual practice, all hypnosis is self-hypnosis – you can't be hypnotised unless you are willing. Hypnotherapy is simply a way of using trance to help with problems. Nothing mystical involved at all.

Of course, the results of good clinical hypnotherapy may *seem* like magic once you are rapidly relieved of your problem, or achieve your goal with ease!

You're Under the Power of the Hypnotherapist

This misconception is related to the one that says hypnosis is magical and mystical. The idea is probably influenced by stage hypnotists who *appear* to have power over those they hypnotise. Just keep in mind that people in stage hypnosis acts are willing participants. Hypnosis is really just self-hypnosis and the participants in a stage hypnosis show choose to join in – even if they appear not to.

It is simply not true that a hypnotist has any control over you. No hypnotherapist can make you do anything that you don't want to do, or anything that is not in character.

Hypnosis Is Dangerous

Hypnosis in itself is not dangerous. You are particularly safe when working with qualified hypnotherapists. You are always in control and can come out of trance whenever you want.

One caveat we offer is to avoid personal involvement with unqualified hypnotherapists and stage hypnotists. Unscrupulous people, who have had only minimal instruction in trance induction, often set themselves up as hypnotists without understanding the complexities of psychological problems. This is not the type of practitioner you want to seek help from. (See Chapter 12 for tips on choosing a qualified hypnotherapist.) A qualified hypnotherapist will ensure that you are taken care of emotionally and will treat you with care, dignity, and respect.

Hypnosis Makes You Cluck like a Chicken and Lose Control

Now is the time to draw distinctions between stage hypnosis and clinical hypnotherapy. Stage hypnosis is about entertainment and laughs. Clinical hypnotherapy is about helping you with problems, or achieving goals. A stage hypnotist simply uses hypnosis for a laugh. A clinical hypnotherapist is serious about working with *your* stated goals.

Keep in mind that the stage hypnotist carefully selects who comes up on stage. Usually compliant extrovert types are ideal for a stage hypnotist. The people chosen are willing to do any silly things suggested to them.

Stage hypnotists may vary in their qualifications and hypnosis experience. Some may even be qualified hypnotherapists, but a stage hypnotist will never treat you with the individual respect and attention you get within the context of one-on-one clinical hypnotherapy.

You Have to Keep Your Eyes Closed and Stay Completely Still

Anyone can move while in a hypnotised state. You may need to scratch an itch, and that's perfectly all right. It doesn't break the trance state.

Although a lot of trance induction involves closing your eyes and being in a relaxed state, this is not always the case.

Athletes are often in trance while competing in sports. An athlete seeking hypnotherapy in order to enhance her sporting performance, will not be asked to close her eyes or to relax. A hypnotist works with such an athlete by bringing about an *alert trance*. This type of trance is more about recalling past peak performances while the eyes are open and movement is occurring. Relaxation and improved sporting performance are not compatible! Can you imagine running a race or playing any competitive sport in a super-relaxed state? You need the 'edge' to perform well.

Similarly, children who come for hypnosis can go into trance even when their eyes are wide open and they're moving around. (Chapter 9 is devoted to children and hypnotherapy).

Also, clients for whom eye closure or relaxation is a threatening occurrence, such as those who suffer panic attacks or have issues of severe trauma, may not be given suggestions to relax or close their eyes because this may invoke the very state of fear that they are seeking treatment for.

Hypnosis Is Therapy

Hypnosis is not therapy, it is a therapeutic technique. Hypnosis can be used as a tool, or a complement, to various types of therapy and counselling.

Hypnotherapy is the therapeutic aspect of hypnosis. Hypnotherapy can be combined to work very powerfully with a range of counselling approaches – even forms that are contradictory in their approach such as behavioural therapies, which don't recognise the concept of the unconscious, and psychodynamic approaches, which do.

You May Not Wake Up from Trance

What wakes you up in the morning? If you said 'My alarm clock', you're missing the point. You always wake up from each night's sleep – even when your alarm clock doesn't ring. Similarly, you always awaken from trance. Remember, trance is not like being in a coma and is not sleep. Trance is a natural state that you enter several times a day while you daydream, exercise, or focus intently on a problem at work. You return to a 'normal' state of non-trance after each trance state. So, if you think about it, you have a daily practice of awakening from trance states – several times a day!

We admit that it's a bit of a contradiction to use the word *awaken* for a state that is not sleep. However, this is common terminology that hypnotherapists also use, even though all are aware that hypnosis isn't the same state as sleep. It's just one of the widespread paradoxes that has become commonplace!

Likewise, you can come out of a hypnotic trance state at anytime that you wish. A qualified hypnotherapist will look after you and carefully bring you out of trance.

You Go to Sleep during a Hypnosis Session

Don't worry, your hypnotherapist won't let you fall asleep. You remain quite aware of your surroundings, even in trance, and may even hear sounds both inside and outside the room you're in – a fact that can help you feel safe and allow yourself to enter trance.

You may be surprised that you clearly recall what was said to you during the session.

Some People Can't Be Hypnotised – Even if They Want to Be

Most people can be hypnotised – except those who really don't want to be. Sometimes fear and misconceptions about hypnosis can create an unconscious resistance. This is why a qualified hypnotherapist will take a lot of time, the first time you meet, to answer your questions and earn your trust before any hypnosis takes place.

You Don't Need a Hypnotist – You Can Hypnotise Yourself

The main thing we emphasise in this book is the need to work with a hypnotherapist before trying self-hypnosis. Even then we would not wholeheartedly recommend – as other books do – that you practise hypnotherapy on yourself.

It is practically impossible to work on your own unconscious problems unaided. Even experienced hypnotherapists seek help from others to work on their deeper psychological issues.

However, once you experience hypnosis with a hypnotherapist, you are in a stronger position to decide when, and when not, to apply self-hypnosis. (For more information on self-hypnosis, turn to Chapter 14.)

Chapter 17

Ten Pioneers of Hypnosis

*I*t is difficult to say exactly *who* started hypnosis. Most researchers and historians agree that all cultures have induced trance in some form since humans began communicating.

Especially popular is the idea that hypnosis has always had a connection with religion, as it was possible through hypnosis to create a sensation of religious ecstasy through suggestion. In these cases, the aim was not about giving up smoking or losing weight, but rather to be filled with spiritual bliss!

Hypnosis techniques can be observed in many modern day religious and political practices with particularly enthusiastic or charismatic speakers. After reading this book, you will be an astute observer of trance induction, and capable of spotting when and how a speaker induces a trance within an audience. This style was employed by early practitioners, especially Franz Mesmer, who was very 'showbiz' in his style.

This chapter concentrates on ten prominent individuals who influenced hypnotherapy as we apply it today in clinical/therapeutic applications. Many of the early contributions involved legitimising hypnosis – removing its occult or entertainment associations – and making it more acceptable to a scientific community. So it's no surprise that most of the people in this list are doctors or psychologists.

Franz Mesmer (1734–1815)

Frederick (Franz) Anton Mesmer was an Austrian physician who, in 1766, wrote 'The Influence of the Stars and Planets on the Human Body'. This essay developed the concept of *animal magnetism* – a belief that the planets, stars, and the moon affect not only the tides of the earth's waters but the predominantly liquid substance in humans, and in all plants and animals, through an invisible, magnetic energy.

The terms *mesmerism* and *mesmerise*, which refer to the act or condition of being enchanted or fascinated, come into the language through Franz Mesmer.

Mesmer believed that placing magnets directly on a person provided his many medical successes. His technique also involved stroking the patient's entire body until the 'animal magnetism' was transferred from the 'operator' to the 'subject', sometimes using a wand to release the energy. Mesmer actually hypnotised people through direct suggestions to heal themselves.

People would easily go into trance given Mesmer's over-the-top, flamboyant style – a bit like fainting to escape an overwhelming experience.

Due to his crowd-pleasing act and his success in healing, Mesmer became very popular with patients. Needless to say, this bizarre new type of healing was not as popular with the medical professionals of the day, and in 1778 he was struck off the medical register and run out of Vienna. However, he moved to Paris, where he became even more famous and even received the patronage of Marie Antoinette.

James Braid (1796–1860)

James Braid initiated the legitimisation of hypnosis with the British and European medical professions. Braid was a surgeon who, like most of his medical colleagues, was initially a sceptic of mesmerism. He accidentally discovered that, by getting patients to fix their view on a single point, he could induce a hypnotic trance. He later achieved trance by asking his patients to stare at his shiny scalpel case. He would move the shiny case in all directions before the patient's eyes, while insisting the client keep his head still and follow the case with his eyes only. This method of inducing hypnosis through fixed focal concentration is still in use today.

As Braid began to understand his accidental discovery of hypnotic trance induction, he came to the conclusion that mesmerism was not a valid concept. He published attacks on Mesmer's ideas about animal magnetism energies having curative powers. Braid wanted to give his understanding of this healing process a more scientific basis.

In 1842, Braid invented the word *hypnotism* in a paper he wrote to discredit mesmerism and animal magnetism (see the earlier section on Franz Mesmer). However, his paper, titled 'Practical Essay on the Curative Agency of Neuro-Hypnotism', was rejected by the British Medical Association. He nevertheless persisted to present his ideas in the form of a series of lectures and public demonstrations.

In 1843, Braid published *Neurypnology, or the Rationale of Nervous Sleep*. In this book he proposed that the phenomenon be called *neurohypnotism* rather than mesmerising. He also mistakenly referred to hypnosis as a 'condition of nervous sleep'. This is actually inaccurate as hypnosis is not the same condition as sleep, producing different types of brain waves. However, Braid's most important contribution was that he moved the world away from practice of animal magnetism and towards hypnosis.

Hippolyte Bernheim (1837–1919)

Bernheim, a French physician, incorrectly viewed hypnosis as a special form of sleeping, in which the patient focused on the suggestions made by the hypnotist. His important contribution is that he emphasised the psychological nature of hypnosis, thereby moving it away from its occult and magic associations and more towards a psychological and medical model – a crucial step in the legitimisation of hypnosis.

James Esdaile (1808–59)

Esdaile, a Scottish physician with the East India Company, was the first to document the use of hypnosis as a surgical anaesthetic in 1845. As the head of the Native Hospital in Hooghly, Bengal, he performed hundreds of surgical operations using hypnosis as the sole anaesthetic. Many of the surgical procedures were quite serious, including amputations and the removal of large tumours. His method of induction would last anywhere from two to eight hours. Sadly, this property of hypnosis fell into disuse and was forgotten with the invention of modern anaesthetic drugs.

Jean-Martin Charcot (1825–93)

Charcot, a brilliant French physician and neurologist, was named as the Superintendent of Salpêtrière Hospital in 1862, then the largest hospice in Europe with a population of over 5,000 'incurables'. He raised the profile of hypnosis within the medical profession by his extensive clinical work in neurology at the hospital. He hypnotised his patients in order to deliberately develop hysteria within them and thus document the treatability and psychological nature of the illness. However, he also got it badly wrong. He thought hypnosis was a symptom of a mental illness, which he termed *hysteria*. Freud hung out at his psychiatric hospital for a while and learned a limited form of hypnosis from observing Charcot's work.

Pierre Janet (1859–1947)

French philosopher, physician, and psychologist Pierre Janet was personally selected by Charcot (see the preceding section) to serve as Director of the Laboratory of Pathological Psychology at the hospital at Salpêtrière. He later served as Professor of Experimental and Comparative Psychology at the College of France.

Janet made important discoveries and contributions in the study of hysterical neuroses with the use of hypnosis. He viewed hypnosis as a helpful investigative and therapeutic tool in helping his patients with dissociative conditions. He thought hypnosis itself was a form of dissociation. He found that patients who could retrieve troublesome memories of their past were often freed of the negative effects associated with the actual event.

Unlike Freud, who gave up on hypnosis after only a few years, Janet believed in it strongly and promoted its benefits during his entire career. He was one of the first to point out the enormous role of suggested beliefs in hysteria. His work led to the theory of neurosis and psychosis by the subconscious persistence of emotional trauma. Janet is also the founder of the analytic tradition in psychology that greatly influenced Freud's psychoanalytic ideas (see the next section).

Janet also contributed significantly to the work of Sigmund Freud. Janet and Freud developed Freud's post-hypnosis ideas. In particular, after Freud abandoned hypnosis, he developed – with Janet's help – his Big Idea, which became known as 'free association'. This technique involved invoking a dream-like state in hysterical patients to allow them to speak directly from their unconscious about whatever came to their minds – especially in relation to their psychological problems. Although this technique is usually attributed to Freud, Janet's influence was considerable.

Sigmund Freud (1856–1939)

Sigmund Freud is best known for developing psychoanalysis. He placed the concept of *dual consciousness* – the idea that each person has conscious and unconscious minds – into modern Western thought and thereby made an important contribution to the field of hypnosis.

Before Freud developed his theory of psychoanalysis, he visited a clinic in Nancy, France, to watch experimental treatments using hypnosis being conducted on psychiatric patients who had been diagnosed as hysterical – mostly women. (Interestingly, the term 'hysteria' is no longer used by psychiatrists.)

Freud was greatly impressed by the fact that hypnosis could help difficult patients access powerfully repressed emotions they otherwise would not have been aware of, or able, to articulate. Freud observed that by recalling some forgotten traumatic experience under hypnosis, many patients seemed to be cured of the emotional problems associated with the experience. In 1895 he and another doctor, Josef Breuer, wrote a book about hypnosis called *Studies in Hysteria*.

At this stage Freud was very keen on hypnosis, but he later abandoned the practice. By his own admission Freud was not very good as a hypnotist. He simply gave up when he had a few failures and was unable to get clients to talk about traumatic events. He didn't have access to the techniques that most hypnotherapists use today to build rapport and make a patient feel safe before recalling – let alone discussing – traumatic events from the past. Freud also realised that simply recalling forgotten memories connected to a current problem did not necessarily remove the patient's problem.

He chose to abandon hypnosis and focus on the patient's avoidance of pain and study how the mind represses difficult feelings. He did this by developing the more active approach of talking to patients that is common in counselling and psychotherapy today. Freud's preference of psychoanalysis over hypnosis dealt a temporary blow to hypnosis . . . at least in Europe.

Clark L. Hull (1884–1952)

Meanwhile, in America, psychologist Clark Hull was conducting extensive experiments in hypnosis in the 1920s and 1930s. Hull greatly de-mystified hypnosis and described it as a normal part of human nature. Hull viewed trance states as a natural part of normal consciousness, no different from daydreaming or reverie. Hull wrote that the patient's imagination played an important role in invoking the trance state. He put forward the idea that some people were more responsive to hypnosis than others. Hull's writings were a major influence on the godfather of modern hypnosis, Milton Erickson.

Milton Erickson (1901–80)

Milton Erickson resurrected and reinvented modern hypnosis after Freud buried it. He is considered the founder of modern hypnotherapy.

Erickson is a fascinating figure, both in his life story as well as the hypnotherapeutic advances he singly developed. He grew up in a rural Midwest American community, partially disabled from polio. He hypnotised himself to overcome the intense pain he experienced as a result of the disease. He also devoured dictionaries (not literally!) and learned the nuances of words.

He later trained as a psychiatrist, but his love of language helped him to develop a conversational style of hypnosis – termed the *permissive style* – that was the antithesis of the old-fashioned authoritarian hypnosis.

Erickson found it easy to hypnotise his patients by letting them talk first about their lives and interests. An expert listener with strong observational skills, Erickson noticed the content and style of speech of his patient and could induce trance simply by adopting a similar style of speech. His therapy sometimes included made-up stories or metaphors that he invented based on the patient's interests.

Erickson was a kindly figure, but he was also very versatile with an extremely unconventional approach to hypnosis. He used authoritarian techniques if that is what the patient could most benefit from. (Don't forget that, like Freud, Erickson was also a psychiatrist, and many people during Erickson's day *expected* their medical men to dominate them.)

Erickson is essentially the cornerstone for the study of modern hypnosis. It would be difficult to meet a hypnotherapist today who was not in some way influenced by Erickson's writings, teachings, audio/video recordings, and methods.

Ernest Rossi (1933–present)

Rossi is an American psychotherapist and teacher who focuses on the mind-body connection in healing. Rossi worked closely with Erickson on several publications.

He is also a widely published author of books and scientific papers on hypnotherapy and healing. His ideas are pioneering in terms of how hypnosis can influence the body even at a cellular level.

Chapter 18

Ten Qualities to Look For in a Hypnotherapist

In This Chapter

▶ Going for certain qualities

▶ Understanding how these qualities can help your therapy

*I*f you are thinking of going to visit a hypnotherapist you want to know that you are going to see someone who is doing their utmost to help get you through whatever issue it is that you are seeing them for. Unfortunately, out there in the big wide world there are many charlatans purporting to be hypnotherapists but who are, in fact, just after your money. Fortunately, there are many others who are professional, well trained, and who offer an exemplary service (and we like to include ourselves in this category!).

Here is a list (in no particular order) of some of the qualities to look for in your hypnotherapist. By taking these into consideration when searching for your therapist, you can separate the wheat from the chaff.

Confidentiality

What is said to your therapist stays with your therapist. In other words, your therapist does not go around telling all and sundry about what went on in the therapy room during your sessions. If your therapist does need to talk to others about your case she'll do so in such a fashion that your identity remains protected.

So, how do you know that your therapist is confidential? A legitimate therapist will be a member of a bona fide ethical organisation and subscribe to the organisation's ethical code of conduct. Ask to see your therapist's ethical code of conduct (check the Appendix for a sample). If she doesn't have one, or subscribe to one that doesn't emphasise confidentiality, then say 'Thanks, but no thanks!'

Honesty

Honesty is the cornerstone on which trust is built. Before you can do therapeutic work, both the therapist and patient need to feel that their communication is open and truthful. Both parties need to feel okay about each other for effective change to occur.

Also, from another angle, honesty is important when understanding the qualifications and experience of your hypnotherapist. Beware of those who claim to hold professional qualifications that they don't really have. Your hypnotherapist should be honest and upfront about her training, experience, and your therapy.

If you have any concerns about what your therapist is saying or claiming, contact her training institution or professional body, and check her out. If your therapist won't let you know the contact details then just say goodbye and seek out a more reputable one.

Well-Trained

Make sure that your therapist is appropriately trained. That means that she has attended a prolonged classroom-based training, balancing theory with practise. Beware the therapist who learned their profession through correspondence courses, or through a single weekend of training, or a similar short course. After all, would you let a doctor loose on your body who had trained in this manner?

Don't be afraid to ask your potential therapist about their training. If they are not forthcoming then beware. Any therapist worth their salt lets you know about it (after all, they are proud of their own achievement) and are more than happy to furnish you with details of their training institution so that you can check them out.

Empathy

Your therapist should be able to understand what you are experiencing with regard to your problem. That means she understands your experience and your feelings and always offers you a professional service reflecting this understanding. Of course, your therapist is not you and only you fully understand your experience. However, through empathy your therapist is able to show a genuine positive regard for you and whatever issue you are seeing them for.

Ethics

Your therapist should always work in an ethical way. That means that their conduct is always appropriate. Your therapist should:

- ✔ Tell you their fee and availability in advance.
- ✔ Explain the process of therapy to you.
- ✔ Answer your questions honestly.
- ✔ Not prolong therapy unnecessarily.
- ✔ Ensure that you are as comfortable as possible during the therapy process.
- ✔ Show a professional regard towards other therapists and therapies.
- ✔ Work within their own level of competence.
- ✔ Ensure the confidentiality of anything that you may tell them.

On top of this, they will always keep their relationship with you at a professional level. In other words, they should neither become friend nor lover! If this happens, then stop seeing them for therapy. What you do afterwards is entirely up to you.

As we repeat throughout this book, all responsible hypnotherapists subscribe to a professional code of ethics, as determined by a professional body or training institution. If you want to know what your therapist's ethical code of conduct is, just ask to see it. The Appendix has a sample code of ethics from the British Society of Clinical Hypnosis.

Experience

How experienced in general is your therapist? How long have they been in practice? How much experience have they had treating your particular symptom? These are all questions you may want to ask. However, length of time in practice on its own does not a good therapist make. You should also find out about their experience of training (see the previous 'Well-Trained' section), what their experience of clinical supervision is and, wherever possible, the experience of other patients. The last point can only be done through talking to someone you know who has been to see your particular therapist. (As a matter of confidentiality your therapist NEVER gives you details of others who have been to see them!).

All helping professionals (counsellors, hypnotherapists, psychotherapists, and the like) undergo *clinical supervision*, which involves going to see another professional in order to discuss cases.

Professionals need to be supported and receive new perspectives on the work they do with their patients. Clinical supervision also ensures that the therapist continues to improve their clinical work to provide the best treatments possible for patients. No matter how experienced a professional, your hypnotherapist should be involved in regular supervision. It's okay to ask if they are.

You may be thinking that it is better to see a seasoned therapist than to see a newly qualified one. Well, that is not necessarily the case. If your therapist has been trained properly, then there will be little difference. However, do take into consideration everything else in this chapter.

Tidiness

Your therapist should be of a smart appearance and keep a tidy therapy room. By doing so, they help you feel comfortable, confident, and at ease, both with them and the process of therapy. Not feeling comfortable in your surroundings results in an adverse effect on your ability to go into trance and enjoy good therapy.

Punctuality

Your hypnotherapist should be punctual for appointments (and that goes for you too!). Obviously, for one reason or another there may be an occasional slight delay to your appointment – we have to be realistic here. But on the whole, you should be able to see your hypnotherapist at the time you have booked. If they are constantly late in starting your appointments, then perhaps question the professional regard they have for you.

Oh, and if you are late for an appointment then don't be surprised if you only get the remaining time allocated for therapy. Don't expect your therapist to delay another patient on your behalf.

Non-Judgemental

Your therapist is not there to judge you! No matter how embarrassing you think your symptom is your therapist has heard it all before. A good therapist listens to what you have to say with genuine empathy (see the previous 'Empathy' section). After all, she is there to help you.

Active Listening

Listening may seem to be an obvious quality to look for in your therapist, as you are talking and your therapist should be listening. However, it is something that is worth highlighting. When listening to what you have to say your therapist should be doing so in an active manner. In other words, she will look as if she is paying attention to you rather than picking her nails or gazing off into space! At the same time, she will be encouraging you to talk further by asking appropriate questions and acknowledging your replies.

Beware the therapist who just loves to talk about herself. Obviously, a little bit of personal banter and history is important and may be relevant, but if she keeps on and on about how wonderful she is and that stunning holiday she just had in Mauritius, then she is not focusing on you and that means that your therapy is more than likely to be less effective.

Chapter 19

Ten Tips for Choosing a Hypnotherapy Training Programme

*P*erhaps you have been for hypnotherapy and your experience has so inspired you that you now want to become a hypnotherapist yourself. Or perhaps you are reading this book because you want to find out about this thing called hypnotherapy before you commit yourself to some training. Either way, this chapter is for you.

If you are thinking of becoming a hypnotherapist, it is important that you choose the right institution to train you. The following list will give you important pointers in helping to make the right decision. After all, you will be parting with your hard-earned money and time, and will want to invest them wisely!

Making Sure the Institution Is Accredited

The institution you are thinking of training with should be accredited by an outside body. Accreditation means that the institution meets a certain standard in training that follows established guidelines.

The sponsorship of some programmes is obvious – for instance, those that fall within the university or government system. Others may be more obscure, but offer genuine and valid accreditation. Whilst others will be bogus, simply taking money so that any Tom, Dick, or Harry can get their course *validated*.

Don't be afraid to investigate what the accrediting body is all about by phoning them up, looking them up on the internet, and so on.

Training for Clinical Hypnosis, NOT Stage Hypnosis!

Remember, you want to train as a clinical hypnotherapist *not* a stage hypnotist. Question the validity of any course that teaches this obnoxious branch of hypnosis. You want to train to help people, not to have others laugh at them!

Of course, many institutions explain the ins and outs of stage hypnosis because you will have to be able to explain it to your patients.

Looking at Length of Training

Find out how long the training takes. If the claim is that you'll be a fully qualified therapist after only one or two weekends, you're wasting your money if you sign on for such a programme. Most bona fide institutions offer training that takes at least a couple of years to reach full qualification.

If you are feeling a little disheartened reading this, don't be. The 'quick route to becoming a therapist' schools are only interested in your money, not in your integrity as a professional therapist. Ask yourself this question: 'Would I be happy seeing a doctor who had only learnt medicine over a couple of weekends?' If your answer is no, then don't go anywhere near these institutions. If your answer is yes, then we think that perhaps you need to pay a visit to a hypnotherapist (a properly trained one at that!).

Going through the Interview Procedure

The institution should interview you before accepting you for training. This is to ensure that you are the right type of person to become a therapist (in other words, not barking mad or a serial killer!). Be upfront about any personal issues you may have, because the interviewer also ensures that training is safe for you. Very few issues would prevent you from training – your interviewer will be able to go over these with you.

Don't forget that the interview is also an opportunity for you to interview your prospective training institution. You need to make sure that the institution's approach is the right one for you. Many institutions allow you to sit in on a lecture to get the feel of the course that you're considering attending. If this courtesy isn't offered, don't be shy about asking for it.

Watch out for those institutions that make wild claims that you can be earning thousands a week by the time you finish training. This is just a ploy to get you to part with your money. The only one making thousands will be the institution! Building a practice takes time and effort, as any reputable training organisation will point out.

Sitting Still for Classroom-Based Training

Correspondence courses are anathema to all genuine therapists! Your training must be classroom based. That means that by far the majority of your training is through lectures and practical sessions, held in a classroom environment by professional therapists and lecturers. Classroom training allows you to question and understand the theory whilst practising in a very safe environment.

Of course, you're also given homework in the form of assignments and required or recommended reading. This is to give you a wider insight and understanding of the material and techniques taught in the classroom.

Checking the Experience, Background, and Variety of Lecturers

Your lecturers are your most important source of knowledge. Find out about their backgrounds and experience as therapists. Most institutions only employ active therapists (and rightly so), as they will be able not only to teach you the theory and techniques, but also give you a wide variety of case examples that put things into context for you.

Having a range of lecturers is also useful, because each therapist has their own individual approach to the way they do therapy. Being taught by different people exposes you to varying styles, helping you to develop as a therapist in your own right.

Getting Help from Tutorials

A very useful addition to any training is the tutorial system, in which you meet up with a tutor outside the classroom to go over course material in order to make sure that you understand it. A session with a tutor also gives you a chance to practise the variety of techniques you have been taught so far.

Tutorials offer a very personal addition to your training, and give you an opportunity to cover aspects of your learning experience that may not be appropriate, or possible, to do in class. Many institutions now have tutorials as a compulsory part of the course curriculum.

Talking to Previous and Current Students

If you want to, your institution should allow you to get in contact with their students or graduates, so that you can get an unbiased opinion of the course you are considering undertaking.

Offering Continuing Professional Development

Look at the training opportunities your prospective training institution offers, for after you have qualified. Continuing professional development is very important, because it allows you to remain fresh and informed throughout your career as a hypnotherapist.

Make sure that the institution you choose offers short courses that allow you to keep abreast of developments in hypnotherapy, or courses that allow you to examine aspects of hypnotherapy in much greater detail.

Supporting You After Training

A respectable institution provides support for its graduates through telephone, Web sites, or clinical supervision. That means that you can always access help on hand to guide you through every difficult case that you have in your therapy room – no matter how long it was since your graduation.

Appendix

Resources

● ●

*T*his Appendix is a little box of delights; a mishmash of useful information that will take your interest in hypnotherapy to the next level.

Hypnotherapy Organisations

These resources are grouped by country, in no particular order.

United Kingdom

British Association of Medical Hypnosis, Suite 296, 28 Old Brompton Road, London SW7 3SS. Tel: 020 8998 4436. Web site: www.bamh.org.uk

The British Society of Clinical Hypnosis has the largest number of highly qualified hypnotherapists in the United Kingdom. 125 Queensgate, Bridlington, North Humberside YO16 7JQ. Tel: 01262 403 103. Web site: www.bsch.org.uk

National Association of Counsellors, Hypnotherapists and Psychotherapists, PO Box 719, Burwell, Cambridge, CB5 0NX. Tel: 0870 850 5383. Web site: www.nachp.org

United States

American Society of Clinical Hypnosis is an interdisciplinary organisation that includes psychologists, psychiatrists, clinical social workers, marriage and family therapists, mental health counsellors, medical doctors, masters-level nurses, and dentists. 140 N. Bloomingdale Road, Bloomingdale, IL 60108-1017, USA. Fax: 630/351-8490. Web site: www.asch.net

American Psychotherapy and Medical Hypnosis Association, 1100 Kittitas Street, Wenatchee, WA 98801, USA. Tel: (509)662-5131. Web site: apmha.com

International Medical and Dental Hypnotherapy Association, 4110 Edgeland, Suite 800, Royal Oak, MI 48073-2285, USA. Tel: (248) 549-5594/(800) 257-5467. Web site: www.imdha.com

National Guild of Hypnotists, PO Box 308, Merrimack, NH, 03054, USA. Tel: (603) 429-9438. Fax: (603) 424-8066. Web site: www.ngh.net

Canada

Canadian Federation of Clinical Hypnosis. Web site: www.csch.org (The organisation is in formative stage so no contact addresses or telephone numbers are available at the moment.)

Professional Board of Hypnotherapy, The Excel Center for Mental Health, #203, 4909 B-48th Street, Red Deer, Alberta, Canada T4N-1S8 Tel: (403) 347-9019 / 1 (888) 686-6163. Web site: www.hypnosiscanada.com

Australia

Australian Society of Clinical Hypnotherapists, PO Box 471, Eastwood, NSW, 2122. Tel: 612 988 4997. Web site: www.asch.com.au

Training Institutions

As hypnotherapy training is usually taught through private colleges in most countries, you won't find many nationally-based schools. If we haven't mentioned a school close to you, then contact the relevant society listed in the previous section, for further details of training being held in your area.

Have a look at Chapter 19 for further tips on what you should be looking for when choosing a hypnotherapy college.

United Kingdom

London College of Clinical Hypnosis (LCCH) holds training courses throughout the United Kingdom. Tel: 020 7486 3939. Web site: www.lcch.co.uk E-mail: info@lcch.co.uk

The **National College of Hypnosis and Psychotherapy** holds training courses in London, Glasgow, Liverpool, and Oxford. Tel: 01282 699378. Web site: www.hypnotherapyuk.net E-mail: info@btconnect.com

United States

Hypnosis Maryland Institute holds training courses in Maryland. Tel: 301-540-6225. Web site: www.hypnosismaryland.com E-mail: lwest52365@aol.com

Hypnotherapy Academy of America holds training courses in Santa Fe. Tel: 505 983 1515. Web site: www.hypnotherapyacademy.com E-mail: info@hypnotherapyacademy.com

Hypnotherapy Training Institute holds training courses in California. Tel: 800 256 6448. Web site: www.hypnotherapy.com E-mail: info@hypnotherapy.com

Midwest Hypnosis Institute holds training courses in Kansas City. Tel: 785-218-9380. Web site: www.midwest-hypnosis.com E-mail: sgriffeth@sunflower.com

Canada

The Orca Institute holds courses in Vancouver, Kelowna, Chase, Victoria, and Calgary. Tel: 1 800 665 6722. Web site: www.orcainstitute.com E-mail: info@orcainstitute.com

Australia

The NSW School of Hypnotic Sciences holds training courses in New South Wales. Tel: 00 61 2 9874 0667. Web site: www.hypnoticsciences.com.au E-mail: nswschhyp@hypnoticsciences.com.au

Malaysia

LCCH Malaysia. Tel: 00 60 (3) 2092 3950. Web site: www.hypnosis-malaysia.com E-mail: info@hypnosis-malaysia.com

Portugal

LCCH Portugal. Tel: 00 351 933 371 32 23. Web site: www.hipnose.net
E-mail: lcchinter@netcabo.pt

Spain

LCCH Iberia. Courses held in Barcelona. Tel: 351 933 371 32 23. Web site:
www.hipnosis-espana.com E-mail: lcchinter@netcabo.pt

Useful Books

The books here are the ones that inspired us and still seem inspirational.
We try to cover a range of hypnosis subjects.

Not all the books in this list are introductory books; some are for people who
have a basic understanding already – perhaps after having read this book and
experienced hypnotherapy for yourself.

The Handbook of Hypnotic Metaphors and Suggestions

Author: D. Corydon Hammond (W W Norton & Co Ltd, 1990).

This is the hypnotherapy bible for many working professionals. Frequently
referred to simply as 'Hammonds', it is without peer and is the most complete reference book available, giving an overview of hypnotherapeutic
scripts and areas of potential treatment. The book has a huge number of
chapters and range of topics.

The book is unique in that it offers a collection of articles written exclusively
by American hypnotherapists (who tend to be all PhDs), who all belong to
the American Society of Clinical Hypnosis (ASCH), which is the main body of
clinical hypnotherapists in America.

The scripts explore a range of techniques and approaches, and many exam-
ples are given under a single chapter heading. Some of the topics include,
'Pain Management', 'Dental Hypnosis', 'Paediatric hypnosis', 'Performance
Enhancement', 'Surgical hypnosis', and many more.

The Wisdom of Milton Erickson: The Complete Volume

Author: Ronald Havens (Crown House Publishing, 2004).

Milton Erickson is the granddaddy of modern hypnosis. Erickson was such a prolific writer that you may find it difficult to know where to begin when reading his works. This book provides an excellent overview to Erickson's writings. It is developed extremely well under a number of topics, and provides many excerpts of Erickson's thinking.

Part One and Two on Human Behaviour and Psychotherapy describe Erickson's thinking and methods. Part Three, 'Hypnosis & Hypnotherapy', discusses Erickson's ideas about hypnotherapy, emphasising the role of the unconscious.

Hartland's Medical and Dental Hypnosis, 3rd Edition

Editor: David Waxman (Bailliere Tindall, 1989).

This is a comprehensive book written by a physician/hypnotist covering the treatment of medical and psychological problems. It is clearly written from the perspective of a medical practitioner, yet uses plain English and avoids the use of medical terminology. For that reason this is a unique book for medical and non-medical hypnotherapists.

It has had subsequent rewritings, but make sure that you obtain the third edition, which was the last edition that sticks to what the original author had written. Although a bit dated, this is required reading in many hypnotherapy training courses.

Hidden Depths: The Story of Hypnosis

Author: Robin Waterfield (Pan Publishers, 2004).

Probably the best researched and most detailed book on the history of hypnosis. The writing is both witty and illuminating. The author delves into a variety of topics, with a particularly interesting examination of Freud's hypnotism apprenticeship and subsequent failing as a hypnotherapist.

Training Trances: Multi-Level Communication in Therapy and Training

Authors: John Overdurf, Julie Silverthorn (Crown House Publishing, 2004).

Want to hypnotise yourself just by reading a book? *Training Trances* is literally the text from a four-day hypnotherapy workshop. The authors describe their express intention to hypnotise the course participants as well as you, the reader, as you follow the book's ingenious use of bold, normal, and italicised text.

And it works – you can feel yourself coming in and out of trance as you read the text!

Besides its novelty aspect, the book is full of excellent insights on hypnosis and advanced techniques. It delves deeply into the explanation of Erickson's thinking. Some have described this as one of the best training manuals on Ericksonian hypnosis.

Patterns of the Hypnotic Techniques of Milton Erickson, Volume 1

Authors: John Grinder, Richard Bandler (Metamorphous Press, 1997).

Essential and unique reading, this book approaches Erickson's linguistic patterns that he used so powerfully in hypnotherapy. These authors went on to develop Neuro-linguistic Programming from their further analysis of therapists Fritz Perls and Virginia Satir. An ingenious book, if not always an easy read. You will be greatly rewarded if you persevere with this book.

Hypnosis and Hypnotherapy with Children, 3rd Edition

Authors: Karen Olness, Daniel Kohen (The Guilford Press, 1996).

There is little competition in terms of books on the subject of hypnotherapy with children. Olness and Kohen write for an academic/practitioner readership, which may put some new to hypnosis completely off, but the material is comprehensive and excellently structured. A must-read for any hypnotherapists wanting to review the evidence and approaches in this area.

Time Distortion in Hypnosis: An Experimental and Clinical Investigation

Authors: Linn Cooper, Milton Erickson (Crown House Publishing, 2002).

This is a special interest topic. Time distortion is one of the most powerful hypnotic techniques and there are few books on the subject. Time distortion is the technique of hypnotically slowing down or speeding up perceived time. Some of the most fascinating case examples in the hypnosis canon are contained within this book. The writing is dated and was written when Milton Erickson was still a young medical student. It therefore has a curious style, which is a combination of an academic and an investigative detective. These authors were trailblazing a radical subject and what has now become a standard and accepted technique amongst hypnotherapists.

Ericksonian Approaches

Authors: Rubin Battino, Thomas L. South (Crown House Publishing, 2005).

If you want to read a book about the ins and outs of the Ericksonian approach to hypnosis, then this is the one for you. It is a very readable book that takes you from the basic concepts through to advanced techniques. A complete manual in its own right, it is recommended reading for many hypnotherapy training courses.

Clinical and Experimental Hypnosis

Author: William S. Kroger (J.B. Lippincott Company, 1978).

Another classic, one that again is required reading for those who are training in hypnotherapy. Kroger takes perhaps a more in-depth look at hypnotherapy than Hartland (see above), and is more for the intermediate to advanced level of reader. *Clinical and Experimental Hypnosis* provides a wealth of background information about the classical approach to hypnosis, as well as a variety of other therapeutic approaches, such as behaviourism, that have leant their techniques to hypnotherapy. Read Hartland's, then Kroger and you will have a core knowledge of the traditional approach to hypnotherapy.

Code of Ethics

The following is an extract taken from the British Society of Clinical Hypnosis Code of Ethics, with their kind permission, as an example of how a code of ethics may look. You can expect the code of ethics for all hypnotherapy societies throughout the world to be very similar:

- *Members engaged in the practice of Clinical Hypnosis shall at all times conduct their professional activities with the propriety and dignity becoming that of a servant of the public. They shall not, under any circumstances, infringe the code of morality becoming their profession and shall not commit any breach of conduct that would adversely reflect upon themselves, the BSCH, the LCCH, or upon their fellow practitioners.*

- *Members shall never enter into a sexual relationship with a patient under their care nor shall they exploit their patients' past, present or future financially or emotionally.*

- *Members shall work in ways that will promote patient autonomy and well-being and maintain respect and dignity for the patient. Hypnotherapy is a non-exploitative therapy.*

- *Members shall not, under any circumstance, offer or promise cures for any conditions.*

- *Members shall not give any performance or display that presents hypnosis as a means of entertainment (e.g. Stage Hypnosis) or engage in activities likely to bring the profession into disrepute.*

- *Members are required to take appropriate action in accordance with the Complaints Procedure with regard to the behaviour of a colleague, which may be deemed detrimental to the profession and or other members.*

- *Members shall not claim to have qualifications or credentials they have not earned. Neither shall they use designated letters to which they are not entitled. The title 'Dr.' shall not be used unless they have a bona fide Medical or Academic Qualification from a Medical or Educational Establishment.*

- *Members are required to disclose qualifications when requested and evidence of such qualification should be made available for inspection when necessary.*

- *Members shall disclose their terms and conditions and where appropriate their method of practice at the very beginning of therapy. The fees and length of therapeutic session(s) shall be disclosed even if the patient does not enquire about them at the first point of contact.*

Index

• *N* •

• O •

• P •

Notes

Notes

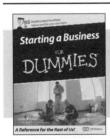
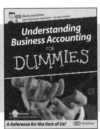

FOR DUMMIES®

A world of resources to help you grow

HOBBIES

Poker
0-7645-5232-5

Sewing
0-7645-6847-7

Drawing
0-7645-5476-X

Also available:

Art For Dummies
(0-7645-5104-3)

Aromatherapy For Dummies
(0-7645-5171-X)

Bridge For Dummies
(0-7645-5015-2)

Card Games For Dummies
(0-7645-9910-0)

Chess For Dummies
(0-7645-8404-9)

Crocheting For Dummies
(0-7645-4151-X)

Improving Your Memory
For Dummies
(0-7645-5435-2)

Massage For Dummies
(0-7645-5172-8)

Meditation For Dummies
(0-471-77774-9)

Photography For Dummies
(0-7645-4116-1)

Quilting For Dummies
(0-7645-9799-X)

Woodworking For Dummies
(0-7645-3977-9)

EDUCATION

Cooking Basics
0-7645-7206-7

The Koran
0-7645-5581-2

Anatomy & Physiology
0-7645-5422-0

Also available:

Algebra For Dummies
(0-7645-5325-9)

Astronomy For Dummies
(0-7645-8465-0)

Buddhism For Dummies
(0-7645-5359-3)

Calculus For Dummies
(0-7645-2498-4)

Christianity For Dummies
(0-7645-4482-9)

Forensics For Dummies
(0-7645-5580-4)

Islam For Dummies
(0-7645-5503-0)

Philosophy For Dummies
(0-7645-5153-1)

Religion For Dummies
(0-7645-5264-3)

Trigonometry For Dummies
(0-7645-6903-1)

PETS

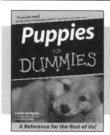

Puppies
0-7645-5255-4

Dog Training
0-7645-8418-9

Cats
0-7645-5275-9

Also available:

Labrador Retrievers
For Dummies
(0-7645-5281-3)

Aquariums For Dummies
(0-7645-5156-6)

Birds For Dummies
(0-7645-5139-6)

Dogs For Dummies
(0-7645-5274-0)

Ferrets For Dummies
(0-7645-5259-7)

German Shepherds
For Dummies
(0-7645-5280-5)

Golden Retrievers
For Dummies
(0-7645-5267-8)

Horses For Dummies
(0-7645-9797-3)

Jack Russell Terriers
For Dummies
(0-7645-5268-6)

Puppies Raising & Training
Diary For Dummies
(0-7645-0876-8)

8666_p2

FOR DUMMIES®

The easy way to get more done and have more fun

LANGUAGES

0-7645-5194-9

0-7645-5193-0

0-7645-5196-5

Also available:

Chinese For Dummies
(0-471-78897-X)

Chinese Phrases
For Dummies
(0-7645-8477-4)

French Phrases For Dummies
(0-7645-7202-4)

German For Dummies
(0-7645-5195-7)

Italian Phrases For Dummies
(0-7645-7203-2)

Japanese For Dummies
(0-7645-5429-8)

Latin For Dummies
(0-7645-5431-X)

Spanish Phrases
For Dummies
(0-7645-7204-0)

Spanish Verbs For Dummies
(0-471-76872-3)

Hebrew For Dummies
(0-7645-5489-1)

MUSIC AND FILM

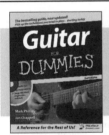

0-7645-9904-6

0-7645-2476-3

0-7645-5105-1

Also available:

Bass Guitar For Dummies
(0-7645-2487-9)

Blues For Dummies
(0-7645-5080-2)

Classical Music For Dummies
(0-7645-5009-8)

Drums For Dummies
(0-7645-5357-7)

Jazz For Dummies
(0-471-76844-8)

Opera For Dummies
(0-7645-5010-1)

Rock Guitar For Dummies
(0-7645-5356-9)

Screenwriting For Dummies
(0-7645-5486-7)

Songwriting For Dummies
(0-7645-5404-2)

Singing For Dummies
(0-7645-2475-5)

HEALTH, SPORTS & FITNESS

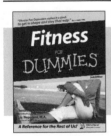

0-7645-7851-0

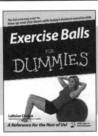

0-7645-5623-4

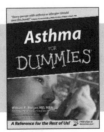

0-7645-4233-8

Also available:

Controlling Cholesterol
For Dummies
(0-7645-5440-9)

Dieting For Dummies
(0-7645-4149-8)

High Blood Pressure
For Dummies
(0-7645-5424-7)

Martial Arts For Dummies
(0-7645-5358-5)

Menopause For Dummies
(0-7645-5458-1)

Power Yoga For Dummies
(0-7645-5342-9)

Weight Training
For Dummies
(0-471-76845-6)

Yoga For Dummies
(0-7645-5117-5)

FOR DUMMIES®

Helping you expand your horizons and achieve your potential

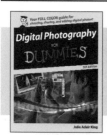

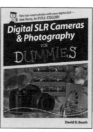